conditional form	potential form	volitional form	-te form	-ta form
会えば (あ)	会える (あ)	会おう (あ)	会って (あ)	会った (あ)
書けば (か)	書ける (か)	書こう (か)	書いて (か)	書いた (か)
行けば (い)	行ける (い)	行こう (い)	行って (い)	行った (い)
およげば	およげる	およごう	およいで	およいだ
けせば	けせる	けそう	けして	けした
まてば	まてる	まとう	まって	まった
しねば	しねる	しのう	しんで	しんだ
よべば	よべる	よぼう	よんで	よんだ
飲めば (の)	飲める (の)	飲もう (の)	飲んで (の)	飲んだ (の)
帰れば (かえ)	帰れる (かえ)	帰ろう (かえ)	帰って (かえ)	帰った (かえ)
あれば	——	——	あって	あった
できれば	——	——	できて	できた
あければ	あけられる	あけよう	あけて	あけた
食べれば (た)	食べられる (た)	食べよう (た)	食べて (た)	食べた (た)
見れば (み)	見られる (み)	見よう (み)	見て (み)	見た (み)
おりれば	おりられる	おりよう	おりて	おりた
来れば (く)	来られる (こ)	来よう (こ)	来て (き)	来た (き)
すれば	できる	しよう	して	した

conditional form	potential form	volitional form	-te form	-ta form (plain, past, aff.)
大きければ (おお)	——	——	大きくて (おお)	大きかった (おお)
便利なら（ば）(べんり)	——	——	便利で (べんり)	便利だった (べんり)
本なら（ば）(ほん)	——	——	本で (ほん)	本だった (ほん)

JAPANESE FOR BUSY PEOPLE II

JAPANESE FOR BUSY PEOPLE

Revised 3rd Edition

II

Association for Japanese-Language Teaching
AJALT

KODANSHA INTERNATIONAL
Tokyo • New York • London

The Association for Japanese-Language Teaching (AJALT) was recognized as a nonprofit organization by the Ministry of Education in 1977. It was established to meet the practical needs of people who are not necessarily specialists on Japan but wish to communicate effectively in Japanese. In 1992 AJALT was awarded the Japan Foundation Special Prize. AJALT maintains a website at www.ajalt.org.

Illustrations by Shinsaku Sumi.

CD narration by Yuki Minatsuki, Aya Ogawa, Yuri Haruta, Koji Yoshida, Tatsuo Endo, Sosei Shinbori, and Howard Colefield.

CD recording and editing by the English Language Education Council, Inc.

PHOTO CREDITS: © Sachiyo Yasuda, 1, 49, 99, 128, 149, 199.

Distributed in the United States by Kodansha America, Inc., and in the United Kingdom and continental Europe by Kodansha Europe Ltd.

Published by Kodansha International Ltd., 17–14 Otowa 1-chome, Bunkyo-ku, Tokyo 112–8652, and Kodansha America, Inc.

ISBN 978-4-7700-3010-8

First published 1990
Second edition 1995
Third edition 2007
15 14 13 12 11 10 09 08   12 11 10 9 8 7 6 5 4 3

CONTENTS

PREFACE XII

INTRODUCTION XIII

UNIT 1 SOUVENIR SHOPPING   1

UNIT 2 BUILDING RAPPORT WITH COLLEAGUES   49

UNIT 3 RETURNING TO JAPAN FOR WORK   99

UNIT 4 PLANNING A VACATION   149

UNIT 5 SOLVING PROBLEMS   199

SUPPLEMENT TO THE TEXT 253

   TRANSLATIONS OF READING TASKS 255

   ANSWERS TO EXERCISES AND QUIZZES 261

   JAPANESE-ENGLISH GLOSSARY 276

   ENGLISH-JAPANESE GLOSSARY 287

   INDEX 298

UNIT 1		GRAMMAR	

LESSON 1

ASKING FOR ADVICE ABOUT A GIFT 2

I. Referring to Indefinite Places, Things, or People   4
⇨ どこか、なにか、だれか

II. Stating and Asking Preference and Soliciting Suggestions   5
⇨ 何が いいですか／いいでしょうか

III. Making Comparisons (1): Expressing the Comparative Degree   6
⇨ 〜の ほうが 〜より 〜です

IV. Making Comparisons (2): Expressing the Superlative Degree   8
⇨ 〜で 〜が いちばん 〜です

V. "Doing Something to See How It Goes"   9
⇨ 〜てみます

LESSON 2

CHOOSING A YUKATA 18

I. Getting Information or Advice: "I'd Like to . . . But . . . ?"   20
⇨ 〜たいんですが

II. Making Comparisions (3): Singling Out an Item for Comparison   21
⇨ 〜は 〜より 〜です
⇨ 〜は いちばん 〜です

III. Stating Decisions   23
⇨ 〜に します

LESSON 3

SEARCHING FOR A LOST ITEM 32

I. Connecting Related Sentences   34
⇨ 〜で、〜／〜くて、〜

II. Describing Ongoing Actions or States in Effect   36
⇨ 〜ています

III. "Going Somewhere to Do Something"   38
⇨ 〜に 行きます

QUIZ 1 (Lessons 1–3) 46

UNIT 2		GRAMMAR	

LESSON 4

CLOCKING IN EARLY 50

I. Plain Forms of Verbs (1): Present-affirmative and Present-negative Tenses   53
⇨ 行く／行かない

II. Asking for and Offering Explanations (1)   55
⇨ Verb (Plain Form) + んです

III. Expressing Frequency   58
⇨ 〜に 〜回

COMMUNICATIVE SKILLS	READING & WRITING

COMMUNICATIVE SKILLS

- Consulting Someone about What to Buy as a Souvenir
- Asking Somone Their Preference for Food, Drink, etc.
- Stating or Asking for an Opinion about Two or More Items in Comparison with One Another

READING & WRITING

Reading Task: おにぎり　プロジェクト　　13
　　　　　(The Rice Ball Project)

Kanji Practice　　14

来 週 行 今 年 何 人 気 一 二
三 四 五 六 七 八 九 十 百 千

- Stating the Size or Characteristics of an Item You Wish to Buy
- Asking a Clerk to Gift-wrap an Item
- Indicating Your Preferred Method of Payment
- Talking about Your Family, Their Interests, and the Kinds of Gifts that Make Them Happy

Reading Task: ミルズさんの　あたらしい　　29
　　　　　パソコン
　　　　　(Mr. Mills's New Computer)

Kanji Practice　　30

大 小 私 高 安 用 店 員 父 母

- Describing a Lost Item
- Describing the Characteristics of a Person, Place, or Thing

Reading Task: かいぎしつの　わすれもの　　43
　　　　　(Items Left Behind in a Conference Room)

Kanji Practice　　44

分 前 後 午 白 中 入 火 水 金

COMMUNICATIVE SKILLS	READING & WRITING

COMMUNICATIVE SKILLS

- Talking about Routines and Habits
- Talking about Interests and Things You Want to Learn
- Explaining Why You Are Doing Something out of the Ordinary

READING & WRITING

Kanji Practice　　67

毎 朝 時 間 半 日 月 土 回 部

LESSON 5

INVITING A COLLEAGUE TO A HOT SPRING 69

I. Plain Forms of Verbs (2): Past-affirmative and Past-negative Tenses 71
⇨ 行った／行かなかった

II. Talking about Past Experiences 72
⇨ ～た　ことが　あります

LESSON 6

CLOCKING OUT EARLY 82

I. Using the Adverbial Forms of Adjectives to Modify Verbs ⇨ ～く／～に 84

II. "Going Somewhere to Do Something and Coming Back" 85
⇨ ～てきます

III. Making Strong Suggestions 86
⇨ ～た／～ない　ほうが　いいです

IV. "Not Yet" ⇨ まだ　～していません 87

V. Asking for and Offering Explanations (2) 88
⇨ Noun/Adjective + んです

QUIZ 2 (Lessons 4–6) 96

UNIT 3 | **GRAMMAR**

LESSON 7

GREETING A NEW EMPLOYEE 100

I. Expressing a Sequence of Events (1): "Before" 103
⇨ ～前に

II. Expressing a Sequence of Events (2): "After" 104
⇨ ～てから

III. "When" (1) 106
⇨ 学生の　とき／さむい　とき

LESSON 8

RUNNING INTO AN OLD ACQUAINTANCE 115

I. Describing a Change in State (1) 117
⇨ ～く／～に　なります

II. "When" (2) 119
⇨ 行く　とき／行った　とき

III. Plain Forms of Adjectives and of Nouns + です 121
⇨ おいしい／便利だ／あめだ

IV. Using Direct and Indirect Quotation 122
⇨ ～と　言っていました

LESSON 9

JOINING A CIVIC ORCHESTRA 132

I. Forming Modifying Clauses 134
⇨ パーティーに　来た　人

II. Nominalizing Sentences 136
⇨ 仕事が　終わるのは　～

QUIZ 3 (Lessons 7–9) 146

- Talking about Traveling in Japan and Japanese Cultural Experiences
- Reporting the Time and Pressing Someone to Do Something
- Gathering Information about What You Want to Do or Where You Want to Go
- Inviting a Colleague to Go Somewhere with You

Reading Task: ききゅうツアー (A Balloon Tour)   79

Kanji Practice   80

帰 本 木 課 事 仕 昼 夜 見 食

- Complaining about Your Health
- Showing Concern for the Health of Others
- Stating or Confirming the Progress of Preperations

Reading Task: ごそうだん (Consultation)   93

Kanji Practice   94

薬 買 飲 休 会 議 書 読 国 先

COMMUNICATIVE SKILLS

READING & WRITING

- Talking about Someone's Personal History
- Giving a Detailed Self-introduction

Reading Task: 佐々木さんの　けいれき   112
さ さ き
(Ms. Sasaki's Personal History)

Kanji Practice   113

学 生 校 支 社 終 語 子 男 女

- Talking about Changes that Have Come Over a Town
- Talking about an Old Aquaintance and How They Have Changed

Reading Task 1: ホームステイの　おもいで   127
(Reminiscences of a Homestay)

Reading Task 2: 原宿 物 語 (The Story of Harajuku)   128
はらじゅくものがたり

Kanji Practice   130

東 京 西 南 北 便 利 言 夕 空

- Describing a Building's Facilities
- Describing Your Personal Effects
- Describing Someone's Personality

Reading Task 1: マルタンさんの　ブログ   141
(Ms. Martin's Blog)

Reading Task 2: アメリカ人かぞくの　ブログ   142
じん
(The Blog of an American Family)

Kanji Practice   144

去 友 作 長 方 度 山 川 花 田

UNIT 4	GRAMMAR	
LESSON 10 ASKING FOR TIME OFF 150	I. Giving a Reason (1) ⇨ 〜ので	152
	II. Expressing Potentiality ⇨ 行けます	154
LESSON 11 SELECTING A VACATION PLAN 164	I. Expressing Volition: "I Am Thinking about . . ." ⇨ 〜う／ようと　思っています	166
	II. Giving a Reason (2) ⇨ 〜て／〜で	168
	III. Forming Indirect Questions ⇨ 〜か／〜か　どうか	170
LESSON 12 RESERVING A ROOM AT AN INN 180	I. Expressing Uncertainty ⇨ 〜かもしれません	182
	II. Talking about Future Events Coming into Being ⇨ 〜たら	184
QUIZ 4 (Lessons 10–12)　196		

UNIT 5	GRAMMAR	
LESSON 13 TALKING ABOUT PRODUCTIVITY 200	I. Describing a Change in State (2) ⇨ 〜てきました	202
	II. Making Hypothetical Statements ⇨ 〜たら	204
LESSON 14 COMPUTER TROUBLE 217	I. Stating the Result of an Action or Event ⇨ 〜たら　〜ました	219
	II. Indicating That an Action or Event Has Been Completed ⇨ 〜てしまいました	220
	III. Making Conditional Statements ⇨ 〜ば	222
LESSON 15 GIVING DIRECTIONS 234	I. Speaking of Natural or Habitual Results ⇨ 〜と	236
	II. Expressing Necessity ⇨ 〜なければ　なりません	238
QUIZ 5 (Lessons 13–15)　250		

COMMUNICATIVE SKILLS	READING & WRITING	

- Talking about Schedules
- Talking about the Services Available at a Department Store

Reading & Writing Task: おさそい (Invitations) — 160

Reading Task: かんそう (Impressions) — 161

Kanji Practice — 162

両 親 初 始 出 予 定 目 末 思

- Stating What You Are Thinking about Doing in the Near Future
- Expressing Your Feelings and Giving Reasons for Them
- Talking about Possible Scenarios That Could Occur in the Near Future

Kanji Practice — 178

旅 多 少 屋 約 聞 新 古 発 着

- Calling for Teamwork When Hosting a Barbecue
- Confirming the Details of a Trip
- Telling Someone over the Phone That You Do Not Have Time to Talk and Will Call Them Back Later

Reading Task 1: しんぱいしょうの 人の 話 — 191
(Words from a Worrywart)

Reading Task 2: 富士山 (Mt. Fuji) — 192

Kanji Practice — 194

館 名 泊 円 意 電 話 番 号 駅

COMMUNICATIVE SKILLS	READING & WRITING	

- Talking about Changes in Sales/Productivity
- Talking about Your Dreams for the Future
- Talking about What to Do in the Event of a Disaster

Reading Task: 3おく円 あたったら — 214
(If I Won 300 Million Yen)

Kanji Practice — 215

売 上 下 倍 万 特 別 口 雨 車

- Talking about Problems and Explaining Solutions
- Asking for Suggestions about How to Solve Problems

Reading Task: ミルズさんの にっき — 231
(Mr. Mills's Diary)

Kanji Practice — 232

動 自 待 打 合 急 内 外 雪 天

- Giving Directions
- Using Intransitive and Transitive Verbs
- Giving a Reason for Rejecting an Invitation

Reading Task 1: けいたいメール (Text Messaging) — 245

Reading Task 2: 私の すんでいる まちの ごみの 出し方 — 247
(How to Put Out the Trash in the Town I Live in)

Kanji Practice — 248

専 階 右 左 側 失 礼 手 足 立

PREFACE
TO THE REVISED 3RD EDITION

For busy working adults, progressing to the next step beyond "survival Japanese" is not easy. Books II and III of the *Japanese for Busy People* series were first published in 1990 for learners seeking intermediate to advanced proficiency in Japanese. Yet even with the aid of these volumes, many people still found it difficult to master complicated Japanese syntax and vocabulary in the few hours they had available outside of other commitments. Over the years, we at AJALT have continued to look for new ways to help learners overcome this barrier, and in the process we have developed and implemented numerous improvements to our lesson plans and supplementary teaching materials. Such experience is put to full use in this extensively revised edition of *Japanese for Busy People II*, designed to better enable adult learners to pursue their study of Japanese to the point of intermediate fluency.

Japanese for Busy People II, Revised 3rd Edition incorporates many new ideas developed carefully over time by a committee of twenty-one working AJALT instructors. Of the group of twenty-one, a team of five teachers compiled the text.

We hope that busy people will find this textbook an enjoyable tool for learning Japanese.

Acknowledgments for *Japanese for Busy People II, Revised Edition* (1990)
Four AJALT teachers wrote this textbook. They are Miyako Iwami, Shigeko Miyazaki, Masako Nagai, and Kimiko Yamamoto. They were assisted by two other teachers, Kumiko Endo and Chikako Ogura.

Acknowledgments for *Japanese for Busy People II, Revised 3rd Edition*
This textbook was written by five AJALT teachers—Emiko Arai, Kaori Hattori, Reiko Sawane, Junko Shinada, and Emiko Yamamoto—with the assistance of Miyuki Fujiwara, Yuko Harada, Ajiko Ietomi, Eiko Ishida, Mitsuyoshi Kaji, Rosa Maekawa, Mariko Mishima, Tomoko Mitaki, Emiko Nakachi, Makiko Nakano, Mikiko Ochiai, Minako Saito, Sadao Sakano, Yuko Takagahara, Keiko Takegami, and Yoriko Yoshida.

Special thanks are owed to Martin and Pamela Murray, who contributed the blog on pp. 142–43.

INTRODUCTION   *For adults*

Aims

Like Book I, Book II is intended for busy people who wish to efficiently master beginning-level Japanese. It may be used in the classroom or outside it.

Book I dealt with "survival Japanese" for tourists and other short-term travelers and newcomers to Japan. Book II, meanwhile, turns to the basics of Japanese syntax. The book is by no means only about grammar, however. Rather, it is designed to help learners consolidate their understanding of syntactical structure through lessons that focus on how to talk about topics relevant to daily life.

In addition to serving learners continuing from Book I, Book II will benefit those who have already studied beginning Japanese to some extent but wish to brush up on syntax.

Major Features of *Japanese for Busy People II, Revised 3rd Edition*

Japanese for Busy People II, Revised 3rd Edition will enable learners to progress smoothly through the equivalent of the latter half of a typical first-year Japanese course while gradually building speaking and listening skills.

Learners approaching mid-beginner status often find themselves suddenly faced with syntax and vocabulary much more complex than what they have studied before. Such grammar and vocabulary do not appear as frequently in everyday conversation as those words and structures they have learned up to this point, necessitating that they spend ample time on review. Moreover, learners at this stage are expected to become familiar with verb tense and aspect, time expressions, conditional clauses, and other topics that require them to have a solid grasp of context and speaker intent if they are to fully understand the differences in meaning conveyed by each. Such points cannot be mastered by reading through grammatical explanations alone. In short, the mid-beginner level is a difficult one for many adult learners who, unlike students in school, have neither time nor opportunities to take repeated tests or to otherwise gauge their progress.

Japanese for Busy People II, Revised 3rd Edition helps overcome the above obstacles through grammar and content topics carefully selected to be appropriate to learners at this level of Japanese proficiency. The book is designed so that by practicing talking about each topic, learners will gradually and effectively acquire sentence patterns and vocabulary related to that topic. Like Book I, Book II is organized into several large units, each covering topics grouped under a particular theme. In this way, the book enables learners to achieve a well-balanced understanding of grammar, sentence structure, and context.

Themes and lesson objectives of the five units in Book II are as follows.

Unit 1: Souvenir Shopping

Following up on Book I, Unit 1 presents survival Japanese related to shopping, thus providing learners with a thorough review of simple clauses. The unit also goes beyond what was covered in Book I by showing ways of asking someone's opinion while shopping, making comparisons between items, and describing an item's characteristics. The overall theme is "picking souvenirs," a subject that should be relevant to learners both in Japan and abroad. The verbal skills and dialogue patterns studied here may be applied not only to shopping but also more broadly to any situation that involves choosing between options.

Unit 2: Building Rapport with Colleagues

This unit introduces the plain forms of verbs—a crucial component of Japanese compound sentences—along with several sentence-final elements that make use of these forms. Topics are selected from among those that typically come up when interacting with people from work. Covered are constructions for indicating interest in another's actions, inviting someone to do something outside of work, asking for help or offering advice, and otherwise interacting with people in ways that help build relationships of trust and understanding.

Unit 3: Returning to Japan for Work

This unit explains how to build sentences using temporal clauses, direct and indirect quotation, and attributive modifiers. Through talking about factual events in one's life history or in that of a particular neighborhood, learners will study how to relate an event in chronological sequence, compare the way something is now to how it was in the past, and describe facilities and other things around them.

Unit 4: Planning a Vacation

Along with sentences with clauses for stating reasons or reporting questions, this unit covers sentence-final elements used to express indefiniteness, for example wish or probability. Topics deal with verbal skills necessary for planning and carrying out activities in cooperation with others, including explaining reasons or circumstances, expressing probability, and indicating desire. The overall theme is that of planning and going on a trip to a unique place in Japan.

Unit 5: Solving Problems

The focus of this unit is on forming conditional clauses. Topics include preparing for earthquakes or other disasters, discussing dreams for the future, solving problems, helping someone who is lost, and other situations that call on learners to talk about what might happen in the future, discuss options for solving problems, and give instructions or explain steps for doing something.

The Structure of the Units

Each of the five units listed above is divided into three lessons. The lessons, in turn, are organized into the following parts:

Target Dialogue
Grammar & Pattern Practice
Practice (1, 2, 3 . . .)
Reading Task
Kanji Practice

Using *Japanese for Busy People II*

Work through the textbook following the steps below.

1. *Target Dialogue*. Scan the target dialogue for an overview of the structures you will be learning in the lesson. The underlined parts are the lesson's key sentences, and page references direct you to where they are explained in detail. At this stage it is not important to understand the Target Dialogue in its entirety, since you will be returning to it after working through the Practice pages (see step 4 below).

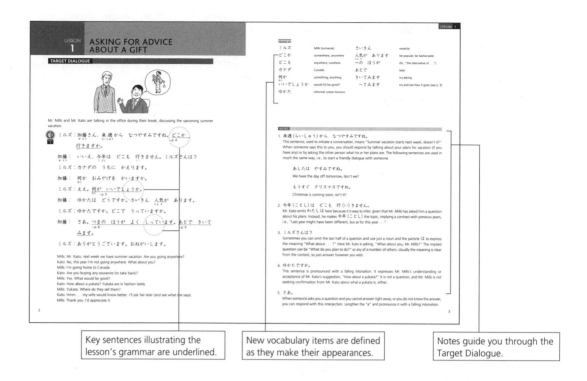

Key sentences illustrating the lesson's grammar are underlined.

New vocabulary items are defined as they make their appearances.

Notes guide you through the Target Dialogue.

2. *Grammar & Pattern Practice*. This section takes up the lesson's grammatical points and sentence patterns one by one, explaining forms and meanings and offering exercises for trying out the patterns. After reading the explanations, turn to the exercises to see whether you can construct sentences following the rules described. The important thing is not only to say the answers out loud but to practice actually writing them down. Answers are given in the back of the book.

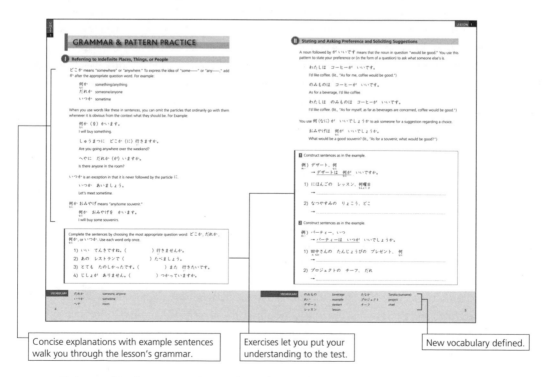

Concise explanations with example sentences walk you through the lesson's grammar.

Exercises let you put your understanding to the test.

New vocabulary defined.

To internalize the constructions and put them to full use requires much more than merely understanding the grammar behind them. It requires that you study them in context, which the Practice pages (to follow) and Target Dialogue allow you to do.

3. *Practice.* Once you understand the meanings and forms of the sentence patterns covered in Grammar & Pattern Practice, it is time to practice using them in conversation.

The Practice pages fall into one of several types: Word Power combined with Speaking Practice; Speaking Practice only; and Phrase Power (in Units 2, 3, 4, and 5) and Speaking Practice.

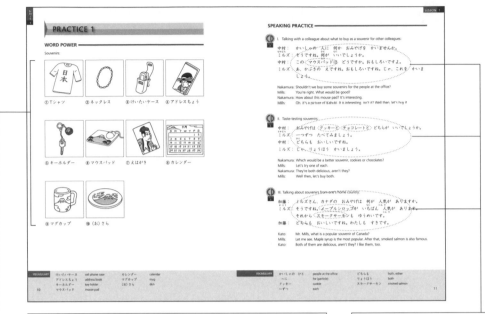

> The Word Power pages in this text are not limited to new vocabulary but include, for review, words you have already learned. Try substituting the words presented here with the ones in the dialogues at right.

> The dialogues in Speaking Practice are thematically linked with the vocabulary presented in the Word Power section at left.

Begin by studying the words and/or expressions in Word Power or Phrase Power. The vocabulary here will be necessary for dealing with the conversation topics covered in the lesson. Study the characters and pronunciation for each one while also referring to the illustrations and glosses. If you feel there are too many, focus on the ones you are most interested in. While the ideal is to become able to recall the Japanese just from looking at the illustrations or glosses, this does not have to happen right away. Once you have spent some time over the meanings and pronunciations, proceed to the Speaking Practice even if you have not finished memorizing everything. While practicing, simply look back at the list for any words you do not remember. You will gradually become more familiar with the words as you use them.

The Speaking Practice is made up of a series of sample dialogues. First listen to each dialogue on the CD to see how much you can comprehend on your own. It will also help to try repeating the words after the speaker or writing them down. Next, read the script in the textbook (and the translation, as necessary) to confirm your understanding. Then read the script out loud. If you have a learning partner, practice acting out the dialogues together, switching roles as neccessary.

Some of the Speaking Practice sections in the latter half of the textbook (Units 4 and 5) also come with exercises that call on you not only to memorize and use set vocabulary, but also to make up dialogues based on additionally provided material. As you come to these parts, work through them according to the instructions given.

After going through the sample dialogues, practice conversing more freely, adjusting the topic to suit you and using the words and expressions that you just learned. If you have a learning partner, talk to that partner. There is no need to stick closely to the examples or to worry about small errors. Simply talk and ask questions about the topic as you like. If you have a native Japanese speaker close by or are otherwise in a position to speak Japanese in real life, then be sure to take the opportunity to try out what you have learned in actual conversation with that person.

Finally, try writing down what you said in the free conversation practice above. Ask an instructor or a Japanese acquaintance to point out your mistakes.

4. *Target Dialogue*. When you finish with the Practice pages, turn back to the Target Dialogue at the beginning of the lesson and study it along with the CD. Carefully go over and review any parts you find difficult to understand. Listen to the CD many times and practice repeating the words after the speaker until you are able to speak the dialogue with natural intonation and speed.

Most of the dialogues begin with expressions typically used to strike up conversations. Try using these in real life when the opportunity presents itself.

5. *Reading Task*. In this section, you will be exposed to short reading material intended also to serve as a lesson review. Written Japanese differs from spoken forms of the language, which tend to abbreviate various syntactic elements. Read the text in order to accustom yourself to expository Japanese that is not part of conversational give-and-take but is instead directed one-way, from writer to reader. Since the materials here are written much less formally than Japanese prose normally would be, however, they may also be used as templates for such oral tasks as giving explanations or making speeches. Once you have read and understood the text, practice explaining the content in your own words. (A few of the texts are written in full prose style.) Questions sometimes accompany the Reading Tasks to encourage you to do this. Translations of all the texts as well as sample answers to the questions can be found at the back of the book.

6. *Kanji Practice*. Each lesson concludes with a Kanji Practice page. This section takes up ten characters (twenty in Lesson 1), most of them from vocabulary appearing in the lesson's Target Dialogue. In all, the textbook introduces 160 basic kanji, selected primarily from those covered in level 4 of the Japanese-Language Proficiency Test.

The meanings of the kanji are given below the character, usage examples and writing instructions to the right of it. The examples, too, are taken mostly from the the lesson's Target Dialogue and are limited to vocabulary appearing in the textbook (albeit sometimes with kanji components introduced in a later lesson). Asterisks indicate frequently used words that are written with kanji not covered in the textbook but that are nevertheless given because they are words you should already be familiar with.

Appearing in small letters below the usage examples are the readings for the kanji, called in Japanese *furigana*. Although kanji dictionaries typically distinguish between Japanese and Chinese readings by setting the former in hiragana and the latter in katakana, in this textbook they are all given in hiragana. Verbs and adjectives are listed in their dictionary forms (except in Unit 1; see p. 52 for an explanation of plain forms, of which the dictionary form is an example). The non-kanji endings on verbs and adjectives (e.g., the ます in 来 (き) ます are called *okurigana* (verbal suffixes). In general, the stem of a word is written in kanji while the inflected parts appear in hiragana as verbal suffixes, e.g., 来 (く) る, 来 (き) ます, 来 (こ) ない, 来 (き) て. There are many exceptions to this rule, however, and so the suffixes are best memorized individually.

The Kanji Practice comes with blanks for writing out the characters. Try writing each one, paying careful attention to the order and direction of the strokes.

Throughout this text we introduce kanji gradually, and always with furigana so that you know how to pronounce them. In addition to words from the Target Dialogue, we also present in kanji (for recognition purposes only) proper nouns—that is, place names and names of people.

Note About Kanji

Kanji came into Japan from China roughly 1,500 years ago. Kanji also became the basis of the hiragana and katakana syllabaries later developed to better represent sounds in Japanese. Japanese today is written primarily with kanji and hiragana, supplemented as necessary by katakana, Arabic numerals, and romanization.

Kanji are logographic (i.e., each character has a meaning) unlike hiragana, which are phonographic (i.e., like English letters, they represent only sounds). For this reason, kanji have the advantage of allowing readers to infer the meaning of a text simply by scanning and understanding the characters.

Readings for kanji fall broadly into one of two types, *on'yomi* (Chinese reading) or *kun'yomi* (Japanese reading). Some kanji have only one reading, others several. In general, a kanji is given a Japanese reading when used by itself as a word, and a Chinese reading when used in combination with other characters as a compound. There is only one set way of reading a kanji in a particular word.

The body of kanji regularly used in Japanese publications such as newspapers and magazines is referred to as *jōyō kanji* (kanji in common use). There are 1,945 characters in the list of *jōyō kanji* officially designated by the Ministry of Education, Culture, Sports, Science and Technology, of which about 500 appear most frequently. These 500 make up 70 to 80 percent of all the kanji used in newspapers and other prose. Thus learners who master these characters will become able to read most Japanese writing while looking up the other 20 to 30 percent in a dictionary.

Introducing the Cast

The following characters feature in this textbook.

ジョン・ミルズ

John Mills (35 years old), a Canadian, is a member of ABC Foods' sales department. He is single.

マリー・マルタン

Marie Martin (25 years old) is from Paris, France. A member of ABC Foods' sales department, she used to live in Japan as an exchange student.

シカ・チャンドラ

Shika Chandra (30 years old) is a member of ABC Foods' systems department. She is from Mumbai, India.

佐々木 恵子
ささき けいこ

Keiko Sasaki (53 years old), a Japanese, is the manager of ABC Foods' sales department. She is married and has a daughter, Aiko.

加藤 明
か とう あきら

Akira Kato (46 years old), a Japanese, is the section chief of ABC Foods' sales department. He is married.

中村 まゆみ
なかむら

Mayumi Nakamura (26 years old), a Japanese, works as a secretary to Ms. Sasaki. She is single.

鈴木 大介
すず き だいすけ

Daisuke Suzuki (24 years old), a Japanese, is a member of ABC Foods' sales staff. He is single.

メイ・チャン

Mei Chan (30 years old) is from Hong Kong. She works in ABC Foods' sales department. She is single.

フランク・グリーン

Frank Green (56 years old), an American, is the president of the Tokyo branch of ABC Foods. He lives in Tokyo, with his wife.

山本 一郎
やまもと いちろう

Ichiro Yamamoto (45 years old), a Japanese, is the president of the Kyoto branch of ABC Foods.

Sachiko Nakajima (Marie Martin's former homestay mother) and Emi Morita (the teenage daughter of the Nakajimas' next-door neighbors, the Moritas) also appear in this book, as do Kyojiro Yamakawa (organizer of a civic orchestra) and a host of others.

SOUVENIR SHOPPING

It is sometimes said that Japanese people are not very good about making up their minds on their own. Seen from another perspective, however, this means that the Japanese language is rich in expressions for involving others in decision-making, among them the sentence-ending でしょうか covered in this unit. Learn to use this and other expressions to discuss choices with others in such familiar situations as picking gifts or souvenirs.

ASKING FOR ADVICE ABOUT A GIFT

TARGET DIALOGUE

Mr. Mills and Mr. Kato are talking in the office during their break, discussing the upcoming summer vacation.

ミルズ： 加藤さん、来週から　なつやすみですね。どこか
　　　　 　かとう　　 らいしゅう　　　　　　　　　　　　　　　　→p. 4

　　　　 行きますか。
　　　　 い

加藤：　 いいえ、今年は　どこも　行きません。ミルズさんは？
　かとう　　　　　　 ことし　　　　　　い

ミルズ： カナダの　うちに　かえります。

加藤：　 何か　おみやげを　かいますか。
　　　　 なに

ミルズ： ええ。何が　いいでしょうか。
　　　　 　なに　→p. 5

加藤：　 ゆかたは　どうですか。さいきん　人気が　あります。
　　　　　　　　　　　　　　　　　　　　　 にんき

ミルズ： ゆかたですか。どこで　うっていますか。

加藤：　 さあ。つまの　ほうが　よく　しっています。あとで　きいて
　　　　 　　→p. 6　　　　　　　　　　　　　　　　　　 →p. 9

　　　　 みます。

ミルズ： ありがとうございます。おねがいします。

Mills: Mr. Kato, next week we have summer vacation. Are you going anywhere?
Kato: No, this year I'm not going anywhere. What about you?
Mills: I'm going home to Canada.
Kato: Are you buying any souvenirs (to take back)?
Mills: Yes. What would be good?
Kato: How about a yukata? Yukata are in fashion lately.
Mills: Yukata. Where do they sell them?
Kato: Hmm . . . my wife would know better. I'll ask her later (and see what she says).
Mills: Thank you. I'd appreciate it.

VOCABULARY

ミルズ	Mills (surname)	さいきん	recently
どこか	somewhere, anywhere	人気が　あります	be popular, be fashionable
どこも	anywhere, nowhere	〜の　ほうが	(lit., "the alternative of . . .")
カナダ	Canada	あとで	later
何か	something, anything	きいてみます	try asking
いいでしょうか	would (it) be good?	〜てみます	try and see how it goes (see p. 9)
ゆかた	informal cotton kimono		

NOTES

1. 来週（らいしゅう）から　なつやすみですね。

This sentence, used to initiate a conversation, means "Summer vacation starts next week, doesn't it?" When someone says this to you, you should respond by talking about your plans for vacation (if you have any) or by asking the other person what his or her plans are. The following sentences are used in much the same way, i.e., to start a friendly dialogue with someone.

あしたは　やすみですね。

We have the day off tomorrow, don't we?

もうすぐ　クリスマスですね。

Christmas is coming soon, isn't it?

2. 今年（ことし）は　どこも　行（い）きません。

Mr. Kato omits わたしは here because it is easy to infer, given that Mr. Mills has asked him a question about his plans. Instead, he makes 今年（ことし）the topic, implying a contrast with previous years, i.e., "Last year might have been different, but as for this year . . ."

3. ミルズさんは？

Sometimes you can omit the last half of a question and use just a noun and the particle は to express the meaning "What about . . . ?" Here Mr. Kato is asking, "What about you, Mr. Mills?" The implied question can be "What do you plan to do?" or any of a number of others. Usually the meaning is clear from the context, so just answer however you wish.

4. ゆかたですか。

This sentence is pronounced with a falling intonation. It expresses Mr. Mills's understanding or acceptance of Mr. Kato's suggestion, "How about a yukata?" It is not a question, and Mr. Mills is not seeking confirmation from Mr. Kato about what a yukata is, either.

5. さあ。

When someone asks you a question and you cannot answer right away, or you do not know the answer, you can respond with this interjection. Lengthen the "a" and pronounce it with a falling intonation.

GRAMMAR & PATTERN PRACTICE

I Referring to Indefinite Places, Things, or People

どこか means "somewhere" or "anywhere." To express the idea of "some——" or "any——," add か after the appropriate question word. For example:

何か	something/anything
だれか	someone/anyone
いつか	sometime

When you use words like these in sentences, you can omit the particles that ordinarily go with them whenever it is obvious from the context what they should be. For example:

何か（を）かいます。
I will buy something.

しゅうまつに　どこか（に）行きますか。
Are you going anywhere over the weekend?

へやに　だれか（が）いますか。
Is there anyone in the room?

いつか is an exception in that it is never followed by the particle に.

いつか　あいましょう。
Let's meet sometime.

何か　おみやげ means "any/some souvenir."

何か　おみやげを　かいます。
I will buy some souvenirs.

Complete the sentences by choosing the most appropriate word: どこか, だれか, 何か, or いつか. Use each word only once.

1) いい　てんきですね。（　　　　　）行きませんか。

2) あの　レストランで（　　　　　）たべましょう。

3) とても　たのしかったです。（　　　　　）また　行きたいです。

4) じしょが　ありません。（　　　　　）つかっていますか。

VOCABULARY

だれか	someone, anyone
いつか	sometime
へや	room

II Stating and Asking Preference and Soliciting Suggestions

A noun followed by が いいです means that the noun in question "would be good." You use this pattern to state your preference or (in the form of a question) to ask what someone else's is.

わたしは　コーヒーが　いいです。

I'd like coffee. (lit., "As for me, coffee would be good.")

のみものは　コーヒーが　いいです。

As for a beverage, I'd like coffee.

わたしは　のみものは　コーヒーが　いいです。

I'd like coffee. (lit., "As for myself, as far as beverages are concerned, coffee would be good.")

You use 何（なに）が　いいでしょうか to ask someone for a suggestion regarding a choice.

おみやげは　何が　いいでしょうか。

What would be a good souvenir? (lit., "As for a souvenir, what would be good?")

---

1 Construct sentences as in the example.

例）デザート、何
れい
　→ デザートは　何が　いいですか。
　　　　　　　なに

1) にほんごの　レッスン、何曜日
　　　　　　　　　　　　なんようび
　→ ....

2) なつやすみの　りょこう、どこ
　→ ....

2 Construct sentences as in the example.

例）パーティー、いつ
れい
　→ パーティーは　いつが　いいでしょうか。

1) 田中さんの　たんじょうびの　プレゼント、何
　たなか　　　　　　　　　　　　　　　　　なに
　→ ....

2) プロジェクトの　チーフ、だれ
　→ ....

VOCABULARY			
のみもの	beverage	たなか	Tanaka (surname)
れい	example	プロジェクト	project
デザート	dessert	チーフ	chief
レッスン	lesson		

III Making Comparisons (I): Expressing the Comparative Degree

の ほうが … より is the pattern to use to describe two things or people in comparison with each other. Things that are superior precede の ほうが, "the alternative of," and things that are inferior precede より, "than."

> ワインの ほうが ビールより たかいです。
>
> Wine is more expensive than beer.

To ask which of two things or people is "more" in some respect, use と … と どちらが … ですか. If the second noun in the answer (what comes before より) is obvious from the context, you can leave it out, together with より, as in the following example.

> Q：ワインと ビールと どちらが たかいですか。
>
> A：ワインの ほうが (ビールより) たかいです。

> Q: Which is more expensive, wine or beer?
> A: Wine is more expensive (than beer).

¥600　¥500

---

1 Look at the menu and make up questions and answers as in the example.

例) コーヒー、こうちゃ、たかい
れい

　→ Q：<u>コーヒーと こうちゃと どちらが たかいですか。</u>

　　　A：<u>こうちゃの ほうが たかいです。</u>

1) こうちゃ、ジュース、やすい

　→ Q：..

　　　A：..

2) アイスクリーム、ケーキ、たかい

　→ Q：..

　　　A：..

---

2 Compare the countries in the table and make up questions and answers based on the information given, as in the example.

Countries of the world by area (km²)

ロシア	17,075,000	アメリカ	9,628,400	ブラジル	8,512,000
カナダ	9,976,100	中国 ちゅうごく	9,600,000	オーストラリア	7,686,800

例）中国、アメリカ
れい　ちゅうごく

→ Q：<u>中国と　アメリカと</u>　どちらが　おおきいですか。
　　　ちゅうごく

A：<u>アメリカの　ほうが</u>　おおきいです。

1) カナダ、ブラジル

→ Q：...

A：...

2) 中国、オーストラリア
　ちゅうごく

→ Q：...

A：...

3 Compare the countries in the table and make up questions and answers based on the information given, as in the example.

Consumption of wine by country (liters per capita per annum)

フランス	58.2	ポルトガル	49.1	アルゼンチン	33.5
イタリア	52.7	スペイン	35.2	ルーマニア	23.1

例）イタリア人、フランス人
れい　　　　じん　　　　　　　じん

→ Q：<u>イタリア人と　フランス人と</u>　どちらが　たくさん　ワインを
　　　　　　じん　　　　　　じん
のみますか。

A：<u>フランス人の　ほうが</u>　たくさん　のみます。
　　　　　じん

1) スペイン人、ポルトガル人
　　　　じん　　　　　　じん

→ Q：...

A：...

2) アルゼンチン人、ルーマニア人
　　　　　　じん　　　　　　じん

→ Q：...

A：...

Ⅳ Making Comparisons (2): Expressing the Superlative Degree

To say that one person or thing is "the most" or "the best" among several, you use a noun followed by の なかで, followed by another noun and が いちばん. The word いちばん, "number one," expresses the superlative degree of comparison, i.e., "the most," "the ——est." For example, いちばん すき means "most likeable," and いちばん きれい means "prettiest," "most beautiful."

スポーツ（の　なか）で　サッカーが　いちばん　人気が　あります。
<small>にん き</small>

Soccer is the most popular of all sports.

Note that you can omit の なか, "among."

To ask, "Which is the most?" or "Which is the ——est?" you use the same basic pattern but with a question word such as 何（なに）, どれ, だれ, どこ, or いつ.

Q：スポーツ（の なか）で　何が　いちばん　すきですか。
　　　　　　　　　　　<small>なに</small>
A：サッカーが　いちばん　すきです。

Q:　What sport do you like best?
A:　I like soccer best.

Note that you use どれ, "which one," instead of 何（なに）, "what," to ask which item among a limited selection of three or more is "the most" or "the ——est."

Q：サッカーと　テニスと　ゴルフ（の　なか）で　どれが　いちばん　すきで
　　すか。
A：サッカーが　いちばん　すきです。

Q:　Which (sport) among soccer, tennis, and golf do you like best?
A:　I like soccer best.

---

1 Fill in the blanks with the appropriate question word.

1) Q：ごかぞくで　（　　　　　）が　いちばん　よく　ほんを　よみますか。
　　A：ははが　いちばん　よく　ほんを　よみます。

2) Q：日本の　おみやげで（　　　　　）が　いちばん　人気が　ありますか。
　　　<small>に ほん</small>　　　　　　　　　　　　　　　　　　　<small>にん き</small>
　　A：ゆかたが　いちばん　人気が　あります。
　　　　　　　　　　　　　　　<small>にん き</small>

3) Q：リストの　ほんの　なかで　（　　　　　　）が　いちばん　おもしろ
　　　いですか。
　　A：この　ほんが　いちばん　おもしろいです。

VOCABULARY		
	いちばん	number one
	ごかぞく	family
	ご〜	(honorific prefix)
	リスト	list

2 Look at the graph and make up questions and answers as in the example.

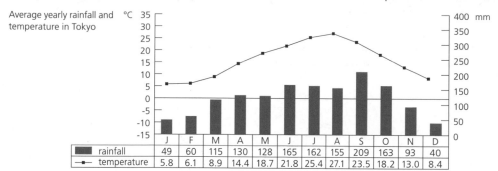

Average yearly rainfall and temperature in Tokyo

		J	F	M	A	M	J	J	A	S	O	N	D
▬	rainfall	49	60	115	130	128	165	162	155	209	163	93	40
-■-	temperature	5.8	6.1	8.9	14.4	18.7	21.8	25.4	27.1	23.5	18.2	13.0	8.4

例) いちばん　あつい

　　→ Q：1年の　なかで　なんがつが　<u>いちばん　あついですか</u>。

　　　 A：<u>8がつが　いちばん　あついです</u>。

1) いちばん　さむい

　　→ Q：...

　　　 A：...

2) いちばん　あめが　おおい

　　→ Q：...

　　　 A：...

3) いちばん　あめが　すくない

　　→ Q：...

　　　 A：...

V "Doing Something to See How It Goes"

You use the -*te* form followed by みます to express the idea of "do something and see how it goes" or "try and . . ." For example, きいてみます means "I'll ask and see what she says."

Change the form of the verbs to 〜てみます as in the example.

例) たべます　　　　　→ <u>たべてみます</u>

1) くつを　はきます　→ ....

2) コートを　きます　→ ....

PRACTICE 1

WORD POWER

Souvenirs:

① Tシャツ

② ネックレス

③ けいたいケース

④ アドレスちょう

⑤ キーホルダー

⑥ マウスパッド

⑦ えはがき

⑧ カレンダー

⑨ マグカップ

⑩ (お) さら

VOCABULARY	けいたいケース	cell phone case	カレンダー	calendar
	アドレスちょう	address book	マグカップ	mug
	キーホルダー	key holder	(お) さら	dish
10	マウスパッド	mouse pad		

SPEAKING PRACTICE

I. Talking with a colleague about what to buy as a souvenir for other colleagues:

中村： かいしゃの 人に 何か おみやげを かいませんか。

ミルズ： そうですね。何が いいでしょうか。

中村： この マウスパッドは どうですか。おもしろいですよ。

ミルズ： あ、かぶきの えですね。おもしろいですね。じゃ、これを かいま
しょう。

Nakamura: Shouldn't we buy some souvenirs for the people at the office?
Mills:　　　You're right. What would be good?
Nakamura: How about this mouse pad? It's interesting.
Mills:　　　Oh, it's a picture of Kabuki. It is interesting, isn't it? Well then, let's buy it.

II. Taste-testing souvenirs:

中村： おみやげは クッキーと チョコレートと どちらが いいでしょうか。

ミルズ： 一つずつ たべてみましょう。

中村： どちらも おいしいですね。

ミルズ： じゃ、りょうほう かいましょう。

Nakamura: Which would be a better souvenir, cookies or chocolates?
Mills:　　　Let's try one of each.
Nakamura: They're both delicious, aren't they?
Mills:　　　Well then, let's buy both.

III. Talking about souvenirs from one's home country:

加藤： ミルズさん、カナダの おみやげは 何が 人気が ありますか。

ミルズ： そうですね。メープルシロップが いちばん 人気が あります。
それから スモークサーモンも ゆうめいです。

加藤： どちらも おいしいですね。わたしも すきです。

Kato:　　　Mr. Mills, what is a popular souvenir of Canada?
Mills:　　　Let me see. Maple syrup is the most popular. After that, smoked salmon is also famous.
Kato:　　　Both of them are delicious, aren't they? I like them, too.

VOCABULARY	かいしゃの　ひと	people at the office	どちらも	both, either
	〜に	for (particle)	りょうほう	both
	クッキー	cookie	スモークサーモン	smoked salmon
	〜ずつ	each (particle)		

11

PRACTICE 2

SPEAKING PRACTICE

TRACK
5

I. Concluding that shopping is best done on weekdays:

加藤：　しゅうまつは　どこか　行きましたか。
ミルズ：ええ、デパートに　行って　いろいろ　かいものを　しました。
　　　　加藤さんは？
加藤：　うちに　いました。しゅうまつは　どこも　こんでいますから。
ミルズ：そうですね。かいものは　へいじつの　ほうが　べんりですね。

Kato:　　Did you go anywhere over the weekend?
Mills:　Yes, I went to a department store and shopped for all sorts of things. What about you?
Kato:　　I was at home. On weekends it's crowded everywhere.
Mills:　That's right. As far as shopping goes, weekdays are more convenient.

TRACK
6

II. Having a guest at a party choose a drink:

ミルズ：よく　いらっしゃいました。こちらへ　どうぞ。何か　のみませんか。
加藤：　ありがとうございます。何が　ありますか。
ミルズ：のみものは　ワインと　ビールと　コーラが　あります。どれが　い
　　　　いですか。
加藤：　ワインが　いいです。
ミルズ：ワインは　あかと
　　　　しろと　どちらが
　　　　いいですか。
加藤：　あかを　おねがいします。

Mills:　Welcome. Right this way. Would you like something to drink?
Kato:　　Yes, thank you. What do you have?
Mills:　The beverages (that we have) are wine, beer, and cola. Which would you prefer?
Kato:　　I'd like wine.
Mills:　Which wine would you prefer, red or white?
Kato:　　Red, please.

VOCABULARY	いろいろ	in various ways	かいもの	shopping	あか	red
	どこも	everywhere	へいじつ	weekday	しろ	white
	こんでいます	be crowded	こちら	here (where I am)		
	こみます	become crowded	コーラ	cola		

READING TASK

おにぎり　プロジェクト

　ジョン・ミルズさんは　ＡＢＣフーズの　しゃいんです。ミルズさんは　日本の　たべものが　だいすきですが、その　なかで　おにぎりが　いちばん　すきです。かいがいでは　おにぎりより　おすしの　ほうが　ゆうめいです。ＡＢＣフーズは　かいがいむけの　おにぎりの　かいはつプロジェクトを　つくりました。ミルズさんは　その　プロジェクトの　チーフです。

Answer the following questions:

　1) ミルズさんは　日本の　たべものの　なかで　何が　いちばん　すきですか。
　2) かいがいでは　おにぎりと　おすしと　どちらが　ゆうめいですか。
　3) ＡＢＣフーズは　どんな　プロジェクトを　つくりましたか。
　4) その　プロジェクトの　チーフは　だれですか。

VOCABULARY

しゃいん	company employee
たべもの	food
だいすき（な）	like very much
おにぎり	rice ball
かいがい	overseas
（お）すし	sushi
〜むけ	geared toward, for (suffix)
かいはつ	development

KANJI PRACTICE

来	来ます き 来週 らいしゅう	二	仁	厂	平	平	来	来
come		来	来					

週	来週 らいしゅう	リ	刀	月	円	用	周	周
week		周	周	调	週	週	週	

行	行きます い *銀行 ぎんこう	ク	タ	彳	行	行	行	行
go		行						

今	今 いま 今週 こんしゅう 今年 ことし	ク	八	今	今	今	今	
now								

年	年 ねん 今年 ことし 来年 らいねん	ク	仁	气	仁	年	年	年
year		年						

何	何 なに 何年 なんねん	�ノ	イ	广	仟	何	何	何
what		何	何					

人	人 ひと 何人 なんにん カナダ人 じん	ノ	人	人	人			
person								

気	人気 にんき	�ノ	广	气	气	気	気	気
spirit mind		気						

一	一つ ひと 一 いち	一	一	一				
one								

二	二つ ふた 二 に	二	二	二				
two								

三	三つ みっ 三 さん	一	三	三	三	三		
three								

四	四つ よっ 四十 よんじゅう 四 よん／し	丨	冂	四	四	四	四	四
four								

五	五つ いつ 五 ご	一	丆	万	五	五	五	
five								

六	六つ むっ 六 ろく	丶	亠	六	六	六	六	
six								

七	七つ なな 七 なな／しち	一	七	七	七			
seven								

八	八つ やっ 八 はち	ノ	八	八	八			
eight								

九	九つ ここの 九 きゅう／く	ノ	九	九	九			
nine								

十	十 とお 十 じゅう	一	十	十	十			
ten								

百	二 百 に ひゃく 三 百 さんびゃく 六 百 ろっぴゃく	一	一丁	丆	万	百	百	百
hundred		百						

千	二千 に せん 三千 さんぜん 八千 はっせん	ン	二	千	千	千		
thousand								

TARGET DIALOGUE

Mr. Mills is looking for a yukata at a kimono shop.

店員：　いらっしゃいませ。

ミルズ：ゆかたを　かいたいん
　　　　→p. 20
　　　　ですが。

店員：　プレゼントですか。

ミルズ：はい、いもうとに。

店員：　こちらは　いかがですか。

ミルズ：あのう、もっと　大きいのは　ありませんか。いもうとは　私
　　　　　　　　　　　　おお　　　　　　　　　　　　　　→p. 21　　　　　わたし

　　　　より　せが　高いんです。このぐらいです。
　　　　　　　　　　たか

店員：　ああ、大きい　かたですね。こちらが　いちばん　大きい　サイ
　　　　　　　　おお　　　　　　　　　　　　　　　　　　　　おお

　　　　ズです。

ミルズ：じゃ、それに　します。プレゼント用に　つつんでください。
　　　　　　→p. 23　　　　　　　　　　　　よう

salesperson: May I help you?
Mills: 　　　I'd like to buy a yukata.
salesperson: Is it a present?
Mills: 　　　Yes, for my younger sister.
salesperson: How about this one?
Mills: 　　　Uh, do you have a bigger one? My younger sister is taller than me, you see. About like this.
salesperson: Oh, she's a tall person. This here is our largest size.
Mills: 　　　Well then, I'll take it. Please wrap it up as a present.

VOCABULARY

店員 てんいん	salesperson, clerk	このぐらい	about like this
かいたいんですが	I would like to buy . . .	ああ	oh, I see
こちら	this, this one (here) (polite)	かた	person (polite form)
あのう	uh . . . , hmm . . .	サイズ	size
もっと	more	それに　します	I will take that one
～の	(particle; see Note 3 below)	プレゼント用 よう	for use as a present
せが　高い たか	tall	～用 よう	for use as
せ	height, stature	つつみます	wrap
高い たか	tall, high		

NOTES

1. 「プレゼントですか」「はい、いもうとに」
   You can omit certain parts of a sentence if the meaning is clear without them. Here ゆかたは is dropped from both the question and the answer, and the verb おくります, "to send," or あげます, "to give," is omitted from the answer, leaving only いもうとに, "for my younger sister." Japanese people often use sentence fragments like these when asking and answering questions.

2. あのう
   You use あのう when hesitating before speaking. Here Mr. Mills uses it to soften his request for a larger yukata in response to the salesperson's recommendation, "How about this one?"

3. もっと　大 (おお) きいのは　ありませんか。
   The particle の in this case functions as a noun modified by 大 (おお) きい. Thus, もっと　大 (おお) きいの means "a bigger one."

4. いもうとは　私 (わたし) より　せが　高 (たか) いんです。
   せ means "height" or "stature." The sentence いもうとは せが 高 (たか) いです means "My sister is tall in stature" and is a neutral, matter-of-fact statement. But notice that Mr. Mills uses んです here instead of です. This makes it clear that he is trying to explain something or make a point. The point he is trying to make, of course, is that he needs a larger yukata. For other basic usages of んです, see Unit 2, Lesson 4, p. 57.

5. このぐらいです。
   Mr. Mills uses this expression while indicating his sister's height with his hand.

6. 大 (おお) きい　かた
   かた, "person," is a politer form of 人 (ひと). Salespeople use polite language when talking to customers, or when talking about people or things connected with them. 大 (おお) きい, which ordinarily means "large," also can mean "tall."

7. (それを) プレゼント用 (よう) に　つつんでください。
   プレゼント + 用 (よう) means "for use as a present." Literally, then, Mr. Mills is saying, "Please wrap it up as a present." Other noun + 用 (よう) combinations include こども用 (よう), "for children," 大人用 (おとなよう), "for adults," and so on.

GRAMMAR & PATTERN PRACTICE

Ⅰ Getting Information or Advice: "I'd Like to . . . But . . . ?"

The phrase かいたいです means "I want to buy." If you use たいんですが instead of たいです, the implication is that you would like information or advice from the other party. You use かいたいんですが in a store, for example, to imply that you are about to make a request, such as asking where an item can be found. かいたいんですが and other たいんですが sentences often conclude with an expression you learned in Lesson 1: 何（なに）が いいでしょうか.

おみやげを　かいたいんですが、何が　いいでしょうか。
なに

I'd like to buy a souvenir, but what would be a good one?

Construct sentences as in the examples.

例1）　えいがを　みます、何
れい　　　　　　　　　　　　なに
　　　→ えいがを　みたいんですが、何が　いいでしょうか。
　　　　　　　　　　　　　　　　　　なに

　1）　おんせんに　行きます、どこ
　　　　　　　　　い
　　　→ ....

　2）　プロジェクトの　かいぎを　します、いつ
　　　→ ....

例2）　おみやげを　かいます、　おかし、えはがき、どちらが　いい
れい
　　　→ おみやげを　かいたいんですが、おかしと　えはがきと　どちらが
　　　　いいでしょうか。

　3）　くうこうに　行きます、でんしゃ、タクシー、どちらが　はやい
　　　　　　　　　い
　　　→ ....
　　　　..

　4）　あたらしい　けいたいを　かいます、Aしゃ、Bしゃ、どちらが　べんり
　　　→ ....
　　　　..

VOCABULARY

はやい　　　　　　　　fast

Aしゃ　　　　　　　　Company A (The names of Japanese companies often end in しゃ, "company.")

▌▌ Making Comparisons (3): Singling Out an Item for Comparison

In Lesson 1 you learned the patterns の ほうが . . . より (to form the comparative degree) and （の なか）で . . . が いちばん (to form the superlative degree). Here we revisit these same basic patterns but with the topic marker は coming before them. By using は, you single out a person or thing as the topic of the sentence.

ゆかたは　きものより　安いです。

Yukata are cheaper than kimono.

Aホテルは　東京で　いちばん　ゆうめいです。

Hotel A is the most famous in Tokyo.

¥10,000　　¥300,000

---

1 Pretending you are Mr. Mills, construct sentences in which you compare your younger sister to yourself. Say that your sister is in various ways superior to you, as in the example.

例）せが　高いです。

→ いもうとは　私より　<u>せが　高いです</u>。

1) ゴルフが　じょうずです。

→ ....

2) よく　べんきょうします。

→ ....

3) ともだちが　おおいです。

→ ....

4) たくさん　ほんを　よみます。

→ ....

---

2 Construct sentences comparing Hotel A and Hotel B. Stay that Hotel A is better than Hotel B in some respect.

例）きれい
_{れい}
　　→ Aホテルは　Bホテルより　きれいです。

1）しずか

　　→ ....

2）へやが　ひろい

　　→ ....

3）サービスが　いい

　　→ ....

4）えきから　ちかい

　　→ ....

5）チェックインが　かんたん

　　→ ....

Aホテル

Bホテル

3 Construct sentences stating that Hotel A is "the most" or "the ——est" in Tokyo, as in the example.

例）ゆうめい
_{れい}
　　→ Aホテルは　東京で　いちばん　ゆうめいです。
　　　　　　　　_{とうきょう}

1）あたらしい

　　→ ....

2）人気が　あります
　　_{にんき}
　　→ ....

3）がいこくじんの　おきゃくさんが　おおいです

　　→ ....

4）べんりな　ところに　あります

　　→ ....

VOCABULARY			
ひろい	spacious	がいこくじん	foreigner
サービス	service	がいこく	foreign country
チェックイン	check-in		
かんたん（な）	simple		

USAGE NOTE

The word もっと also expresses the comparative degree. For example, もっと 大（おお）きい means "bigger."

もっと 大きいのは ありませんか。
<small>おお</small>
Do you have a bigger one?

To state or ask how much bigger, you use other words.

ワンサイズ 大きいのは ありませんか。
<small>おお</small>
Do you have one that is a size bigger?

もっと is not needed before the adjective or adverb that follows より in a sentence of the のほうが . . . より type (see Lesson 1, p. 6) as it makes the sentence sound redundant.

III Stating Decisions

You use に します after a noun to state your decision when choosing something from among several available alternatives. Be careful not to confuse this phrase with が いいです, which indicates preference (see Lesson 1, p. 5).

Q：デザートは どれに しますか。

A：アイスクリームに します。

Q: Which one of the desserts will you have?
A: I'll have the ice cream.

Make up questions and answers as in the example.

例）たんじょうびの プレゼント、コーヒーカップ
<small>れい</small>
　→Q：たんじょうびの プレゼントは 何に しましたか。
<small>なに</small>
　　A：コーヒーカップに しました。

1) おくさんの おみやげ、ネックレス
　→Q：...
　　A：...

2) かいぎの ひ、げつようび
　→Q：...
　　A：...

PRACTICE 1

WORD POWER

Adjectives:

① 高い
　たか

② ひくい

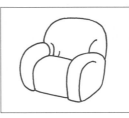

③ やわらかい

④ かたい

⑤ ふとい

⑥ ほそい

⑦ ながい

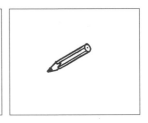

⑧ みじかい

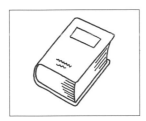

⑨ あつい

⑩ うすい

⑪ かるい

⑫ おもい

⑬ はでな

⑭ じみな

⑮ かわいい

⑯ シンプルな

VOCABULARY

ひくい	low, short	ながい	long	おもい	heavy
やわらかい	soft	みじかい	short	はで (な)	colorful, gaudy
かたい	hard	あつい	thick	じみ (な)	plain, subdued
ふとい	wide	うすい	thin (of cloth, paper, etc.)	かわいい	cute
ほそい	thin, narrow	かるい	light, lightweight	シンプル (な)	simple

14

SPEAKING PRACTICE

I. Trying on clothes in a store:

きゃく：　これ、きてみても　いいですか。

店員：　はい、しちゃくしつは　あちらです。
てんいん

．．．．．．．．．．．．．．．．

店員：　いかがですか。

きゃく：　もう　すこし　小さいのは　ありませんか。
　　　　　　　　　　　　　ちい

店員：　もうしわけございませんが、これが　いちばん　小さい　サイズです。
てんいん　　　　　　　　　　　　　　　　　　　　　　　　　　ちい

きゃく：　そうですか。じゃ　いいです。

customer:　May I try this on?
salesperson: Yes, the fitting room is over there.
・・・・・・
salesperson: How is it?
customer:　Do you have a slightly smaller one?
salesperson: I'm very sorry, but this is the smallest size.
customer:　Oh. Never mind, then.

II. Asking for the same garment in another size:

きゃく：　これと　おなじ　いろの　Mサイズは　ありませんか。

店員：　Mサイズは　うりきれです。来週　はいります。
てんいん　　　　　　　　　　　　　　　　らいしゅう

きゃく：　じゃ、来週　また　来ます。
　　　　　　らいしゅう　　　き

customer:　Do you have the same color as this in a medium?
salesperson: I'm very sorry. The mediums are sold out. They'll be coming in next week.
customer:　Well then, I'll come back next week.

III. Buying a computer:

きゃく：　もう　すこし　ディスプレイが　大きいのは　ありませんか。
　　　　　　　　　　　　　　　　　　　　　おお

店員：　では　こちらは　いかがですか。
てんいん

きゃく：　ああ　いいですね。　じゃ、これ、おねがいします。

店員：　おしはらいは　げんきんですか、クレジットカードですか。

きゃく：　カードで　おねがいします。

customer:　Do you have one with a slightly larger display?
salesperson: In that case, how about this one?
customer:　Oh, this one is fine. I'll take this one.
salesperson: Will you be paying in cash or with a credit card?
customer:　With a credit card.

VOCABULARY					
しちゃくしつ	fitting room	うりきれ	sold out	げんきん	cash
いいです	never mind	はいります	go/come in, enter	クレジットカード	credit card
おなじ	same	ディスプレイ	display		
Mサイズ	medium (size)	（お）しはらい	payment		

PRACTICE 2

WORD POWER

I. Family:

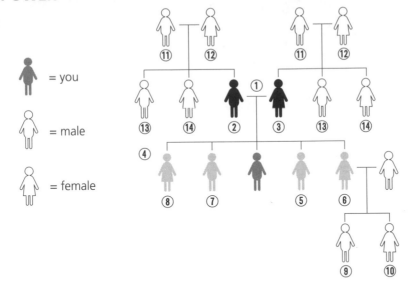

= you

= male

= female

① りょうしん（ごりょうしん）　② 父（お父さん）　　　　③ 母（お母さん）
④ きょうだい（ごきょうだい）　⑤ あに（おにいさん）　　⑥ あね（おねえさん）
⑦ おとうと（おとうとさん）　　⑧ いもうと（いもうとさん）⑨ おい（おいごさん）
⑩ めい（めいごさん）　　　　　⑪ そふ（おじいさん）　　⑫ そぼ（おばあさん）
⑬ おじ（おじさん）　　　　　　⑭ おば（おばさん）

NOTE: The words in parentheses are used primarily to refer to family members or relatives of other people. Do not use them when talking to other people about your own family.

II. Colleagues:

① どうりょう
② じょうし
③ ぶか
④ アシスタント

III. Others:

① マンションの　かんり人
② となりの　人
③ 日本ごの　せんせい

VOCABULARY					
りょうしん	parents	そぼ	grandmother	ぶか	junior staff
きょうだい	siblings, brothers and sisters	おじ	uncle	アシスタント	assistant
おい	nephew	おば	aunt	マンションの　かんりにん	apartment manager
めい	niece	どうりょう	colleague	となりの　ひと	next-door neighbor
そふ	grandfather	じょうし	superior	せんせい	teacher

SPEAKING PRACTICE

I. Showing photographs of family to colleagues:

私の　りょうしんです。バンクーバーの　こうがいに　すんでいます。父は
ぎんこうに　つとめていましたが、きょねん　しごとを　やめて　今　うちに
います。まいにち　つりや　ガーデニングを　しています。母は　りょうりを
おしえています。母の　レシピは　とても　人気が　あります。今は　父より
いそがしいです。

私の　きょうだいです。あねの　ダイアナと　いもうとの　アンです。二人とも
とても　せが　高いです。いもうとは　私より　せが　高いですが、あねより
ひくいです。あねは　きょうだいの　なかで　いちばん　せが　高いです。あねは
バスケットボールせんしゅです。いもうとは　モデルです。

(These are) my parents. They live in the suburbs of Vancouver. My dad worked in a bank, but last year he quit his job and now he is at home. Everyday, he goes fishing or does the gardening. My mom teaches cooking. My mom's recipes are very popular. These days she is busier than my dad.

(These are) my sisters. My older sister Diana and my younger sister Anne. They are both very tall. My younger sister is taller than me but shorter than my older sister. My older sister is the tallest among us. My older sister is a basketball player. My younger sister is a model.

バンクーバー	Vancouver	ガーデニング	gardening	ふたりとも	both of them
こうがい	suburbs	レシピ	recipe	バスケットボールせんしゅ	basketball player
やめます (R2)	quit	ダイアナ	Diana	せんしゅ	player, athlete
つり	fishing	アン	Anne	モデル	model

II. Choosing a souvenir for one's father:

ガイド：おみやげですか。

ミルズ：ええ、父に。はなの　えはがきを　かいたいんですが。

ガイド：これは　いかがですか。北海道の　しきの　はなです。

ミルズ：ああ、いいですね。これに　します。

guide:	Are you looking for a souvenir?
Mills:	Yes, for my father. I'd like to buy postcards of flowers.
guide:	How about these? The flowers of Hokkaido in the four seasons.
Mills:	Oh, these are nice, aren't they? I'll take these.

III. Choosing a souvenir for one's mother:

ミルズ：母に　日本りょうりの　レシピを　かいたいんですが、どこに
　　　　ありますか。

店員：　これは　いかがですか。えいごの　日本りょうりの　ほんです。

ミルズ：あついですね。うわあ、おもいです。もっと　うすいのは　ありませんか。

店員：　では、この　日本りょうりしょうかいの　ＤＶＤは　いかがですか。か
　　　　るいですよ。

ミルズ：ああ、これは　いいです。これを　ください。

Mills:	I'd like to buy some Japanese recipes for my mother. Where can I find them?
salesperson:	How about this? It's an English-language book about Japanese cuisine.
Mills:	It's thick, isn't it? Wow, it's heavy! Do you have a thinner one?
salesperson:	Well, how about this DVD that presents Japanese cuisine? It's lightweight.
Mills:	Oh, this is nice. I'll take this.

VOCABULARY	しき	the four seasons
	うわあ	wow
	～しょうかい	that presents

READING TASK

ミルズさんの　あたらしい　パソコン

　ミルズさんは　せんしゅう　秋葉原に　行って　あたらしい　パソコンを
かいました。その　パソコンは　スクリーンが　とても　大きいですが、ふ
るい　パソコンより　かるいです。ミルズさんは　しゅうまつに　パソコン
で　DVDを　みました。パソコンの　スクリーンは　テレビより　いろが
きれいでした。ミルズさんは　レンタルショップに　行って　DVDを　た
くさん　かりました。

Answer the following questions:

1) ミルズさんは　どこで　パソコンを　かいましたか。
2) ミルズさんは　しゅうまつに　何を　しましたか。
3) パソコンの　スクリーンと　テレビの　スクリーンと　どちらが　いろが
　　きれいでしたか。
4) ミルズさんは　レンタルショップで　何を　かりましたか。

VOCABULARY

秋葉原	Akihabara (district in Tokyo)
スクリーン	screen
レンタルショップ	rental shop
かります	borrow, rent

KANJI PRACTICE

大	大きい おお 大学 だいがく 大人 おとな	一	ナ	大	大	大		
big								

小	小さい ちい 小学校 しょうがっこう	亅	刂	小	小	小		
small								

私	私 わたし	一	二	千	禾	禾	私	私
I **private**		私	私					

高	高い たか 高校 こうこう	亠	亠	宀	宀	宁	宁	高
tall **expensive**		高	高	高	高	高		

安	安い やす	丷	丷	宀	宀	安	安	安
cheap		安						

用	〜用 よう	リ	冂	月	月	用	用	用
for								

店	店 みせ 店員 てんいん	丶	亠	广	庁	庐	庐	店
shop		店	店	店				

員	店員 てんいん	丶	冂	口	尸	吊	目	目
member		員	員	員	員	員		

父	父 ちち お父さん とう	ク	バ	父	父	父	父	
father								

母	母 はは お母さん かあ	乚	乜	母	母	母	母	母
mother								

SEARCHING FOR A LOST ITEM

TARGET DIALOGUE

Mr. Mills realizes that he has left a bag of chocolates at the store where he was shopping, so he rings up the store to see if it is still there.

店員：　　(answering the phone) はい。「えどや」でございます。
てんいん

ミルズ：すみません。３０分ぐらい
　　　　　さんじゅっぷん

　　　　前に　そちらに　かみぶくろを
　　　　まえ

　　　　わすれました。

店員：　どんな　ふくろでしょうか。

ミルズ：白くて　大きい　かみぶくろで、中に　チョコレートが　いく
　　　　しろ　　　おお　→pp. 34–37　　　なか

　　　　つか　入っています。レジの　あたりに　ありませんか。
　　　　　　はい

店員：　のぞみデパートの　ふくろでしょうか。

ミルズ：はい、そうです。　ああ、よかった！　今から　とりに　行き
　　　　　　　　　　　　　　　　　　　　　　いま　→p. 38　　　　い

　　　　ます。

…………………

ミルズ：ありがとうございました。

店員：　この　チョコレート、きれいで　おもしろい　パッケージですね。

ミルズ：ＡＢＣフーズの　しんしょうひんです。一つ　どうぞ。
　　　　　　　　　　　　　　　　　　　　　　ひと

salesperson: Yes, this is Edoya.
Mills:　　　Excuse me, but about thirty minutes ago, I left (lit. "forgot") a paper bag at your store.
salesperson: What kind of bag might it be?
Mills:　　　It's a large, white paper bag, and inside it there are several boxes of chocolates. Is it not near the cash register?
salesperson: Is it a bag from Nozomi Department Store?
Mills:　　　Yes, it is! Oh, good! I'll come and get it right away.
. . . . . .
Mills:　　　Thank you.
salesperson: These chocolates are in a pretty, interesting package, aren't they?
Mills:　　　It's a new product of ABC Foods. Please have a box.

VOCABULARY

えどや	Edoya (fictitious store)
前に	before
かみぶくろ	paper bag
かみ	paper
ふくろ	sack, bag
わすれます	forget, leave behind
いくつか	some, a number of, several
入っています	be in/inside
レジ	cash register
～の　あたり	near, in the general area of
あたり	general area

～でしょうか	might it be?
ああ、よかった	oh, good! (speaking to oneself)
今から	from now, right away
とりに　行きます	come and get (lit., "go to get")
とります	take, get
パッケージ	package
しんしょうひん	new product
しん～	new (prefix)

NOTES

1. そちらに　かみぶくろを　わすれました。
You use そちら to mean "there (where you are)" when speaking over the telephone to a person with whom you are not particularly close. The particle に as used in this sentence indicates the location where Mr. Mills left his bag.

2. どんな　ふくろでしょうか。
A sentence ending with ですか is a straightforward question, while one ending with でしょうか is less direct and softer-sounding.

3. レジの　あたり
あたり, "in the general area," is a vague way of indicating a location when you do not remember it exactly. Its meaning is similar to that of ちかく, which you learned in Book I, but ちかく, literally meaning "vicinity," emphasizes that the location in question is nearby.

4. この　チョコレート、きれいで　おもしろい　パッケージですね。
Here the salesperson has omitted the topic marker は after チョコレート. Often in everyday speech you leave out は and go straight into your comment about the topic.

GRAMMAR & PATTERN PRACTICE

I Connecting Related Sentences

The particle で after a noun can serve as a conjunction equivalent in meaning to the -te form. You use it to connect a sentence ending in です to another, related sentence. You can connect two sentences in this way even when they have different subjects or topics, as in:

ミルズさんは　カナダ人で、加藤さんは　日本人です。

Mr. Mills is a Canadian and Mr. Kato is a Japanese.

or:　（わすれものは）　白い　かみぶくろで、中に　チョコレートが　入っています。

It's a white paper bag, and inside it there are chocolates.

---

1 Construct sentences as in the example.

例）アナさんは　スイス人です。（アナさんは）渋谷に　すんでいます。
　　→　<u>アナさんは　スイス人で、渋谷に　すんでいます。</u>

1) 佐藤さんはべんごしです。（佐藤さんは）ミルズさんの　ともだち　です。
　　→　..

2) これは　いちばん　大きい　サイズです。（これは）いちばん　高いです。
　　→　..

3) アナさんは　スイス人です。ミルズさんは　カナダ人です。
　　→　..

4) こちらは　中国の　おかしです。そちらは　日本の　おかしです。
　　→　..

VOCABULARY　　わすれもの　　thing left behind
　　　　　　　　　アナ　　　　　Anna

The -te (or -de) form of an adjective, too, can act as a conjunction. For -i adjectives, you get the -te form by dropping the final い from the modifying form and adding くて, e.g.:

白い　→　白くて
しろ　　　しろ
white　→　white and . . .

For -na adjectives, you drop な from the modifying form and add で.

べんりな　→　べんりで

convenient　→　convenient and . . .

Examples:

この　かみぶくろは　白くて　大きいです。
しろ　　　おお
This paper bag is white and big.

ちかてつは　べんりで　安いです。
やす
The subways are convenient and cheap.

You connect two or more adjectives with the -te form when they are both/all either positive in meaning or negative. When you want to connect a positive adjective with a negative one, as in the following example, you have to use the particle が.

この　ケーキは　おいしいですが　高いです。
たか
This cake is delicious but expensive.

---

2 Complete the sentences as in the example.

例）かるい、うすい
れい
　　→ この　けいたいは　かるくて　うすいです。

1) あたらしい、きれい
　　→ この　けいたいは ....

2) べんり、安い
やす
　　→ この　けいたいは ....

3) きれい、人気が　ありません
にんき
　　→ この　けいたいは ....

II   Describing Ongoing Actions or States in Effect

The -*te imasu* form of a verb indicates an ongoing action, e.g.,

水を　のんでいます。
みず
I am drinking water.

or a state that is in effect, e.g.,

コートを　きています。

I am wearing a coat.

The precise meaning—ongoing action or state in effect—depends on the meaning of the verb. If the verb expresses a process—for example, "to drink"—then -*te imasu* with that verb will typically indicate an ongoing action. If, on the other hand, the verb describes something that happens more or less instantaneously—"put on a coat," for instance—the meaning of -*te imasu* will be that the action has been completed and a state is in effect as a result.

ネクタイを　しています。

I am wearing a tie.

ぼうしを　かぶっています。

I am wearing a hat.

くろい　くつを　はいています。

I am wearing black shoes.

かさと　しんぶんを　もっています。

I am carrying an umbrella and a newspaper.

たっています。

I am standing.

すわっています。

I am sitting.

エレベーターに　のっています。

I am riding in an elevator.

VOCABULARY

（ネクタイを）します	put on (a necktie)
かぶります	put on (a hat)
すわります	sit

Two highly frequent verbs that well exemplify the "state in effect" meaning of -te imasu are 入（は
い）ります, "to go inside," and つきます, "to attach to," "to come with."

グラスに　ワインが　入っています。
はい

Wine is in the glass.

バッグに　はなが　ついています。

A flower is attached to the bag.

Describe the pictures below by using the appropriate verb.

1) はこに ....

2) きんこに ....

3) キャビネットに ....

4) かばんに ....

5) スーツケースに ....

6) シャツに ....

7) サンドイッチに ....

8) アパートに ....

1) ネクタイ　　　2) お金　　　3) しょるい　　　4) Nothing
かね

5) なふだ　　　6) ポケット　　　7) フライドポテト　8) バルコニー

VOCABULARY					
グラス	glass	キャビネット	cabinet	なふだ	tag
バッグ	bag	スーツケース	suitcase	フライドポテト	french fry
つきます	attach (to), come with	シャツ	shirt	バルコニー	balcony
はこ	box	アパート	apartment		
きんこ	safe	しょるい	document		37

III "Going Somewhere to Do Something"

You use the -*masu* stem of a verb, followed by に 行 (い) きます, に 来 (き) ます, or に かえり ます, to express the idea of "coming," "going," or "returning" to do something.

今から　とりに　行きます。
_{いま}　　　　　　_い
I'll come and get it right away.

Note that although the verb in this sentence is 行 (い) きます, "to go," in natural English you usually say "come" if you are imagining yourself to be where the other person is.

---

1 Change the sentences as in the example.

例)　ひるごはんを　たべます。　→　<u>ひるごはんを　たべに　行きます。</u>
_{れい}　　　　　　　　　　　　　　　　　　　　　　　　　　　　_い

1) えいがを　みます。　　　→　..

2) ビールを　のみます。　　→　..

3) おべんとうを　かいます。　→　..

2 Read the following sentences aloud while considering their meanings, and repeat them until you have memorized them.

1) 何か　たべに　行きませんか。
　_{なに}

2) こんど　うちに　あそびに　来てください。
　　　　　　　　　　　　　　　_き

3) ゆうびんきょくに　きってを　かいに　行きます。
　　　　　　　　　　　　　　　　　　　_い

4) ゆうびんきょくに　にもつを　とりに　行きます。
　　　　　　　　　　　　　　　　　　　_い

5) うちに　わすれものを　とりに　かえります。

VOCABULARY

（お）べんとう	box lunch
こんど	next time
あそびます	visit (lit., "play")

PRACTICE 1

WORD POWER

I. Belongings:

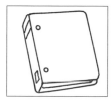   

① めがね　② さいふ　③ かさ　④ スーツケース　⑤ てぶくろ

⑥ しょるい　⑦ マフラー　⑧ かばん　⑨ コート　⑩ カメラ
　 ぶくろ

⑪ ファイル　⑫ うでどけい　⑬ てちょう　⑭ けいたい　⑮ かぎ

II. Materials:

① プラスチック　　④ かみ
② かわ　　　　　　⑤ ウール
③ ビニール　　　　⑥ ナイロン

III. Locations:

① テーブルの　うえ　　④ デスクの　後ろ
② ひきだしの　中　　　⑤ ほんだなの　前
③ いすの　した　　　　⑥ にわの　いすの　あたり

VOCABULARY					
めがね	glasses	プラスチック	plastic	デスク	desk
てぶくろ	glove	かわ	leather	ほんだな	bookshelf
しょるいぶくろ	document envelope	ビニール	vinyl		
マフラー	scarf	ウール	wool		
うでどけい	wristwatch	ナイロン	nylon		

SPEAKING PRACTICE

I. On the telephone with a taxi company's lost and found office:

中村：　　　　　　　すみません。タクシーに　くろい　かわの　コート
なかむら　　　　　　を　わすれました。

タクシーがいしゃの　人：なんじごろに　どこから　どこまで　のりましたか。
ひと

中村：　　　　　　　けさ　９じごろ　渋谷で　のって　六本木で　おり
しぶや　　　　　　　ろっぽんぎ
ました。

タクシーがいしゃの　人：しょうしょう　おまちください。

Nakamura:　　　　　　　　　　　Excuse me. I left a black leather coat in a cab.
person from the taxi company: About what time did you ride with us, and from where to where?
Nakamura:　　　　　　　　　　　This morning at about nine o'clock I got on in Shibuya and got off
in Roppongi.
person from the taxi company: Please wait a moment.

II. In a coffee shop, asking whether one's forgotten umbrella has turned up:

ミルズ：　すみません。こちらに　かさの　わすれものが　ありませんでしたか。
店の　人：どんな　かさですか。
みせ　ひと
ミルズ：　あおい　おりたたみの　かさで、Mの　マークが　ついています。
さっき　まどの　ちかくの　せきに　すわりました。いすの　したに
ありませんか。
店の　人：おまちください。
・・・・・・・・・・・・・・・・・
店の　人：すみません。さがしましたが、ございません。
ミルズ：　そうですか。どうも。

Mills:　　　　Excuse me. Was an umbrella left behind here?
shopkeeper:　What kind of umbrella?
Mills:　　　　It was a blue folding umbrella marked with the letter *M*. Just a while ago I was sitting
in a seat near the window. Is it under the chair?
shopkeeper:　Please wait.
・・・・・・
shopkeeper:　I'm sorry. I looked for it, but it isn't there.
Mills:　　　　Oh. Thank you.

VOCABULARY		
けさ	this morning	ございません　　it is not there (polite form)
しょうしょう	a little (polite form)	
おまちください	please wait (polite form)	
おりたたみ	fold-up, folding	
マーク	mark	
さっき	just now, only a moment ago	
せき	seat	

PRACTICE 2

WORD POWER

I. Parts of the body:

① くび
② うで
③ むね
④ ひじ
⑤ ウエスト
⑥ ひざ

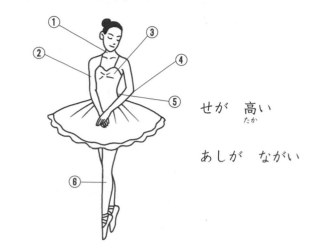

せが　高い
たか

あしが　ながい

II. Parts of the face:

① かみ（のけ）
② ひたい
③ まゆ（げ）
④ はな
⑤ ほお
⑥ ひげ
⑦ みみ
⑧ くち

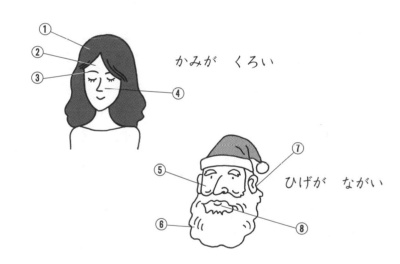

かみが　くろい

ひげが　ながい

II. Personalities:

① あかるい
② つめたい
③ やさしい
④ げんきな
⑤ おとなしい

⑥ まじめな
⑦ おもしろい
⑧ がんこな
⑨ きびしい
⑩ いじわるな

VOCABULARY					
くび	neck	まゆ（げ）	eyebrow	やさしい	gentle, kind
うで	arm	はな	nose	げんき（な）	energetic
むね	chest, breast	ほお	cheek	おとなしい	mild-mannered
ひじ	elbow	ひげ	beard, mustache	まじめ（な）	serious
ウエスト	waist	みみ	ear	がんこ（な）	stubborn
ひざ	knee	くち	mouth	きびしい	strict
かみ（のけ）	hair	あかるい	cheerful	いじわる（な）	mean
ひたい	forehead	つめたい	cold		

41

SPEAKING PRACTICE

I. Talking about a famous person one saw:

中村：　きのう　くうこうで　ゆうめいな　人を　みました。
ミルズ：えっ、だれですか。
中村：　ええと、ええと、ブラジルの　サッカーせんしゅで、めが　大きくて、
　　　　かみが　ながくて……。
ミルズ：わかった。ロナウ、ロナウ何とか。
中村：　そう　そう、その　人です。

Nakamura: Yesterday I saw a famous person at the airport.
Mills:　　Oh? Who?
Nakamura: Uh . . . uh . . . He's a Brazilian soccer player with big eyes and long hair . . .
Mills:　　I know! Ronal, Ronal something or other.
Nakamura: Right! That guy!

II. Talking about an apartment one found:

中村：　やっと　いい　アパートが　みつかりました。
ミルズ：どんな　アパートですか。
中村：　あまり　ひろくないですが、あたらしくて　えきから　ちかくて　小
　　　　さな　テラスが　ついています。こんど　あそびに　来てください。

Nakamura: I finally found a good apartment.
Mills:　　What kind of apartment?
Nakamura: It's not very spacious, but it's new, close to the station, and has a small terrace attached.
　　　　　Please come and visit sometime.

VOCABULARY	えっ	really?	なんとか	something or other	ちいさな	small
	ええと	hmm . . . , uh . . .	そう　そう	that is right	テラス	terrace
	サッカーせんしゅ	soccer player	やっと	at last, finally		

READING TASK

かいぎしつの　わすれもの

　　ミルズさんは　きのう　5じから　かいぎしつで　のぞみデパートの　高橋さんと　しんしょうひんの　PRについて　かいぎを　しました。かいぎは　6じはんに　おわりました。ミルズさんは　かいぎしつの　つくえの　うえに　めがねと　てちょうを　わすれて、1かいの　ロビーに　おきゃくさんを　おくりに　行きました。けさ　かいぎしつに　とりに　行きましたが、ありませんでした。ミルズさんの　めがねは　フレームが　くろくて　かるい　プラスチックです。てちょうは　ちゃいろの　かわの　システムてちょうです。

Answer the following questions:

1) ミルズさんは　きのう　5じから　何を　しましたか。
2) ミルズさんは　かいぎしつに　何を　わすれましたか。
3) ミルズさんは　1かいの　ロビーに　だれを　おくりに　行きましたか。
4) ミルズさんの　めがねは　どんな　めがねですか。
5) ミルズさんの　てちょうは　どんな　てちょうですか。

VOCABULARY

～について	about, concerning
おわります	end, finish
つくえ	table
おくりに　行きます	see (someone) off
おくります	send
フレーム	frame
ちゃいろ	brown
システムてちょう	system notebook

KANJI PRACTICE

分	～分 ふん/ぶん 気分 きぶん 分けます わ	ク	八	分	分	分	分	
minute **part**								

前	前 まえ 前 ぜん 午 ご	丶	✗	丷	广	芀	首	首
		前	前	前	前			
front **before**								

後	後 ろ 後 で うし 後 あと 午 ご	ク	㇅	彳	彳	彳	徉	後
		後	後	後	後			
back **after**								

午	前 ぜん 午 ご 後 ご 午 ご	ク	┕	匚	午	午	午	
noon								

白	白 しろ 白 い しろ	ク	亻	白	白	白	白	白
white								

中
なか
午前中
ご ぜん ちゅう
一年中
いち ねん じゅう

in

| ↓| | � | 冂 | 口 | 中 | 中 | 中 | |

入ります
はい
入れます
い
入口
いり ぐち
入学
にゅう がく

enter

| ノ | 入 | 入 | 入 | | | | |

火
ひ
＊火曜日
か よう び

fire

| ↓ | 丶 | ｿ | 少 | 火 | 火 | 火 | |

水
みず
＊水曜日
すい よう び

water

| ↓丨 | 丁 | 水 | 水 | 水 | 水 | | |

お金
かね
＊金曜日
きん よう び

gold
money

| ノ | 人 | 全 | 仐 | 全 | 金 | 金 |
| 金 | 金 | | | | | |

I Fill in the blanks with the appropriate particle.

1) プレゼントは　何（　　　）　いいでしょうか。

2) 一年の　中（　　　）　なんがつが　いちばん　あついですか。

3) いもうとは　私（　　　）　せが　高いです。

4) グラス（　　　）　ワインが　入っています。

5) スーパーに　のみものを　かい（　　　）　行きます。

II Choose the correct word from among the alternatives (1–4) given.

1) A：しゅうまつに　どこか　行きましたか。

　　B：いいえ、（　　　）　行きませんでした。

　　1.どこで　　2.どこに　　3.どこ　　4.どこも

2) A：のみものは　コーヒーと　こうちゃと（　　　）　いいですか。

　　B：コーヒーを　おねがいします。

　　1.どれが　　2.何が　　3.どちらが　　4.何か

3) A：（　　　）　おみやげを　かいませんか。

　　B：そうですね。じゃ、この　おかしを　かいましょう。

　　1.何が　　2.何か　　3.どんな　　4.どう

4) A：すみません。そちらに　かばんを　わすれました。

　　B：（　　　）　かばんですか。

　　1.どんな　　2.どうして　　3.いつ　　4.どこで

5) A：すしと　てんぷらと　すきやきの　中で（　　　）　いちばん　すきですか。

　　B：すしが　いちばん　すきです。

　　1.どれが　　2.どれか　　3.何か　　4.何を

III Change the form of the word given in parentheses to complete the sentence in a way that makes sense.

1) この　カメラは　（　　　　　　　　）、べんりです。(小さいです)

2) さいふの　中に　クレジットカードが　（　　　　　　　）います。(入ります)

3) この　くつを　（　　　　　　　）みても　いいですか。(はきます)

4) Aホテルは　サービスが　（　　　　　　　）えきから　ちかいです。(いいです)

5) 京都に　おてらを　（　　　　　　　）に　行きました。(みます)

IV Choose the most appropriate word or phrase from among the alternatives (1–4) given.

1) この　ノートは　うすいですね。もう　すこし（　　　　）のは　ありませんか。
   1. あつい　　2. おもい　　3. 高い　　4. ながい
   〔たか〕

2) この　コート、（　　　　）みても　いいですか。
   1. して　　2. きて　　3. はいて　　4. かぶって

3) うけつけ：うけつけです。ここに　スミスさんの　めがねが　ありますよ。
   スミス：　ありがとうございます。後で（　　　　）行きます。
   1. おくりに　　2. さがしに　　3. わすれに　　4. とりに
   　　　　　　　　　　　　　　〔あと〕　　　　　　　　　　　　　　〔い〕

4) これを　ください。プレゼント用に（　　　　）ください。
   1. つかって　　2. つつんで　　3. ついて　　4. つくって
   　　　　　　　　　　　　〔よう〕

5) アパートの（　　　　）に　カナダの　おみやげを　あげました。
   1. どうりょう　　2. じょうし　　3. アシスタント　　4. かんり人
   　　　　　　　　　　　　　　　　　　　　　　　　　　　　　〔にん〕

V Fill in the blanks with the correct reading of each kanji.

1) 大きい　りんごは　一つ　　百えんです。
   （　　　）　　　　（　　　）（　　　　）

2) 今年は　　白い　コートが　人気が　　あります。
   （　　　）（　　）　　　　（　　　　）

3) 午後　　　父の　ともだちが　五人　うちに　来ます。
   （　　　）（　　）　　　　　（　　　）　　（　　　）

2

BUILDING RAPPORT WITH COLLEAGUES

The focus of this unit is, as the title suggests, building rapport. One expression commonly used in daily conversation, and useful in building relationships of trust and understanding, is the sentence-ending んです. This ending carries a variety of nuances depending on how it is used and thus is said to be particularly difficult to master. But one learns best by doing, as the old adage goes; so first listen to how んです is used in the dialogues in this unit, and then try out the expression in real conversations with the Japanese people around you.

CLOCKING IN EARLY

TARGET DIALOGUE

It's seven o'clock in the morning. Mr. Mills comes to the office earlier than usual and to his surprise sees Ms. Nakamura there.

ミルズ：はやいですね。毎朝　この　時間に　来るんですか。
　　　　　　　まいあさ →p. 55　　じかん　く

中村：　いいえ。今日は　これから　ヨガを　するんです。
なかむら　 →p. 55　きょう

ミルズ：ヨガ？

中村：　ええ。週に　２回　システム部の　シカさんに　ならっている
　　　　　しゅう →p. 58 かい　　　　　　ぶ

　　　　んです。

ミルズ：ここで　するんですか。

中村：　ええ。この　ヨガ用の　マットを　つかうんです。
　　　　　　　　　　　よう

ミルズ：へえ。

中村：　(sees *Shika Chandra enter the room*) あ、シカさんが　来ました。
　　　　　　　　　　　　　　　　　　　　　　　　　　　　き

ミルズ：じゃ、がんばって。

Mills:　　　You're early, aren't you? Do you come at this time every morning?
Nakamura: No. Today I'm going to do yoga, starting right now.
Mills:　　　Yoga?
Nakamura: Yes. I'm taking lessons twice a week from Shika of the systems department.
Mills:　　　Do you do it here?
Nakamura: Yes, I use this yoga mat.
Mills:　　　Oh, really?
Nakamura: Oh, here's Shika now.
Mills:　　　Well, enjoy yourselves.

VOCABULARY

はやい	early	２回	twice
来る／来ます	come	〜回	times (counter)
これから	starting now	システム部	systems department
ヨガ	yoga	〜部	department
する／します	do	マット	mat
週に	per week	つかう／つかいます	use
週	week	へえ	oh, really?
〜に	per (particle)	がんばる／がんばります	do one's best

NOTES

1. はやいですね。

   This expression means "It's early, isn't it?" You often use it in the morning to start a conversation. Mr. Mills is surprised that Ms. Nakamura is at the office at 7:00 a.m. and is interested in the reason. However, since it would seem a bit abrupt to ask the reason right away, he starts off by commenting about how early it is, thus indicating that he wants to talk to Ms. Nakamura.

2. シカさん

   You usually address a person by their surname followed by さん, though you can sometimes use their given name and さん depending on the person and how well you know them, or depending on the formality of the situation. Here we can assume Ms. Nakamura knows that Shika Chandra prefers to be called by her given name.

3. シカさんに　ならっているんです。

   There are three points to be made about this sentence:

   (1) The particle に, "from," is used with the verb ならいます, "to learn," after the person from whom one receives lessons, in this case Shika.

   (2) ならっている is the plain, present-affirmative form (to be discussed shortly) of ならっています. Here 〜ている denotes a habitual action.

   (3) By using んです, Ms. Nakamura is offering an explanation of why she is doing yoga at the company. (For the basic usages of んです, see p. 57.)

4. へえ。

   Mr. Mills is showing an interest in his colleague's unexpected answer. This is one of those expressions that comes out almost unconsciously. If you say it either with too much emphasis or indifferently, it sounds sarcastic, so be careful.

5. じゃ、がんばって。

   がんばって is a shortened, less formal form of がんばってください, from the verb がんばります, "to do one's best." Traditionally you used this expression to wish people good luck or encourage them. Nowadays, though, you use it more broadly to mean "take it easy" or "enjoy yourself."

PLAIN FORMS OF VERBS

In Book I you learned the -*masu* form with its variations -*masen*, -*mashita*, -*masendeshita*, and -*mashō*. The -*masu* form represents a standard polite speech style, one that anyone can use in almost any situation without sounding rude. In this lesson you will learn about plain forms, which express another, more casual speech style known as the plain style. As the table below shows, there are plain-form equivalents for the -*masu* form and each of its variations.

tense	-*masu* form	plain-form equivalent	
present aff.	かきます	かく	dictionary form
present neg.	かきません	かかない	-*nai* form
past aff.	かきました	かいた	-*ta* form
past neg.	かきませんでした	かかなかった	-*nakatta* form

Plain forms have two functions. One, as already noted, is to express the plain style, which is used in conversations among intimates (to be discussed in Unit 5) as well as in certain forms of writing (to be discussed in Unit 4). The other is to modify elements in a sentence to create a variety of semantic constructions, among them んです presented in this lesson.

As the table shows, plain forms have two tenses, present and past. However, when a plain form is used to modify another word, its tense does not indicate the tense of the entire sentence, nor does it show the politeness level of the utterance, both of which are determined by the form at the end of the sentence.

There are also plain forms for adjectives and nouns + です. You will learn about these in Unit 3, Lesson 8 (p. 121).

GRAMMAR & PATTERN PRACTICE

❶ Plain Forms of Verbs (1): Present-affirmative and Present-negative Tenses

The conjugation table below will help you to understand how to make some of the plain forms from the -*masu* form.

Verbs have basic conjugated forms that are useful to remember (the -*nai* form, the -*masu* form, the dictionary form, the conditional form, and the volitional form). The plain form corresponding to the present-affirmative -*masu* form is the dictionary form, called that because it is the form in which verbs are listed in dictionaries. The plain form of the -*masen* form is the -*nai* form. In this lesson, you will review the verb forms you learned in Book I and also learn how to make the dictionary form. You will learn about the volitional form in Unit 4, Lesson 11, and the conditional form in Unit 5, Lesson 14.

As you learned in Book I, Japanese verbs are divided into three groups based on their patterns of conjugation. The following table shows how Regular I verbs change their stem vowels (*a-i-u-e-o*) in the various conjugations, while the stems of Regular II verbs do not change. There are two verbs that fit into neither the Regular I nor the Regular II group: 来 (く) る (dictionary form of 来 (き) ます) and する (dictionary form of します). These are the Irregular verbs.

	-*nai* form	-*masu* form	dictionary form	conditional form	volitional form
Regular I	あわない	あいます	あう	あえば	あおう
	かかない	かきます	かく	かけば	かこう
	およがない	およぎます	およぐ	およげば	およごう
	けさない	けします	けす	けせば	けそう
	またない	まちます	まつ	まてば	まとう
	しなない	しにます	しぬ	しねば	しのう
	よばない	よびます	よぶ	よべば	よぼう
	のまない	のみます	のむ	のめば	のもう
	かえらない	かえります	かえる	かえれば	かえろう
Regular II	たべない	たべます	たべる	たべれば	たべよう
	あけない	あけます	あける	あければ	あけよう
	みない	みます	みる	みれば	みよう
	おりない	おります	おりる	おりれば	おりよう
Irregular	来(こ)ない	来(き)ます	来(く)る	来(く)れば	来(こ)よう
	しない	します	する	すれば	しよう

NOTE: The -*nai* form of あります (dictionary form ある, a Regular I verb) is ない.

VOCABULARY	およぎます	swim
	しにます	die

Change the verbs to their dictionary and *-nai* forms, as in the example.

例) かきます   → <u>かく</u>   <u>かかない</u>
れい

Regular I

  1) 行きます   → ....
    い

  2) ききます   → ....

  3) ぬぎます   → ....

  4) はなします   → ....

  5) もちます   → ....

  6) あそびます   → ....

  7) よみます   → ....

  8) あります   → ....

  9) のります   → ....

 10) わかります   → ....

 11) かいます   → ....

 12) ならいます   → ....

Regular II (**NOTE:** R2 indicates a Regular II verb in the vocabulary below.)

 13) います   → ....

 14) きます (wear) → ....

 15) あびます   → ....

 16) でます   → ....

 17) しらべます   → ....

 18) とどけます   → ....

 19) みせます   → ....

 20) おしえます   → ....

 21) わすれます   → ....

Irregular

 22) 来ます   → ....
    き

 23) します   → ....

VOCABULARY	ぬぎます	take off (clothes, shoes)	しらべます (R2)	investigate, look into
	はなします	talk, speak		
	あびます (R2)	take (a shower)		

II Asking for and Offering Explanations (1)

You use んですか to ask about another person's circumstances, and んです to make someone else better understand your own. To get a feel for how these constructions are used, let's take a look at the Target Dialogue again.

ミルズ： はやいですね。毎朝 この 時間に 来るんですか。
中村： いいえ。今日は これから ヨガを するんです。

Mills: You're early, aren't you? Do you come at this time every morning?
Nakamura: No. Today I'm going to do yoga, starting right now.

Here the question ending in んですか shows that Mr. Mills wants to know the reason why Ms. Nakamura has come to the office so early. 毎朝（まいあさ）この 時間（じかん）に 来（き）ますか and 毎朝（まいあさ）この 時間（じかん）に 来（く）るんですか both mean "Do you come at this time every morning?" The difference it that the latter is asking not only for a yes or no, but also the reason. ヨガを するんです gives the reason. The following exchange, also from the Target Dialogue, is similar in terms of the speakers' intent.

ミルズ： ヨガ（をするんですか）？
中村： ええ。システム部の シカさんに ならっているんです。
ミルズ： ここで するんですか。
中村： ええ。この ヨガ用の マットを つかうんです。

Mills: Yoga?
Nakamura: Yes. I'm taking lessons twice a week from Shika of the systems department.
Mills: Do you do it here?
Nakamura: Yes, I use this yoga mat.

Be careful about asking questions with んですか all the time, though, since it can sound as if you are prying. Also, try not to overuse んです in answering people. There is no need to use んです when you are just stating facts or telling someone what you saw just as it happened. Even if someone asks you a question with んですか, you do not have to answer with んです unless you feel some special need to explain your situation.

You can use verbs, adjectives, or nouns in front of んです, but this lesson will deal only with verbs. As the Target Dialogue demonstrates, you use plain forms (the dictionary form, the -nai form, and their past tenses -ta and -nakatta) before んです.

For other basic usages of んです, see p. 57.

Complete the answers to the question as in the example.

Q：はやいですね。毎朝　この　時間に　来るんですか。
　　　まいあさ　　　　　　　　じ かん　　　く

例）これから　かいぎの　じゅんびを　します
れい
　→ A：いいえ。今日は　<u>これから　かいぎの　じゅんびを　するんです。</u>
　　　　　　きょう

1）これから　にほんごの　レッスンが　あります
　→ A：いいえ。今日は ....
　　　　　　きょう

2）これから　ニューヨークししゃと　テレビかいぎを　します
　→ A：いいえ。今日は ....
　　　　　　きょう

3）これから　しごとの　前に　スポーツクラブで　およぎます
　　　　　　　　　　　まえ
　→ A：いいえ。今日は ....
　　　　　　きょう

4）これから　おきゃくさまを　いちばに　あんないします
　→ A：いいえ。今日は ....
　　　　　　きょう

5）これから　くうこうに　おきゃくさまを　むかえに　行きます。
　　　　　　　　　　　　　　　　　　　　　　　　　　　い
　→ A：いいえ。今日は ....
　　　　　　きょう

6）毎日　かいしゃで　朝ごはんを　たべます。
　まいにち　　　　　　あさ
　→ A：ええ。..

7）毎朝　にほんごを　ならっています。
　まいあさ
　→ A：ええ。..

8）この　時間は　ちかてつが　すいています。
　　　　じ かん
　→ A：ええ。..

VOCABULARY			
じゅんびを　します	do preparations	あんない	guidance
じゅんび	preparation	むかえに　いきます	go to meet
テレビかいぎ	teleconference	むかえます (R2)	meet, welcome
おきゃくさま	customer, visitor (polite form)	すいています	be empty
いちば	market	すきます	become empty
あんないします	show (someone) around, guide		

66

USAGE NOTE

Here we summarize the usages of んです introduced in Units 1 and 2. More detailed explanations can be found in the Notes and Grammar & Pattern Practice sections.

(1) as a prelude to a request or an invitation (see pp. 18, 69)

ゆかたを　かいたいんですが（どこに　ありますか）。　　　　(Lesson 2)

I'd like to buy a yukata, but . . . (where can I find one? / will you show me where they are?)

あした　おんせんに　行くんですが、いっしょに　いかがですか。(Lesson 5)

We are going to a hot spring resort tomorrow. Would you like to come along?

As the first example shows, you can sometimes get by with saying only the introductory part of the sentence. That is, you do not have to come out with the question directly.

(2) offering an explanation (see p. 18)

もっと　大きいのは　ありませんか。いもうとは　私より　せが　高いんです。　　　　(Lesson 2)

Do you have a bigger one? My younger sister is taller than me, you see.

(3) asking for or giving an explanation (see p. 50)

ここで（ヨガを）するんですか。　　　　(Lesson 4)
ええ。この　ヨガ用の　マットを　つかうんです。

Do you do (yoga) here?
Yes, I use this yoga mat.

(4) declining an invitation or a suggestion. (see p. 69)

あした　いっしょに　おんせんに　行きませんか。　　　　(Lesson 5)
ざんねんですが、あしたは　用事が　あるんです。

Would you like to go to a hot spring with me tomorrow?
I'm sorry, but I have things to do tomorrow.

(5) stopping in mid-sentence (see p. 82)

薬を　飲んだんですが……。　　　　(Lesson 6)

I took medicine, but . . . (I still feel bad).

III Expressing Frequency

The particle に following a period of time means "per." When a number and the counter 回 (かい),
"times," comes immediately after に, the sentence tells you how many times per period someone
does something or something happens. For example:

週に　２回　ヨガを　ならっているんです。
しゅう　　かい

I'm taking yoga lessons twice a week.

Common periods include:

週 (＝１週間)　　　　　a week
しゅう　　いっしゅうかん

１時間　　　　　　　　an hour
じ かん

１日　　　　　　　　　a day
にち

月 (＝１か月)　　　　　a month
つき　　　いっ か げつ

年 (＝１年)　　　　　　a year
ねん　　　ねん

The same に + number formula but with a period instead of 回 (かい) is also used.

１週間に　１０時間ぐらい　にほんごの　べんきょうを　します。
いっしゅうかん　　　じ かん

I study Japanese about ten hours a week.

To review adverbs for expressing frequency (from Book I):

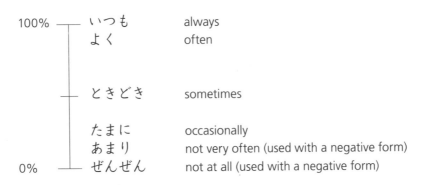

100% ── いつも　　　always
　　　　　よく　　　　often

　　　　　ときどき　　sometimes

　　　　　たまに　　　occasionally
　　　　　あまり　　　not very often (used with a negative form)
0% ──　ぜんぜん　　not at all (used with a negative form)

Examples:

Ａ：よく　ジョギングを　しますか。

Ｂ：ええ。

Ａ：毎日　するんですか。
　　まいにち

Ｂ：毎日では　ありませんが、週に　５日ぐらい　します。
　　まいにち　　　　　　　　　　　しゅう　　いつ か

A:　Do you jog often?

B:　Yes, I do.

A:　Everyday?

B:　Not everyday, but about five days a week.

ほとんど　毎週　どうりょうと　のみに　行きます。

Almost every week I go drinking with colleagues.

Complete the sentences based on the schedule.

Monday	Tuesday	Wednesday	Thursday	Friday	Saturday	Sunday
1 かいぎ （ほんしゃ）	2 にほんごの レッスン	3 ジョギング	4 にほんごの レッスン	5 ジョギング	6 テニス・ スクール	7 ジョギング
8 かいぎ （ほんしゃ）	9 にほんごの レッスン	10 ジョギング	11 にほんごの レッスン	12 ジョギング	13 テニス・ スクール	14 ジョギング

例）週に　１回　ほんしゃで　かいぎが　あります。

1) .... にほんごの　レッスンが　あります。

2) .... テニスを　ならっています。

3) .... ジョギングを　しています。

USAGE NOTE

Especially in long sentences, にほんごの　べんきょうを　します (example at left) is often stated more simply as にほんごを　べんきょうします. Both expressions mean "I study Japanese." Grammatically, べんきょう is a noun followed by the particle を and the verb します, whereas べんきょうします, with を left out, is itself considered a verb. Constructions of the latter type are called する verbs and are extremely frequent in both spoken and written Japanese.

VOCABULARY　ほとんど　　　　almost

PRACTICE 1

WORD POWER

I. The daily grind:

① おきます

② シャワーを
　　あびます

③ かおを
　　あらいます

④ はを　みがきます

⑤ スーツに
　　きがえます

⑥ うちを　でます

⑦ でんしゃを
　　まちます

⑧ でんしゃに
　　のります

⑨ カフェに
　　よります

⑩ しごとを
　　はじめます

⑪ どうりょうと　いざ
　　かやで　(お)さけを
　　のみます

⑫ カラオケで　うた
　　を　うたいます

⑬ うちに
　　かえります

⑭ テレビで　ニュー
　　スを　みます

⑮ (お)ふろに
　　入ります
　　_{はい}

⑯ ねます

VOCABULARY					
おきる (R2)	get up	スーツ	suit	カラオケ	karaoke
シャワー	shower	きがえる (R2)	change (clothes)	うた	song
かお	face	カフェ	café	うたう	sing
あらう	wash	よる	stop off	ニュース	news
は	teeth	はじめる (R2)	begin, start	(お)ふろ	bath
みがく	brush	いざかや	tavern	ねる (R2)	go to bed

II. Things to do on days off:

① そうじを します

② せんたくを します

③ かいものを します

④ ひるごはんを つくります

⑤ バーベキューを します

⑥ かたづけます

⑦ こどもと あそびます

⑧ いぬと さんぽを します

⑨ えいがを みに 行きます

⑩ ともだちと おしゃべりを します

⑪ かぞくと りょこうを します

⑫ ドライブを します

⑬ うちで のんびりします

VOCABULARY			
せんたくを する	do laundry	おしゃべりを する	talk, chat
せんたく	laundry	おしゃべり	talking, chatting
バーベキューを する	have a barbecue	ドライブを する	go for a drive
バーベキュー	barbecue	ドライブ	drive
かたづける (R2)	tidy up	のんびりする	relax

SPEAKING PRACTICE

I. 8:00 a.m., talking to a colleague who is preparing for a trip:

ミルズ：しゅっちょうですか。

チャン：ええ。１１時の　ひこうきで　シンガポールに　行くんです。

ミルズ：シンガポールには　よく　行くんですか。

チャン：ええ、毎月　かいぎが　あるんです。

ミルズ：たいへんですね。気を　つけて。

Mills:　　　Are you going on a business trip?
Chan:　　　Yes, I'm going to Singapore on an eleven o'clock flight.
Mills:　　　Do you often go to Singapore?
Chan:　　　Yes, I have a meeting (there) every month.
Mills:　　　That must be tough. Take care.

II. 12:00 noon, talking to a colleague who is eating lunch:

鈴木：　　　　シカさんは　毎日　おべんとうを　もってくるんですか。

チャンドラ：ええ。毎朝　５時に　おきて　つくるんです。鈴木さんは　りょう
　　　　　　りを　しますか。

鈴木：　　　　いいえ。

チャンドラ：ぜんぜん　しないんですか。

鈴木：　　　　ええ。ほとんど　毎日　がいしょくか　コンビニの　べんとうです。

Suzuki:　　　Shika, do you bring a lunch every day?
Chandra:　　Yes, every morning at 5:00 a.m. I get up and make one. Mr. Suzuki, do you cook?
Suzuki:　　　No.
Chandra:　　Not at all?
Suzuki:　　　That's right. Almost every day it's either eating out or a box lunch from the conve-
　　　　　　nience store.

III. 3:00 p.m., handing out sweets that one's boss has brought to the office as a souvenir:

中村： 京都の　おかしです。どうぞ。佐々木ぶちょうの　おみやげです。

ミルズ：ありがとう。いただきます。

鈴木： ぼくは　いいです。

ミルズ：あれっ、たべないんですか。

中村： ダイエットですか。

鈴木： ちがいますよ。今日は　ともだちと　しゃぶしゃぶ　たべほうだいの
　　　　店に　行くんです。

Nakamura: These are some sweets from Kyoto. Please have some. They're a present from Department Manager Sasaki.

Mills: Thank you. I'll have some.

Suzuki: No thank you. I'm fine.

Mills: What? You won't eat one?

Nakamura: Are you on a diet?

Suzuki: No, it's not that. Today I'm going to an all-you-can-eat shabu-shabu restaurant with a friend.

CULTURE NOTE

It is customary in the Japanese workplace for suppliers to visit the offices of their clients, or for employees to return to their offices after a business trip or vacation, with sweets—usually a specialty product—from some place they have visited. Such confections are usually given out around three o'clock (tea time) to staff seated at their desks.

IV. 5:00 p.m., talking to a colleague who is about to leave the office early for a change:

鈴木： 今日は　ざんぎょうを　しないんですか。

ミルズ：ええ。今　いもうとが　カナダから　来ているんです。これから　いっ
　　　　しょに　カラオケに　行くんです。じゃ。

Suzuki: You aren't going to work overtime today?

Mills: That's right. My sister has come over from Canada. We're going to karaoke together, right now. See you later.

VOCABULARY				
ぶちょう	department manager	ちがう	differ
あれっ	what?	しゃぶしゃぶ	shabu-shabu
ぼく	I/me (informal; used by men and boys)	たべほうだい	all-you-can-eat
いいです	no thank you, I am fine.	ざんぎょうを　する	do overtime work
ダイエット	diet	ざんぎょう	overtime

PRACTICE 2

WORD POWER

I. Interests:

 ① ゴルフ

 ② テニス

 ③ ジョギング

 ④ すいえい

 ⑤ トレーニング

 ⑥ サイクリング

 ⑦ ダイビング

 ⑧ スノーボード

 ⑨ スキー

 ⑩ やまのぼり

 ⑪ ヨガ

 ⑫ じゅうどう

 ⑬ けんどう

 ⑭ からて

 ⑮ いけばな

 ⑯ さどう

 ⑰ 日本りょうり
にほん

 ⑱ え（えを　かく）

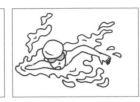 ⑲ ピアノ（ピアノ
を　ひく）

 ⑳ わだいこ（わだい
こを　たたく）

VOCABULARY					
トレーニング	training	やまのぼり	mountain climbing	かく	draw, paint
サイクリング	cycling	やま	mountain	ひく	play (an instrument)
ダイビング	diving	からて	karate	わだいこ	Japanese drum
スノーボード	snowboarding	さどう	tea ceremony	たたく	beat, play (drums)

SPEAKING PRACTICE

I. Talking with a colleague about exercise habits:

鈴木： ミルズさんは 何か うんどうを　していますか。
ミルズ：ええ、週に　2回　ジョギングを　しています。
鈴木： どこを　はしるんですか。
ミルズ：うちの　ちかくです。ちかくに　こうえんが　あるんです。
鈴木： どのぐらい　はしるんですか。
ミルズ：３０分ぐらいです。

Suzuki:	Do you do any kind of exercise, Mr. Mills?
Mills:	Yes, I go jogging twice a week.
Suzuki:	Where do you run?
Mills:	Near my home. There's a park near my home.
Suzuki:	About how long do you run?
Mills:	About thirty minutes.

PARTICLE REVIEW

Take special note of the particles in these sentences:

スポーツクラブで　テニスを　します。	I play tennis at a fitness club.
こうえんに　テニスに　行きます。	I go to a park to play tennis.
こうえんで　ジョギングを　します。	I jog in the park.
青山通りを　はしります。	I run along Aoyama Avenue.
うちの　ちかくを　あるきます。	I walk near my house.
じてんしゃで　まちを　回ります。	I travel around town on bicycle.
やまに　のぼります。	I climb mountains.

VOCABULARY			
うんどうを　する	exercise	〜どおり	street, avenue (suffix)
うんどう	exercise	じてんしゃ	bicycle
はしる	run	まわる	travel around, go around
あおやまどおり	Aoyama Avenue	のぼる	climb, go up (something)

II. At a bus stop, interacting with an elderly neighbor who is carrying a duffle bag:

ミルズ：　　　……

おんなの人：スポーツクラブに　行くんです。

ミルズ：　　どんな　うんどうを　するんですか。

おんなの人：ウエイトトレーニングと　すいえいです。

ミルズ：　　毎日　行くんですか。

おんなの人：週に　3日ぐらいです。

Mills:	. . .
woman:	I'm going to a fitness club.
Mills:	What kind of exercise will you do?
woman:	Weight training and swimming.
Mills:	Do you go (there) every day?
woman:	I go about three times a week.

III. Talking to a colleague who is carrying some flowers:

鈴木：　　チャンさん、いけばなを　ならっているんですか。

チャン：ええ。

鈴木：　　私も　いけばなを　ならいたいんですが、チャンさんは　どこで　ならっているんですか。

チャン：えきの　ちかくの　コミュニティーセンターです。

鈴木：　　クラスは　いつ　あるんですか。

チャン：毎週　2回　月、金の　6時からです。こんどの　金曜日に　いっしょに　行ってみませんか。

鈴木：　　いいですか。よろしく　おねがいします。

Suzuki:	Ms. Chan, are you learning ikebana?
Chan:	Yes.
Suzuki:	I want to learn ikebana, too. Where do you take lessons?
Chan:	The community center near the station.
Suzuki:	When are classes?
Chan:	Two times a week, on Mondays and Fridays from six o'clock. How about going with me this Friday?
Suzuki:	Would it be okay? I look forward to your guidance.

VOCABULARY	ウエイトトレーニング	weight training
	コミュニティーセンター	community center
	げつ（＝げつようび）	Monday
	きん（＝きんようび）	Friday

KANJI PRACTICE

毎 every	毎週 まいしゅう / 毎年 まいとし まいねん	ノ	一	仁	与	勾	毎	
		毎	毎					

朝 morning	朝 あさ / 毎朝 まいあさ / 朝食 ちょうしょく	二	十	十	古	古	直	
		卓	軋	朝	朝	朝	朝	朝

時 time	四時 よじ / 九時 くじ	丨	𠄌	日	日	日	日	時
		時	時	時	時	時		

間 between interval	間 あいだ / 時間 じかん / 一週間 いっしゅうかん / 間に合う まあ	丨	𠄌	𠄌	月	門	門	門
		門	門	閂	間	間	間	間

| 半 half | 四時半 よじはん / 半年 はんとし / 半分 はんぶん / 前半 ぜんはん | ヽ | ヽ | 丷 | 半 | 半 | 半 | 半 |
| | | | | | | | | |

日	日 ひ 毎日 まいにち 今日 きょう ＊日曜日 にちよう び	↓丨	刀	月	日	日	日	
sun								

月	毎月 まいつき 今月 こんげつ 一月 いちがつ ＊月曜日 げつよう び	↓丿	刀	月	月	月	月	
moon								

土	土田 つち だ ＊土曜日 ど よう び	一	十	土	土	土		
ground soil								

回	回る まわ 一回 いっかい	↓丨	冂	冋	冋	回	回	回
turn time		回						

部	システム部 ぶ 部屋 へ や	↓丶	立	宀	立	立	立	音
section part		音	音	部	部	部	部	

LESSON 5

INVITING A COLLEAGUE TO A HOT SPRING

TARGET DIALOGUE

It is almost 11:00 p.m. and Mr. Mills and Mr. Suzuki are still working in the office.

鈴木：　もう　１１時に　なりますよ。

　　　　そろそろ　帰りませんか。

ミルズ：そうですね。

On the train, on the way home:

ミルズ：(*talking to himself*) ああ、つかれた。

鈴木：　ミルズさん、六本木の　おんせんに　行った　ことが　ありますか。
→p. 73

ミルズ：えっ？　六本木に　おんせんが　あるんですか。

鈴木：　ええ。あした　帰りに　課の　人たちと　行くんですが、

　　　　いっしょに　いかがですか。

ミルズ：あしたですか。ざんねんですが、あしたは　用事が　あるんです。

鈴木：　そうですか。じゃ、また　つぎの　きかいに。

The train arrives at Mr. Mills's station.

ミルズ：じゃ、私は　ここで。おつかれさま。

鈴木：　おつかれさま。

Suzuki: It's getting on eleven. Shouldn't we go home soon?
Mills:　Oh, right.
. . . . . .
Mills:　Oh, I'm tired.
Suzuki: Mr. Mills, have you ever been to the hot springs in Roppongi?
Mills:　Huh? There are hot springs in Roppongi?
Suzuki: Yes. Tomorrow I'm going there on my way home with some people from our section. How would you like to come along?
Mills:　Tomorrow. I'm sorry, but I have things to do tomorrow.
Suzuki: Oh? Next time, then.
. . . . . .
Mills:　Well, this is where I get off. Good night.
Suzuki: Good night.

VOCABULARY

〜に　なる	become	課 か	section
〜に	(particle indicating the result of a change)	人たち ひと	people
ああ、つかれた	I am tired (talking to oneself)	〜たち	(suffix added to nouns referring to people to create a plural)
つかれる (R2)	get tired	用事 ようじ	things to do, errands
〜ことが　ある	(see p. 73)	きかい	opportunity, chance
帰り かえ	going home (see Note 3 below)	おつかれさま	good-bye (see Note 7 below)

NOTES

1. １１時（じ）に　なりますよ。

   なります means "become" and １１時（じ）に　なります means "It is getting close to eleven." Mr. Mills has lost track of the time and become absorbed in his work, so Mr. Suzuki starts the conversation by telling him the time in order to urge him to go home.

2. そろそろ

   This is an adverb equivalent in meaning to "in just a short while" or "it's about time." In this case, Mr. Suzuki is trying to urge Mr. Mills to go home, since he is not making any moves to leave, even though it is late. You use そろそろ when you are about to leave or when it is almost time to begin or end a meeting.

3. 帰（かえ）りに

   The -masu stem of a verb—that is, the part of the verb just before -masu—functions as a noun. Here 帰（かえ）り is the -masu stem of 帰（かえ）ります and means "going home." Followed by the particle に, however, the translation becomes "on one's way home."

4. 課（か）の　人（ひと）たちと　行（い）くんですが、いっしょに　いかがですか。

   Like ゆかたを　かいたいんですが from Lesson 2, this んですが is used as an introductory remark. Here, however, it is a preliminary to an invitation.

5. ざんねんですが、あしたは　用事（ようじ）が　あるんです。

   This んです is used to decline an invitation. Mr. Mills has to decline Mr. Suzuki's invitation, but instead of saying no outright, he states only his reason for refusing, adding んです to it. Mr. Suzuki is supposed to understand that Mr. Mills cannot go.

6. 私（わたし）は　ここで。

   It is understood that a verb such as おります, "to get off," or しつれいします, "to take one's leave," follows 私（わたし）は　ここで in this sentence.

7. おつかれさま。

   Originally this was an expression you used to thank a person for his or her service. Nowadays, you use it at work toward colleagues who leave the office before you at the end of the day. It is a courteous way of saying good-bye.

GRAMMAR & PATTERN PRACTICE

I Plain Forms of Verbs (2): Past-affirmative and Past-negative Tenses

The *-ta* form is the plain form of *-mashita* (the past–affirmative form of *-masu*). It follows the same pattern of conjugation as the *-te* form but with *-te* replaced by *-ta*.

	-nai form	-masu form	dictionary form	-te form	-ta form	ending
Regular I	あわない	あいます	あう	あって	あった	-tte/tta
	かかない	かきます	かく	かいて	かいた	-ite/ita
	およがない	およぎます	およぐ	およいで	およいだ	-ide/ida
	けさない	けします	けす	けして	けした	-shite/shita
	またない	まちます	まつ	まって	まった	-tte/tta
	しなない	しにます	しぬ	しんで	しんだ	-nde/nda
	よばない	よびます	よぶ	よんで	よんだ	
	のまない	のみます	のむ	のんで	のんだ	
	帰らない かえ	帰ります かえ	帰る かえ	帰って かえ	帰った かえ	-tte/tta
Regular II	食べない た	食べます た	食べる た	食べて た	食べた た	-te/ta
	あけない	あけます	あける	あけて	あけた	
	見ない み	見ます み	見る み	見て み	見た み	
	おりない	おります	おりる	おりて	おりた	
Irregular	来ない こ	来ます き	来る く	来て き	来た き	-te/ta
	しない	します	する	して	した	

NOTE: 行（い）きます (dictionary form 行（い）く is an exception among the Regular I verbs in that its *-te* and *-ta* forms are 行（い）って and 行（い）った, respectively.

-TE FORM REVIEW

The *-te* form for Regular I verbs is obtained as follows:

final syllable before 〜ます	changes to
い, ち, り	って
に, み, び	んで
き	いて
ぎ	いで
し	して

The plain form of -masendeshita (the past-negative form of -masu) is not given in the tables in this book, but it is formed by replacing -nai with -nakatta. For example:

あわない　　　→　　　あわなかった

食べない　　　→　　　食べなかった

来ない　　　　→　　　来なかった

しない　　　　→　　　しなかった

Change the verbs to their -ta and -nakatta forms, as in the example.

例)かきます　　　→　かいた　　　　　　かかなかった

Regular I

1) 行きます　　　→ ....　...................................

2) あるきます　　→ ....　...................................

3) ぬぎます　　　→ ....　...................................

4) もちます　　　→ ....　...................................

5) かいます　　　→ ....　...................................

6) ならいます　　→ ....　...................................

7) あります　　　→ ....　...................................

8) のぼります　　→ ....　...................................

9) のります　　　→ ....　...................................

10) あそびます　　→ ....　...................................

11) よみます　　　→ ....　...................................

12) けします　　　→ ....　...................................

Regular II

13) います　　　　→ ....　...................................

14) きます (wear)　→ ....　...................................

15) あびます　　　→ ....　...................................

16) かります　　　→ ....　...................................

17) おきます　　　→ ....　...................................

18) ねます　　　　→ ....　...................................

19) でます　　　　→ ....　...................................

20) しらべます　　→ ....　...................................

21) はじめます　　→ ....　...................................

Irregular

22) 来ます　　　　→ ....　...................................

23) します　　　　→ ....　...................................

II Talking about Past Experiences

The -ta form of a verb followed by ことが あります expresses the fact that a person has experienced something before. For example:

六本木の　おんせんに　行った　ことが　あります。
ろっぽんぎ　　　　　　　　い
I have been to the hot springs in Roppongi.

Q：すしを　食べた　ことが　ありますか。
　　　　　　た
A：はい、あります。

　　いいえ、ありません。

Q:　Have you even eaten sushi?
A:　Yes, I have.
　　No, I have not.

Complete the sentences as in the example.

例）見ます →　かぶきを　<u>見た</u>　ことが　あります。
れい　み　　　　　　　　　み

1) のみます →　おさけを ....

2) 行きます →　北海道に ....
　　い　　　　　ほっかいどう

3) のぼります　→　富士山に ....
　　　　　　　　　ふ　じ　さん

4) のります→　しんかんせんに ....

PRACTICE 1

WORD POWER

I. Experiences in Japan:

① （お）しろ

② きもの

北海道
ほっかいどう

沖縄
おきなわ

札幌
さっぽろ

仙台
せんだい

金沢
かなざわ

本州
ほんしゅう

京都
きょうと

東京
とうきょう

大阪
おおさか

福岡
ふくおか

広島
ひろしま

名古屋
なごや

鎌倉
かまくら

四国
しこく

九州
きゅうしゅう

③ すもう

④ だいぶつ

⑤ （お）みこし

⑥ ぼんおどり

⑦ なべりょうり

⑧ おこのみやき

⑨ しょうちゅう

⑩ まっちゃ

SPEAKING PRACTICE

I. Talking to a colleague about experiences climbing in Japan:

加藤： 富士山に のぼった ことが ありますか。
　　　（かとう）（ふじさん）

ミルズ：はい、あります。

加藤： いつ のぼったんですか。

ミルズ：きょねんです。たのしかったですが、とても つかれました。

Kato:　　Have you ever climbed Mt. Fuji?
Mills:　　Yes, I have.
Kato:　　When did you climb it?
Mills:　　Last year. It was fun, but I got very tired.

II. Getting information from a colleague about a place one wants to go:

ミルズ：加藤さん、お台場の おんせんに 行った ことが ありますか。
　　　　（かとう）　　（だいば）　　　　（い）

加藤： ええ。
　　　（かとう）

ミルズ：どうでしたか。

加藤： よかったです。おふろに 入って、それから、ビールを のみました。
　　　　　　　　　　　　　　　（はい）

　　　リラックスしましたよ。

ミルズ：どうやって 行きましたか。
　　　　　　　　　　（い）

加藤： 新橋から ゆりかもめに のりました。品川から シャトルバスも あ
　　　（しんばし）　　　　　　　　　　　　　（しながわ）

　　　りますよ。

Mills:　　Mr. Kato, have you ever been to the hot springs in Odaiba?
Kato:　　Yes.
Mills:　　How were they?
Kato:　　They were good. We bathed, and then we drank beer. We relaxed.
Mills:　　How did you go?
Kato:　　We rode the Yurikamome from Shimbashi. There's also a shuttle bus from Shinagawa.

VOCABULARY	リラックスする	relax
	ゆりかもめ	Yurikamome (name of an automated train in Tokyo that runs from the mainland to Odaiba)
	シャトルバス	shuttle bus

PRACTICE 2

PHRASE POWER

I. Telling the time:

3時です。 It's three o'clock.
3時　ちょうどです。 It's three o'clock exactly.

1時　55分です。 It's 1:55.
2時　5分前です。 It's five minutes to two.
あと　5分で　2時です。 In five minutes it will be two o'clock.
もうすぐ　2時に　なります。 In a few minutes it will be two o'clock.

4時　10分です。 It's 4:10.
4時　10分すぎです。 ┐
 ├ It's ten minutes past four.
4時を　10分　すぎました。 ┘

もうすぐ　9時半です。 In a few minutes it will be 9:30.
9時半に　なります。 It's going to be 9:30.

午前	a.m., in the morning	昼	noon, daytime
午後	p.m., in the afternoon	ゆうがた	evening
朝	morning	ばん／夜	evening, night

ちょうど	exactly, just	～すぎ	past (the hour) (suffix)
～まえ	to . . . , before . . .	すぎる (R2)	pass
あと	later, afterward		

98

SPEAKING PRACTICE

I. Pressing to begin a meeting:

ミルズ：１０時を　すぎました。そろそろ　かいぎを　はじめましょう。

鈴木：　そうですね。
すずき

Mills:　　It's past ten o'clock. It's about time we started the meeting.

Suzuki:　Yes, I agree.

II. Worrying about a colleague who is late for an appointment:

加藤：ミルズさん、おそいですね。もう　やくそくの　時間を　２０分　すぎて
かとう　　　　　　　　　　　　　　　　　　　　　じかん　　　にじゅっぷん
　　　いますよ。

鈴木：そうですね。けいたいに　でんわしてみましょうか。
すずき

Kato:　　Mr. Mills is late, isn't he? It's already twenty minutes past our appointment.

Suzuki: You're right. Shall I try calling him on his cell phone?

III. Deciding when to have an appointment:

加藤：　ミルズさん、今日の　よていは？　フードフェアについて　そうだんした
かとう　　　　　　　きょう
　　　　いんですが。

ミルズ：午後　のぞみデパートで　高橋さんと　やくそくが　ありますが、ゆう
　　　　ごご　　　　　　　　　たかはし
　　　　がた　４時半すぎには　もどります。
　　　　　　よじはん

加藤：　では、午前中に　ちょっと　そうだんしましょうか。
　　　　　　ごぜんちゅう

ミルズ：はい、わかりました。

Kato:　　Mr. Mills, what are your plans for today? I'd like to talk with you about the food fair.

Mills:　　I have an appointment with Mr. Takahashi at Nozomi Department Store in the after-
　　　　　noon, but I'll be back after 4:30 in the afternoon.

Kato:　　Well then, should we discuss the matter this morning?

Mills:　　Yes, that would be fine.

VOCABULARY			
やくそく	appointment, promise	そうだん	consultation
よてい	plan, schedule	もどる	go/come back
フードフェア	food fair	ごぜんちゅう	during the morning
そうだんする	consult	〜ちゅう	during (suffix)

PRACTICE 3

SPEAKING PRACTICE

I. Inviting a colleague to a soccer game:

鈴木： 金曜日の　ばん、ともだちと　サッカーの　しあいを　見に　行くんで
すが、いっしょに　いかがですか。

ミルズ：ざんねんですが、金曜日は　7時から　かいぎが　あるんです。

鈴木： そうですか。じゃ、また　つぎの　きかいに。

Suzuki: Friday night I'm going to see a soccer game with some friends. Would you like to come
            along?
Mills: It's too bad, but I have a meeting on Friday from seven o'clock.
Suzuki: Really? Well then, maybe next time.

II. Inviting a colleague to a sumo match:

鈴木： 土曜日の　すもうの　チケットを　もらったんですが、いっしょに　行
きませんか。

ミルズ：ぜひ　行きたいです。いちど　行ってみたかったんです。

鈴木： じゃ、これ、チケットです。私は　昼ごろから　行っています。
中で　あいましょう。

ミルズ：わかりました。ありがとうございます。

Suzuki: I received some sumo tickets for Saturday. Would you like to go with me (to the match)?
Mills: I definitely want to go. I have been wanting to go at least once (to see what it is like).
Suzuki: Well, this is the ticket. I'll be there from around noon. Let's meet inside.
Mills: Okay. Thank you.

VOCABULARY	チケット	ticket (for an event)
	てみたかったんです	have been wanting to . . .
	なか	inside, middle

READING TASK

ききゅうツアー

　私は　ききゅうに　のった　ことが　あります。おととしの　なつ、ガールフレンドと　いっしょに　トルコに　行きました。そして、カッパドキアで　ききゅうツアーに　さんかしました。はじめ　すこし　こわかったです。でも、ながめは　ほんとうに　すばらしかったです。ぜひ　また　どこかでのりたいです。

VOCABULARY

ききゅう	hot-air balloon
おととし	the year before last
ガールフレンド	girlfriend
トルコ	Turkey
カッパドキア	Cappadocia
ツアー	tour
さんかする	participate
さんか	participation
はじめ	beginning, at first
すこし	a little, a bit
こわい	frightening
ながめ	view
すばらしい	fabulous, fantastic, spectacular

KANJI PRACTICE

帰	帰る かえ 帰り かえ	し	リ	リア	リヨ	リヨ	リヨ	帰
return		帰	帰	帰	帰	帰		

本	本 ほん 日本 に ほん 何本 なんぼん	一	十	オ	木	本	本	本
basis **book**								

木	木 き 六本木 ろっぽん ぎ ＊木曜日 もくよう び	一	十	オ	木	木	木	
tree								

課	課の人 か ひと	ゝ	ニ	言	言	言	言	言
section **lesson**		言	訂	誤	課	課	課	課
課	課	課						

事	仕事 し ごと 用事 よう じ お大事に だい じ	一	一	一	写	写	写	写
affair **abstract thing**		事	事	事				

仕 serve	仕事 しごと	ノ	イ	仁	什	仕	仕	仕

昼 noon daytime	昼 ひる / 昼食 ちゅうしょく	⊃	⊐	尸	尺	尺	尽	昼
		昼	昼	昼	昼			

夜 night	夜 よる	ヽ	亠	广	夲	夜	夜	夜
		夜	夜	夜				

見 see	見る み / 見せる み / 見学 けんがく	⌐	冂	月	目	目	貝	見
		見	見					

食 eat	食べる た / 食事 しょくじ / 朝食 ちょうしょく / 昼食 ちゅうしょく	ノ	𠆢	𠆢	今	今	会	食
		食	食	食	食			

CLOCKING OUT EARLY

TARGET DIALOGUE

Mr. Kato speaks to Mr. Mills, who looks a little pale.

加藤：　かおいろが　よく　ありませんね。かぜですか。

ミルズ：　ええ。じつは　ちょっと　ねつが　あるんです。さっき　薬を
買ってきて　飲んだんですが……。（ハクション）

加藤：　はやく　うちに　帰って　休んだ　ほうが　いいですよ。
　　　→p. 84　　　　　　　　→p. 86

ミルズ：　でも、まだ　きのうの　会議の　レポートを　書いていないん
　　　　　→p. 87　　　　　　　　　　　　　　　　　　　　　　です。

加藤：　むりを　しない　ほうが　いいですよ。　あさってから　中国
　　　→p. 86
しゅっちょうでしょう。

ミルズ：　ええ。（ゴホゴホッ）

After a bad coughing fit:

ミルズ：　じゃ、すみませんが、今日は　お先に　しつれいします。

加藤：　ええ、お大事に。

Kato: You look pale. Do you have a cold?
Mills: Yes. In fact, I have a bit of a fever. I just bought some medicine and took it. Achoo!
Kato: You should go home early and rest.
Mills: But I still haven't written the report of yesterday's meeting.
Kato: You shouldn't push yourself. You leave on a business trip to China the day after tomorrow, right?
Mills: Yes. (cough-cough) . . . Sorry, I'm going to leave early today.
Kato: Yes, take care.

VOCABULARY

かおいろ	complexion	むり（な）	impossible
よく　ありません	not good	〜ない　ほうが　いい	should not . . . , had better not . . .
かぜ	cold		
じつは	actually	〜でしょう	right? (see Note 5 below)
買（か）ってくる	go and buy (lit., "buy and come back")	ゴホゴホッ	(sound of coughing)
ハクション	(sound of sneezing)	お先（さき）に	ahead (of) (polite form)
はやく	quickly, early (see p. 84)	先（さき）	ahead
〜た　ほうが　いい	should . . . , had better . . .	お大事（だいじ）に	take care
むりを　する	force oneself, overdo it	大事（だいじ）（な）	important, precious

NOTES

1. かおいろが　よく　ありませんね。
This means "you look pale." よく　ありません is the same as よく　ないです (introduced in Book I). In fact, ありません or ないです may be used with any adjective to express the negative form; the two are interchangeable. For example, おいしく　ありません and おいしく　ないです both mean "not delicious," and げんきではありません／げんきじゃありません and げんきではないです all mean "not healthy."

2. 薬（くすり）を　買（か）ってきて　飲（の）んだんですが……。
Mr. Mills did not finish his sentence. This stopping in midsentence is one of the usages of んです (see p. 57). Had Mr. Mills continued, he would have stated that he has not gotten better yet or that the medicine he took did not work, or both. Mr. Mills does not say all this, of course, because he knows Mr. Kato can understand him well enough. By ending with んです, you can imply that there is something you do not need to say because it is obvious, or that there is something you hesitate to say.

3. ハクション、ゴホゴホッ
These are *giongo*, or Japanese sound-effect words. ハクション represents sneezing, and ゴホゴホッ represents coughing. There is no custom in Japanese of saying, "bless you" or "gesundheit" after someone sneezes. *Giongo* are typically written in katakana.

4. でも、まだ　きのうの　会議（かいぎ）の　レポートを　書（か）いて　いないんです。
This んです is explaining a situation. Note that you can use んです not only to answer questions of the んですか type but also to give explanations when you feel they are needed. Here Mr. Mills is telling Mr. Kato the reason why he is reluctant to leave early.

5. あさってから　中国（ちゅうごく）しゅっちょうでしょう。
でしょう is an inflection of です. Here Mr. Kato uses it with rising intonation to confirm something he understands to be true. He is trying to persuade Mr. Mills not to push himself too hard, given that he is ill and has a business trip coming up.

6. お大事（だいじ）に
大事（だいじ）な means "important" and 大事（だいじ）に　する means "take good care of." お大事（だいじ）に shows sympathy and consideration for an ill or injured person, or those who have a family member who is ill or injured.

GRAMMAR & PATTERN PRACTICE

1 Using the Adverbial Forms of Adjectives to Modify Verbs

Adjectives can change form to serve as adverbs in Japanese, just as they can in English. -*I* adjectives change their -*i* endings to -*ku*, and -*na* adjectives change their -*na* endings to -*ni,* when they modify verbs. For example:

はやい → はやく　　　はやく　おきました。

I got up early.

きれい → きれいに　　　きれいに　書いてください。
か

Please write it neatly.

---

1 Change the adjectives to their adverbial forms, as in the examples.

例 1) はやい　→ はやく
れい
例 2) きれい　→ きれいに
れい

1) 大きい　→ ....
　　おお

2) 小さい　→ ....
　　ちい

3) 安い　→ ....
　　やす

4) しずか　→ ....

5) しんせつ　→ ....

6) にぎやか　→ ....

2 Change the adjectives to their adverbial forms to construct complete sentences where the adverbs modify the verbs.

例) しずか、あるきます
れい
　　→ しずかに　あるきます。

1) たのしい、食事を　します
　　　　　　しょくじ
　　→ ....

2) きれい、そうじを　します
　　→ ....

3) おそい、おきます
　　→ ....

4) じょうず、うたいます
　　→ ....

▌▌ "Going Somewhere to Do Something and Coming Back"

The -*te* form of a verb followed by きます sometimes has the literal meaning of "go, do something, and return." For example:

薬を　買ってきました。
くすり　　か

I went and bought some medicine
(and came back).

---

1 Change the form of the verbs to 〜てきます as in the example.

例）買います　→　買ってきます
れい　か　　　　　　　　か

1) 書きます　→　...
　　か

2) さがします →　...

3) とどけます →　...

4) とります　→　...

5) 食べます　→　...
　　た

6) 飲みます　→　...
　　の

2 Construct sentences as in the example.

例）パンを　買います。食べます。
れい　　　　か　　　　た

　→　パンを　買ってきて、食べます。
　　　　　　か　　　　　た

1) カタログを　もらいます。せつめいします。

　→　...

2) 本を　かります。読みます。
　　ほん　　　　　　よ

　→　...

3) としょかんで　しらべます。みんなに　おしえます。

　→　...

VOCABULARY

せつめいする	explain
せつめい	explanation
みんな	everyone

85

III Making Strong Suggestions

The -ta or -nai form followed by ほうが いいです expresses a strong suggestion: "should do" or "should not do," respectively.

かぜですか。じゃあ、うちに 帰って 休んだ ほうが いいですよ。

今、むりを しない ほうが いいですよ。

You have a cold? Well then, you should go home and get some rest.

You shouldn't push yourself now.

Because a sentence with ほうが いいです essentially suggests that someone do something (or refrain from doing something) that is better than what they are doing or thinking about doing, it can sound pushy. Therefore, you should not use it all the time.

Complete the strong suggestions posed by B, as in the example.

例) はやく 帰ります

    A：ちょっと ねつが あります。

    → B：じゃあ、<u>はやく 帰った ほうが いいですよ。</u>

1) すぐ こうばんに 行きます。

    A：さいふを おとしたんです。

    → B：じゃあ、..

2) すぐ カードがいしゃに でんわします。

    A：カードが ないんです。

    → B：じゃあ、..

3) すこし 休みます

    A：とても つかれています。

    → B：じゃあ、..

4) たばこを すいません

    A：のどが いたいです。

    → B：じゃあ、..

5) おさけを 飲みません

    A：あした けんこうしんだんが あるんです。

    → B：じゃあ、..

VOCABULARY

じゃあ	well then, in that case	けんこうしんだん	health checkup
おとす	drop, lose	けんこう	health
カードがいしゃ	credit card company	しんだん	checkup

Ⅳ "Not Yet"

The -te form followed by いません sometimes indicates that something has not yet occurred or has not yet been achieved. For example:

Q：もう　レポートを　書きましたか。

A：はい、もう　書きました。

いいえ、まだ　書いていません。

いいえ。レポートは　書きません（でした）。

Q:　Have you already finished your report?

A:　Yes, I have.

No. (I intend to but) I haven't yet.

No, I will not (did not) write it.

---

1 Complete the answers to the questions, as in the example.

例）Q：もう　見ましたか。

→ A：はい、<u>もう　見ました。</u>／いいえ、<u>まだ　見ていません。</u>

1) Q：もう　飲みましたか。

→ A：はい、..／いいえ、..

2) Q：もう　ききましたか。

→ A：はい、..／いいえ、..

3) Q：もう　来ましたか。

→ A：はい、..／いいえ、..

4) Q：もう　食べましたか。

→ A：はい、..／いいえ、..

5) Q：もう　はなしましたか。

→ A：はい、..／いいえ、..

2 Complete the answers to the question as in the example.

Q：ざんぎょうですか。

例) レポートを　書きます
れい　　　　　　　か
　→ A：ええ、<u>まだ　レポートを　書いていないんです。</u>
　　　　　　　　　　　　　　　　か

1) メールの　へんじを　だします
　→ A：ええ、..

2) しりょうを　読みます
　　　　　　　よ
　→ A：ええ、..

3) データを　おくります
　→ A：ええ、..

4) 会議の　じゅんびが　できます
　かい ぎ
　→ A：ええ、..

V　Asking for and Offering Explanations (2)

You use んです after adjectives as follows:

わるいです	→ わるいんです	(-I ADJECTIVE)
わるくないです	→ わるくないんです	
わるかったです	→ わるかったんです	
わるくなかったです	→ わるくなかったんです	
べんりです	→ べんりなんです	(-NA ADJECTIVE)
べんりでは　ありません	→ べんりでは　ないんです	
べんりでした	→ べんりだったんです	
べんりでは　ありませんでした	→ べんりでは　なかったんです	

After nouns, you use な before んです if the tense is present-affirmative.

かぜです	→ かぜなんです
かぜでは　ありません	→ かぜでは　ないんです
かぜでした	→ かぜだったんです
かぜでは　ありませんでした	→ かぜでは　なかったんです

VOCABULARY

へんじ	response, answer
だす	send, issue
データ	data
できる (R2)	get done

PRACTICE 1

WORD POWER

I. Symptoms and conditions:

State your symptoms using the words below. (See p. 41 for names of other body parts.)

| あたま　おなか　のど　は　こし | が　いたいんです。 |

| 気分（き ぶん）　ちょうし　おなかの　ちょうし | が　わるいんです。 |

| かぜ　インフルエンザ　アレルギー　かふんしょう
ふつかよい　ねぶそく　じさぼけ | なんです。 |

ねつが　あるんです。
かぜを　ひいたんです。
つかれているんです。
ねむいんです。

| て　あし　ゆび | に　けがを　したんです。 |

| くしゃみ　せき　はな（みず）　あくび | が　でます。 |

(See p. 41 for names of other body parts.)

VOCABULARY	ちょうし	condition	ねぶそく	sleeplessness	けがを　する	get injured	あくび	yawn
	インフルエンザ	the flu	じさぼけ	jet lag	けが	injury	でる	come out
	アレルギー	allergy	ひく	catch (a cold)	くしゃみ	sneeze		
	かふんしょう	hay fever	ねむい	sleepy	せき	cough		
	ふつかよい	hangover	ゆび	finger	はな（みず）	runny nose		89

SPEAKING PRACTICE

 I. Asking someone whether they have a cold:

中村：　　ハクション……。
なかむら

ミルズ：　かぜですか。

中村：　　いいえ、アレルギーです。ハクション……。日本には　かふんしょう
　　　　　　　　　　　　　　　　　　　　　　　　　　　にほん
　　　　　　の　人が　おおいんですよ。
　　　　　　　ひと

ミルズ：　そうなんですか。

Nakamura: Ah-choo!
Mills:　　 Do you have a cold?
Nakamura: No, allergies. Ah-choo! A lot of people in Japan have pollen allergies.
Mills:　　 Is that so?

 II. Asking someone who has been off with a cold how they are doing:

ミルズ：かぜは　どうですか。

鈴木：　おかげさまで、もう　だいじょうぶです。
すずき

ミルズ：よかったですね。

Mills:　　How is your cold?
Suzuki:　 I'm okay now, thanks.
Mills:　　That's good.

 III. Calling the office to say that one will be late because of an injury:

鈴木：　　鈴木です。今　びょういんに　いるんです。
すずき　　すずき　　いま

中村：　　どうしたんですか。
なかむら

鈴木：　　ちょっと　あしに　けがを　したんです。今日は　午後から　かいしゃ
　　　　　　　　　　　　　　　　　　　　　　　きょう　　　ごご
　　　　　　に　行きます。
　　　　　　　い

中村：　　わかりました。気を　つけて。
　　　　　　　　　　　　き

Suzuki:　　 This is Suzuki. I'm in the hospital right now.
Nakamura: What's wrong?
Suzuki:　　 I sort of injured my foot. Today I'll go to the office in the afternoon.
Nakamura: Okay. Take care.

VOCABULARY	おかげさまで	thanks (lit., "thanks to you")
	だいじょうぶ（な）	okay, all right, fine
	どうしたんですか	what is wrong?

PRACTICE 2

WORD POWER

① 食事会
しょくじかい

② 飲み会
のみかい

③ かんげい会
かい

④ そうべつ会
かい

⑤ しんねん会
かい

⑥ ぼうねん会
かい

⑦ はなみ

⑧ クリスマス
パーティー

SPEAKING PRACTICE

TRACK 39

I. Confirming the details of a dinner party:

加藤：あさっての　食事会は　どこで　するんですか。
かとう　　　　　しょくじかい

鈴木：まだ　きめていないんです。　さっき　パンフレットを　もらってきたん
すずき　　　　　　　　　　　　　ですが、ここは　どうでしょう。

加藤：いいですね。みなさんに　はやく　しらせた　ほうが　いいですよ。

鈴木：はい。よやくして、すぐ　メールします。

Kato:　Where is the day after tomorrow's dinner party going to be held?
Suzuki: We haven't decided yet. I just received this pamphlet; how about this place?
Kato:　Looks nice. You should inform everyone right away.
Suzuki: Right. I'll make a reservation and send out an e-mail (to everyone) immediately.

VOCABULARY

しょくじかい	dinner party	しんねんかい	New Year party	きめる (R2)	decide
のみかい	drinking party	ぼうねんかい	end-of-the-year party	みなさん	everyone
かんげいかい	welcome party	はなみ	cherry blossom viewing	しらせる (R2)	inform
そうべつかい	farewell party	クリスマスパーティー	Christmas party	メールする	send e-mail

91

II. Asking how preparations are going:

TRACK 40

加藤：　しりょうの　じゅんびは　できましたか。

中村：　まだなんです。コピーの　ちょうしが　わるいんです。

加藤：　メンテナンスに　れんらくしましたか。

中村：　いいえ。まだ　していません。

加藤：　はやく　でんわした　ほうが　いいですね。

Kato:　　　How are those materials coming along? (lit., "As for the preparation of the materials, is it done?")

Nakamura:　(They are) not (ready) yet. The copier isn't working well.

Kato:　　　Did you contact Maintenance?

Nakamura: No, I haven't yet.

Kato:　　　You should call them right away.

III. Working even during the lunch break to get things done:

TRACK 41

ミルズ：１２時に　なりますよ。　鈴木さん、昼ごはんは？

鈴木：　どうぞ、お先に。私は　午後の　会議に　でるんですが、まだ　じゅんびが　できていないんです。

ミルズ：そうですか。じゃ、行ってきます。帰りに　何か　買ってきましょうか。

鈴木：　それじゃ、マックのチーズバーガー・セットを　おねがいしても　いいですか。

ミルズ：チーズバーガー・セットですね。わかりました。

Mills:　　It's almost twelve o'clock. What about lunch, Mr. Suzuki?

Suzuki:　Please go on ahead. I'm attending this afternoon's meeting, but I haven't finished preparing for it (lit., "preparations aren't done yet").

Mills:　　Really? Well then, I'll go out for a little bit. Should I buy something for you on the way back?

Suzuki:　In that case, can I ask you to buy me a cheesburger combo from McDonald's?

Mills:　　A cheesburger combo? Okay.

VOCABULARY			
しりょう	material, data	おねがいする	ask a favor of
メンテナンス	maintenance	（お）ねがい	wish, hope
れんらくする	contact, get in touch (with)	マック	McDonald's (short for マクドナルド)
れんらく	contact, connection	チーズバーガー・セット	cheeseburger combo
どうぞ　おさきに	please go ahead	チーズバーガー	cheeseburger
（に）でる (R2)	go to, attend		

READING TASK

ごそうだん

Read the following e-mails. Mr. Oki is working in the Düsseldorf office, in Germany. He gets an e-mail from Ms. Tsuchida, who is coming to the office as a new staff member.

ごそうだん

大木さま
おおき

えいぎょう部の　土田です。
ぶ　　　　つちだ

来年の　4月から　私も　デュッセルドルフじむしょで　仕事を　します。
らいねん　　がつ　　　わたし　　　　　　　　　　　　　　　しごと

たのしみですが、ちょっと　しんぱいです。これから　ひっこしの　じゅんびを

します。いろいろ　おしえてください。

よろしく　おねがいします。

土田
つちだ

RE：ごそうだん

土田さま
つちだ

デュッセルドルフは　とても　いい　ところですよ。ひっこしの　じゅんびは

たいへんですね。

こちらには　あまり　小さい　サイズの　ふくや　くつが　ありませんから、日本から
　　　　　　　　　　ちい　　　　　　　　　　　　　　　　　　　　　　　　　にほん
もってきた　ほうが　いいですよ。薬も　もってきた　ほうが　いいです。こちらの
　　　　　　　　　　　　　　　くすり
薬は　すこし　つよいですから。
くすり

かぐは　こちらで　かりた　ほうが　いいです。かぐつきの　アパートも　あります。

それから、日本で　すこし　ドイツごの　べんきょうを　した　ほうが　いいです。私
　　　　　にほん　　　　　　　　　　　　　　　　　　　　　　　　　　　わたし
は　はじめ　ぜんぜん　わかりませんでしたから、たいへんでした。

来年の　4月が　たのしみです。
らいねん　　がつ

大木
おおき

VOCABULARY

（ご）そうだん	consultation	しんぱい（な）	worried
大木 おおき	Oki (surname)	ひっこし	moving (from one home to another)
土田 つちだ	Tsuchida (surname)	ふく	clothes
デュッセルドルフ	Düsseldorf	つよい	strong
じむしょ	office	かぐつきの	furnished
たのしみ	delight	～つき	with . . . , including . . . (suffix)

KANJI PRACTICE

薬 medicine	薬 くすり	一	十	艹	节	芍	芍	苩
		苩	苩	苩	莁	莁	莁	莝
薬	薬	薬	薬					

買 buy	買 か・う	リ	一	一	四	四	罒	罒
		買	買	買	買	買	買	買

飲 drink	飲 の・む	ク	八	今	今	今	今	食
		食	食	食	飲	飲	飲	飲

| 休 rest | 休 やす・む *昼休み ひるやす | ノ | イ | 仁 | 什 | 休 | 休 | 休 |
| | | 休 | | | | | | |

会 meet gathering	会 あ・う 飲み会 の かい 食事会 しょくじ かい	ノ	八	今	今	会	会	会
		会						

議
discuss
会議
かいぎ

`	ニ	ニ	言	言	言	言
言	言	言	言	言	言	言
謙	議	議	議	議	議	議	議

書
write
書く
か

⏋	⏞	⏞	聿	聿	聿	書
書	書	書	書	書		

読
read
読む
よ

`	ニ	言	言	言	言	言
言	計	詰	読	読	読	読
読	読					

国
country
国
くに
中国
ちゅうごく

｜	冂	冂	冋	国	国	国
国	国	国				

先
ahead
お先に
さき
先週
せんしゅう
先月
せんげつ

| ⺍ | 广 | 牛 | 生 | 歩 | 先 | 先 |
| 先 | | | | | | |

95

Quiz 2 Unit 2 (Lessons 4–6)

I   Fill in the blanks with the appropriate particle.

1) 毎朝 この 時間 （   ） かいしゃに 来るんですか。

2) きょねん 富士山 （   ） のぼりました。

3) もうすぐ 5時 （   ） なります。

4) かぜですか。はやく うちに 帰ったほう （   ） いいですよ。

5) 毎日 うちの ちかく （   ） あるいています。

II   Choose the correct word from among the alternatives (1–4) given. The same word cannot be used twice in the same dialogue.

1) A：えいがを 見に 行くんですが、いっしょに 行きませんか。

    B：ざんねんですが、（   ） にほんごの レッスンが あるんです。

    1. それから　　2. これから　　3. さっき　　4. こんど

2) A：もう 8時ですよ。（   ） 帰りませんか。

    B：（   ） レポートが できていないんです。

    A：じゃ お先に。

    1. さっき　　2. それから　　3. そろそろ　　4. まだ

3) A：どうしたんですか。かおいろが よく ありませんね。

    B：（   ） ねつが あるんです。（   ） びょういんに 行ってきました。

    1. じつは　　　2. さっき　　　3. ぜひ　　　4. これから

III   Change the form of the word given in parentheses to complete the sentence in a way that makes sense.

1) 毎日 おべんとうを （   ）んですか。（もってきます）

2) きのう 何時に （   ）んですか。（帰りました）

3) 北海道に （   ）ことが ありますか。（行きました）

4) かおいろが わるいですね。むりを （   ） ほうが いいですよ。

    （しません）

5) コンビニに 行って、しんぶんを （   ） きます。（買います）

IV Choose the most appropriate word or phrase from among the alternatives (1–4) given. The same word cannot be used twice in the same dialogue.

1) 朝 おきて、シャワーを（　　　）。
   1. みがきます　　2. あびます　　3. あそびます　　4. あらいます

2) ゴホゴホッ。（　　　）。
   1. かぜが あります　　　2. かぜを もっています
   3. かぜを とりました　　4. かぜを ひきました

3) A：あたまが いたいんです。
   B：かぜですか。（　　　）。
   1. お大事に　　2. お先に　　3. がんばって　　4. おつかれさま

4) A：今週の 土曜日に サッカーの しあいを 見に 行きませんか。
   B：ちょっと（　　　）が わるいんです。
   A：そうですか。じゃ、また つぎの（　　　）に。
   1. 気分　　2. つごう　　3. きかい　　4. 用事

V Fill in the blanks with the correct reading of each kanji.

1) 一日に 三回 この 薬を 飲んでください。
   （　　）（　　）（　　）（　　　　）

2) 昼休みに 会議の レポートを 書きました。
   （　　）（　　）　　　（　　　）

3) まだ 中国の れきしの 本を 読んでいません。
   　（　　　）　　　（　　）（　　）

3

RETURNING TO JAPAN FOR WORK

Self-introductions are among the first things you practice when starting to learn Japanese. Taking such introductions one step further, this unit—based on the scenario of someone returning to Japan after a hiatus—explains how to talk about past events in your life, the history of the place you live in, and other subjects you know well, incorporating these topics with discussion of some fairly sophisticated grammatical forms. Learn through this unit to talk more about yourself and your environment in Japanese.

GREETING A NEW EMPLOYEE

TARGET DIALOGUE

Department Manager Sasaki is introducing Marie Martin, who has just been transferred from the Paris branch office.

佐々木： みなさん、ごしょうかいします。こちらは　マリー・マルタ
(ささき)　　ンさんです。

マルタン：はじめまして。マリー・マルタンです。３年前に　大学を　そ
　　　　　　　　　　　　　　　　　　　(ねんまえ)　(だいがく)
　　　　つぎょうして　パリ支社に　入りました。パリでは　マーケティ
　　　　　　　　　　　(ししゃ)　(はい)
　　　　ングの　仕事を　していました。よろしく　おねがいします。
　　　　　　　(しごと)

After the self-introduction:

鈴木： 　日本は　はじめてですか。
(すずき)　(にほん)

マルタン：いいえ。大学に　入る　前に、ホームステイを　した　こと
　　　　　　　　(だいがく)　(はい)　(まえ) →p. 103
　　　　が　あります。

加藤： 　マリーさん、ひさしぶりですね。
(かとう)

マルタン：あ、加藤さん。ごぶさたしています。
　　　　　　(かとう)

佐々木： 　ああ、加藤さんは　パリきんむの　とき、会った　ことが
　　　　　　　(かとう)　　　　→p. 106　　　(あ)
　　　　あるんですね。

加藤： 　ええ、そうなんです。(turning to Ms. Martin) 仕事が　終わってか
　　　　　　　　　　　　　　　　　　　　　(しごと)　(お) →p. 104
　　　　ら　よく　食事に　行きましたね。
　　　　　　　(しょくじ)　(い)

マルタン：ええ。なつかしいですね。

Sasaki: Everyone, I'm going to introduce someone to you. This is Ms. Marie Martin.

Martin: Pleased to meet you. I'm Marie Martin. I graduated from college three years ago and joined the Paris branch office. In Paris I worked in marketing. I look forward to working with all of you.

Suzuki: Is this your first time in Japan?

Martin: No. Before entering college, I did a homestay.

Kato: Marie, it's been a long time!

Martin: Oh, Mr. Kato, I'm sorry I haven't been keeping in touch.

Sasaki: Mr. Kato, you met Ms. Martin when you were working in Paris, didn't you?

Kato: Yes, that's right. We often went out to eat after work, didn't we?

Martin: That's right. I remember those times.

VOCABULARY

ごしょうかいします	I am going to make an introduction (polite form)	ごぶさたしています	I have not been staying in touch
そつぎょうする	graduate	～きんむ	on duty (in)
そつぎょう	graduation	きんむ	job assignment, duties
マーケティング	marketing	とき	time, when (see p. 106)
はじめて	for the first time	～から	after . . . (particle; see p. 104)
ホームステイ	homestay	なつかしい	nostalgic
ひさしぶり（です）	it has been a long time		

NOTES

1. パリでは

The は of パリ では emphasizes the contrast between Ms. Martin's time in Paris and her current assignment in Japan. You can add は to a number of particles, including で, に, と, から, and まで, to express contrast. For example:

加藤さんには　会いましたが、鈴木さんには　会いませんでした。
I met Mr. Kato, but I did not meet Mr. Suzuki.

今日は　ひまですが、あしたからは　いそがしいです。
Today I am free, but from tomorrow I will be busy.

But you cannot add は to が or を. は replaces these particles entirely.

広島の　しゃしんを　見た　ことは　ありますが、行った　ことは　ありません。
I have seen pictures of Hiroshima, but I have never been there.

2. 日本（にほん）は　はじめてですか。

Be careful of the difference between はじめて, "for the first time," and はじめに, "in the beginning," "to begin with."

3. ひさしぶりですね。／ごぶさたしています。

The first phrase means "I haven't seen you for a long time" and you use it as a greeting when you meet someone again after a long hiatus of being apart. ごぶさたしています, "I haven't been keeping in touch," is more formal and you use it when talking to superiors or when writing letters.

4. そうなんです。

Mr. Kato responds with そうなんです, rather than with そうです, to confirm that Ms. Sasaki's interpretation—that he had met Ms. Martin while working in Paris—is correct.

5. 食事（しょくじ）に　行（い）きましたね。

This is the same "go to do something" pattern that you learned about in Unit 1, Lesson 3 (p. 38). With certain nouns that are considered activities such as 食事（しょくじ）, ゴルフ, 買（か）いもの, etc., the noun can be followed directly by に　行（い）く.

6. なつかしいですね。

なつかしい literally means "nostalgic." You say なつかしい when you are reminded of something out of your past, even if you are not particularly nostalgic about it.

GRAMMAR & PATTERN PRACTICE

Ⅰ Expressing a Sequence of Events (1): "Before"

前 (まえ) に means "before." The verb coming before 前 (まえ) に is always in the dictionary form regardless of the tense of the verb at the end of the sentence.

日本に　来る　前に、日本語の　べんきょうを　はじめました。
にほん　く　まえ　にほんご

I began my studies of Japanese before I came to Japan.

However, when the emphasis is not on the order of the actions but on the duration of the previous action, you often omit に.

日本に　来る　前、２年間　日本語の　べんきょうを　していました。
にほん　く　まえ　ねんかん　にほんご

I had studied Japanese for two years before I came to Japan.

Complete the sentences as in the example.

例)　しんかんせんに　のります。
れい

→ しんかんせんに　のる　前に、
まえ

おべんとうを　買います。
か

1) 仕事を　はじめます。
しごと

→ .... 前に、ヨガを　します。
まえ

2) パリに　行きます。
い

→ .... 前に、ガイドブックを　よく　読みます。
まえ　よ

3) 大学を　そつぎょうします。
だいがく

→ .... 前に、会社を　つくりました。
まえ　かいしゃ

4) 会社に　入ります。
かいしゃ　はい

→ .... 前に、１か月　りょこうを　しました。
まえ　いっ　げつ

5) 国に　帰ります。
くに　かえ

→ .... 前に、おみやげを　買いました。
まえ　か

II Expressing a Sequence of Events (2): "After"

The *-te* form of a verb followed by から (hereafter ～てから) means "after ——ing." Do not confuse this form with the から that means "because."

日本に　来てから、日本語の　べんきょうを　はじめました。
<small>に ほん　　き　　　に ほん ご</small>
I began my studies of Japanese after I came to Japan.

～てから can also mean "since . . ." and in this sense it is often accompanied by the adverb ずっと, meaning "the whole time." For example:

日本に　来てから、ずっと　日本語の　べんきょうを　しています。
<small>に ほん　　き　　　　　　　　に ほん ご</small>
I have been studying Japanese ever since I came to Japan.

---

1 Complete the sentences as in the example.

例）しんかんせんに　のります。
<small>れい</small>
　　→ しんかんせんに　のってから、
　　　　おべんとうを　食べます。
<small>た</small>

1) 仕事が　終わります。
<small>し ごと　　お</small>
　　→ .... から、スポーツクラブに　行きます。
<small>い</small>

2) パリに　行きます。
<small>い</small>
　　→ .... から、ホテルを　さがします。

3) 大学を　そつぎょうします。
<small>だいがく</small>
　　→ .... から、会社を　つくりました。
<small>かいしゃ</small>

4) 会社に　入ります。
<small>かいしゃ　はい</small>
　　→ .... から、えいかいわの　レッスンを
　　　　はじめました。

5) 会社に　入ります。
<small>かいしゃ　はい</small>
　　→ .... から、ずっと　えいかいわの
　　　　レッスンを　しています。

VOCABULARY

ずっと	the whole time, ever (since)
えいかいわ	English conversation
かいわ	conversation

6) 中学を　そつぎょうします
　　ちゅうがく
　　→ .... から、ずっと　やきゅうを　していません。

7) 中学に　入ります。
　　ちゅうがく　はい
　　→ .... から　高校を　そつぎょうするまで、
　　　　　　　　　　　　　　　　　　　　こうこう
　　じゅうどうを　していました。

2 Read the following schedules and complete the sentences using either 〜前に or 〜てから,
　　　　　　　　　　　　　　　　　　　　　　　　　　　　　　　　まえ
as in the example.

ミルズさんの　朝　　　　　　　　　マルタンさんの　朝
　　　　　　　あさ　　　　　　　　　　　　　　　　　あさ

5：00 ┬　　　　　　　　　　5：00 ┬
　　　│　おきる　　　　　　　　　│
　　　│　　　　　　　　　　　　　│
6：00 ┼　ジョギングを　する　6：00 ┼　おきる
　　　│　シャワーを　あびる　　　│　シャワーをあびる
7：00 ┼　朝ごはんを　食べる　7：00 ┼　おけしょうを　する
　　　│　あさ　　　　た　　　　　│　メールを　チェックする
　　　│　うちを　でる　　　　　　│　うちを　でる
8：00 ┴　会社に　つく　　　8：00 ┼　朝ごはんを　買う
　　　　　かいしゃ　　　　　　　　│　あさ　　　　か
　　　　　メールをチェックする　　│　会社に　つく
　　　　　　　　　　　　　　　　　│　かいしゃ
　　　　　　　　　　　　　　　　　┴　朝ごはんを　食べる
　　　　　　　　　　　　　　　　　　　あさ　　　　た

例）ミルズさんは　朝ごはんを　<u>食べる　前</u>に、ジョギングを　します。
れい　　　　　　　　あさ　　　　　た　　まえ

1) ミルズさんは　朝ごはんを .... 、うちを　でます。
　　　　　　　　　あさ

2) マルタンさんは　会社に .... 、朝ごはんを　食べます。
　　　　　　　　　　かいしゃ　　　　　　　　　　　　　あさ　　　　　た

3) ミルズさんは　会社に .... 、メールを　チェックします。
　　　　　　　　　かいしゃ

4) マルタンさんは　うちを .... 、メールを　チェックします。

VOCABULARY

チェックする	check	こうこう	senior high school
（お）けしょうを　する	make up (one's face)	そつぎょうするまで	until graduation
（お）けしょう	make-up	〜まで	until
ちゅうがく	junior high school		

105

III "When" (1)

とき by itself means "time," but when it is used after a modifier it means "when." Here you will learn how to use とき in this sense with noun and adjectival modifiers.

Modifier	Example
noun	学生の　とき
-i adjective	さむい　とき
-na adjective	ひまな　とき

Examples:

（私は）　学生の　とき、毎日　１０時間　べんきょうしました。
I studied for ten hours a day when I was a student.

（私は）　ひまな　とき、よく　えいがを　見に　行きました。
I often went to see movies when I had free time.

（私は）　ひまな　とき、よく　えいがを　見に　行きます。
I often go to see movies when I have free time.

NOTE: You will learn about とき with other modifiers (verbs) in Lesson 8.

Complete the sentences as in the example.

例）あかんぼう　　→ あかんぼうの　とき、日本に　すんでいました。

1) 子ども　　　　→ ……………………、毎日　サッカーを　していました。

2) ６さい　　　　→ ……………………、小学校に　入りました。

3) あつい　　　　→ ……………………、アイスクリームを　食べます。

4) げんき　　　　→ ……………………、いえじゅうを　そうじします。

5) あたまが　いたい → ……………………、何も　したくないです。

あかんぼう	baby
～さい	years old (counter for a person's age)
しょうがっこう	elementary/primary school
いえじゅう	the entire house, throughout the house
～じゅう	throughout (suffix)

106

PRACTICE 1

WORD POWER

I. Life:

① 生まれる
　う

② 入学する
　にゅうがく
（学校に　入る）
　がっこう　はい

③ そつぎょうする
（学校を　でる）
　がっこう

④ しけんを　うける

⑤ しゅうしょくする

⑥ てんしょくする

⑦ たいしょくする
（会社を　やめる）
　かいしゃ

⑧ こんやくする

⑨ けっこんする

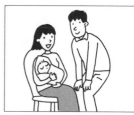

⑩ 子どもが　できる
　こ

⑪ 子どもが　生まれる
　こ　　　　う

⑫ ひっこす

⑬ りこんする

⑭ しぬ

VOCABULARY					
うまれる (R2)	be born	しゅうしょく	getting a job	けっこんする	get married
にゅうがくする	enter school	てんしょくする	change jobs	こどもが　できる	become pregnant
にゅうがく	entrance into school	てんしょく	changing jobs	こどもが　うまれる	have a child
しけんを　うける (R2)	take an exam	たいしょくする	retire	ひっこす	move
しけん	test, exam	たいしょく	retiring	りこんする	get divorced
うける (R2)	receive	こんやくする	get engaged	りこん	divorce
しゅうしょくする	get a job	こんやく	engagement		

107

SPEAKING PRACTICE ━━━━━━━━━━━━━━

I. Asking an actress whether she will continue to work after getting married:

きしゃ： ごこんやく　おめでとうございます。

じょゆう：ありがとうございます。

きしゃ： けっこんしてからも、ずっと　仕事を　つづけますか。

じょゆう：もちろんです。こんやくする　前に、かれと　やくそくしました。

reporter: Congratulations on your engagement.
actress: Thank you.
reporter: Are you going to continue to work even after your get married?
actress: Of course. I made an agreement with him (i.e., my fiancé) before getting engaged.

II. Having lunch in Kyoto with a colleague who is based there:

ミルズ： 山本さんは　ずっと　京都に　すんでいるんですか。

山本： いいえ、5年前までは　東京に　すんでいました。てんきんで　京都に　来たんです。

ミルズ： おくさんは　京都の　かたですか。

山本： ええ、こちらに　来てから、しりあったんです。

Mills: Have you always lived in Kyoto?
Yamamoto: No. I lived in Tokyo until five years ago. I came to Kyoto because I was transferred here.
Mills: Is your wife from Kyoto?
Yamamoto: Yes. I got to know her after coming here.

VOCABULARY			
きしゃ	reporter	かれ	he/him, my boyfriend
（ご）こんやく	engagement	やくそくする	promise
おめでとうございます	congratulations	てんきん	being transferred
じょゆう	actress	〜で	because of (particle)
つづける (R2)	continue with	しりあう	get to know
もちろん	of course		

108

III. Asking the daughter of a colleague about her experience with ballet after seeing her perform:

マルタン：愛子さん、とても　すてきでしたよ。

愛子：　　ありがとうございます。

マルタン：愛子さんは　いつ　バレエを　はじめたんですか。

愛子：　　３さいの　ときです。

マルタン：それから　ずっと　つづけているんですか。

愛子：　　いいえ、高2の　とき、いちど　やめました。じゅけんべんきょう
　　　　　　が　たいへんでしたから。大学に　入ってから、また　はじめたん
　　　　　　です。

Martin:	Aiko, you were lovely.
Aiko:	Thank you.
Martin:	When did you begin doing ballet?
Aiko:	When I was three years old.
Martin:	Have you been doing (lit., "continuing with") it ever since then?
Aiko:	No, I quit once when I was in my second year of senior high. That was because studying to take the university entrance exams was tough. Once I entered college, I began doing it again.

VOCABULARY		
	あいこ	Aiko (given name)
	バレエ	ballet
	こう2	second year of senior high school
	じゅけんべんきょう	studying for entrance exams
	じゅけん	taking entrance exams

PRACTICE 2

WORD POWER

I. Fields of expertise:

① ほうりつ
② けいざい
③ ぶんがく
④ いがく
⑤ けいえい

⑥ ぶつり
⑦ すうがく
⑧ コンピューターサイエンス
⑨ バイオテクノロジー
⑩ こくさいかんけい

$$\int_1^3 x^2\,dx$$

II. Occupations:

① きょうし
② コンサルタント
③ いしゃ
④ かんごし
⑤ けいかん

⑥ プログラマー
⑦ けんちくか
⑧ けんきゅうしゃ
⑨ がいこうかん
⑩ こうむいん

III. Divisions of a company:

① マーケティング
② えいぎょう
③ けいり
④ そうむ
⑤ こうほう

⑥ システム
⑦ かいはつ
⑧ きかく
⑨ 人事
　　じんじ
⑩ しょうひんかんり

SPEAKING PRACTICE

I. Giving a short speech when joining a local soccer club:

　３ちょうめの　さくらマンションの　中田英之です。ヒデと　よんでくだ
さい。サッカーは　高校で　３年、大学で　４年　やりました。ポジション
は　フォワードでした。会社に　入ってからは、ずっと　やっていません。
しんぱいですが、よろしく　おねがいします。

I'm Hideyuki Nakata from Sakura Apartments in District Three. Call me Hide. I played soccer in high school for three years, and in college for four. My position was forward. I haven't played soccer at all since I joined the company I work at now. I'm a bit nervous, but I look forward to playing with all of you.

II. Speaking at an informal gathering for people in different industries:

　のぞみコンサルティングの　井上です。大学を　でてから　ずっと　しょ
うしゃに　いましたが、５年前に　会社を　やめて　コンサルティングの
仕事を　はじめました。のぞみコンサルティングに　入る　前は、さくらコン
サルティングに　いました。よろしく　おねがいします。

I'm Inoue of Nozomi Consulting. After graduating from college, I worked in a trading company for a long time, but five years ago I quit that company and began working as a consultant. Before I joined Nozomi Consulting, I was at Sakura Consulting. I'm glad to have this opportunity to meet all of you.

VOCABULARY

３ちょうめ	third district	いのうえ	Inoue (surname)
〜ちょうめ	district	しょうしゃ	trading company
さくらマンション	Sakura Apartments (fictitious apartment building)	さくらコンサルティング	Sakura Consulting (fictitious company)
なかた	Nakata (surname)		
ひでゆき	Hideyuki (given name)		
ヒデ	Hide (nickname)		
〜と　よんでください	call me . . .		
〜と	(particle used after a quotation)		
やる	do (less formal than する)		
ポジション	position		
フォワード	forward (position in a game)		
のぞみコンサルティング	Nozomi Consulting (fictitious company)		
コンサルティング	consulting		

111

READING TASK

佐々木さんの　けいれき
さ　さ　き

　佐々木　恵子さんは　札幌で　生まれました。１０さいの　とき、東京
さ　さ　き　けいこ　　　さっぽろ　　　う　　　　　　　　　じゅっ　　　　　　　　とうきょう
に　ひっこしました。東京の　大学に　入って、けいざいの　べんきょうを
とうきょう　だいがく　はい
しました。大学を　そつぎょうして、ＡＢＣフーズに　入りました。
だいがく　　　　　　　　　　　　　　　　　はい

　３２さいの　とき、けっこんしました。２年後に　子どもが　生まれまし
ねんご　こ　　　　う
た。子どもが　生まれる　前と　後に　半年ずつ　休みましたが、ずっと
こ　　　う　　　まえ　あと　はんとし　やす
仕事を　つづけています。　佐々木さんは　今　えいぎょう部の　ぶちょう
しごと　　　　　　　　　　　　　　　　　さ　さ　き　　　いま　　　　　　　ぶ
です。ＡＢＣフーズでは　じょせいの　ぶちょうは　佐々木さんが　はじめ
さ　さ　き
てです。

Answer the following questions:

1) 佐々木さんは　何さいの　とき　東京に　ひっこしましたか。
さ　さ　き　　　なん　　　　　　　とうきょう
2) 東京に　ひっこす　前、佐々木さんは　どこに　すんでいましたか。
とうきょう　　　　　　まえ　さ　さ　き
3) 佐々木さんは　大学で　何の　べんきょうを　しましたか。
さ　さ　き　　　だいがく　なん
4) 佐々木さんは　子どもが　生まれる前と　後に　どのぐらい　仕事を　休みま
さ　さ　き　　　こ　　　う　　　まえ　あと　　　　　　　　しごと　やす
したか。

VOCABULARY

けいれき	personal history
２年後 ねんご	two years later
～後 ご	later
半年 はんとし	half a year
じょせい	female, woman

KANJI PRACTICE

学 learn

大学 だいがく
入学 にゅうがく
見学 けんがく

生 be born / student

生まれる う
学生 がくせい
先生 せんせい

校 school

学校 がっこう
小学校 しょうがっこう
高校 こうこう

支 branch

支社 ししゃ

社 company

会社 かいしゃ
本社 ほんしゃ
社員 しゃいん

終	終わる 終わり							
end								

語	日本語 にほんご							
word language								

子	子ども こ							
child								

男	男の人 おとこ ひと							
man								

女	女の子 おんな こ							
woman								

TARGET DIALOGUE

Ms. Martin is about to visit the Nakajimas, her homestay family from seven years ago, at their home. On the way from the station, she meets Emi Morita, the Nakajimas' next-door neighbor.

森田：　　あのう、マリーさん　じゃ
　　　　　ありませんか。

マルタン：えっ、あ、エミちゃん？

森田：　　おひさしぶりです。マリーさん、
　　　　　いつ、こちらに？

マルタン：先月から　東京で　仕事を　しているんです。エミちゃん、
　　　　　　　　　　　　　　　　　　　　　　　　　　→ p. 117
　　　　　大きく　なりましたね。

森田：　　今、中2です。これから　じゅくに　行くんです。

Arriving at the Nakajima home, Ms. Martin gets into a conversation with her former host mother.

マルタン：この　あたり、ずいぶん　にぎやかに　なりましたね。

中島：　　そうでしょう。7年前と　くらべて、だいぶ　便利に　なり
　　　　　ましたよ。

マルタン：ここに　来る　とき、おとなりの　エミちゃんに　会いました。
　　　　　→ p. 119
　　　　　じゅくに　行くと　言っていました。日本の　子どもは　たい
　　　　　→ p. 122
　　　　　へんですね。

Morita:　　Uhhh, aren't you Marie?
Martin:　　Oh, Emi?
Morita:　　It's been a long time. When did you come here, Marie?
Martin:　　I've been working in Tokyo since last month. You've grown, haven't you, Emi?
Morita:　　I'm in my second year of junior high school now. I'm on my way to *juku*.
. . . . . .
Martin:　　This area has certainly come to life (lit., "gotten lively"), hasn't it?
Nakajima:　You can say that again. It's become much more convenient compared to seven years ago, you know.
Martin:　　On my way here, I met Emi from next door. She said she was going to *juku*. Japanese children have it rough, don't they?

VOCABULARY

森田 もりた	Morita (surname)
じゃ　ありませんか	is it not . . . ?, are you not . . . ?
エミ	Emi (given name)
〜ちゃん	(title of courtesy; see Note 2 below)
中２ ちゅう	second year of junior high school
じゅく	cram school
中島 なかじま	Nakajima (surname)
ずいぶん	considerably
〜と　くらべて	compared to . . .
〜と	(particle indicating a standard to which something is compared)
くらべる (R2)	compare
だいぶ	quite a bit

NOTES

1. マリーさん　じゃありませんか。

   Even though Emi Morita thinks that the woman she sees is probably Marie Martin, she is not quite sure, so she uses this sentence pattern to address her. If you have mistakenly identified a stranger as someone you know, all you have to do is apologize with すみません でした. And if someone mistakes you for someone else, you can just say, いいえ、ちがいます, "No, you're mistaken."

2. えっ、あ、エミちゃん？

   Ms. Martin reacts with surprise because Emi has spoken to her without warning and because she has changed a lot in seven years. ちゃん is an informal title of courtesy used mainly toward women younger than oneself, or toward children.

3. いつ、こちらに？

   This is an abbreviation of いつ、こちらに　来（き）たんですか.

4. 中（ちゅう）２

   Compulsory education in Japan consists of six years of elementary school, 小学校（しょうがっこう）, and three years of junior high school, 中学校（ちゅうがっこう）. When talking about a child's year in school, you can use abbreviations such as 中（ちゅう）２ for 中学２年生（ちゅうがく２ねんせい）, "second-year student in junior high school."

5. じゅく

   じゅく are private after-school "cram schools" in which children and teenagers study for junior and senior high school and university entrance exams.

6. ずいぶん、だいぶ

   Both ずいぶん and だいぶ mean "to a large extent," but ずいぶん has the nuance of "more than expected," while だいぶ means "more, but not quite completely."

7. そうでしょう。

   Use this when the other person says something that you, too, believe to be true or strongly agree with. Say it with a rising intonation.

GRAMMAR & PATTERN PRACTICE

I Describing a Change in State (1)

なります means "become" or "get" and indicates a change of state. You use it with adjectives in their adverbial forms (see Unit 2, Lesson 6, p. 84) and with nouns followed by に.

コートや　セーターが　安く　なりました。

Coats and sweaters and the like have become cheaper.

てんきが　よく　なりました。

The weather has gotten better.

マリーさんは　日本語が　じょうずに　なりました。

Marie has gotten better at Japanese. (lit., "As for Mary, her Japanese has become good.")

はるに　なりました。

Spring has come. (lit., "It has become spring.")

きょうしに　なりたいです。

I want to become a teacher.

---

1 Complete the sentences as in the example.

例）　大きい　　　→　大きく　なりました。

1) おいしい　　　→　..................................... なりました。

2) いそがしい　　→　..................................... なりました。

3) くらい　　　　→　..................................... なりました。

4) きれい　　　　→　..................................... なりました。

5) ゆうめい　　　→　..................................... なりました。

6) げんき　　　　→　..................................... なりました。

7) きらい　　　　→　..................................... なりました。

VOCABULARY

はる	spring
くらい	dark
きらい（な）	dislike, be sick of

117

2 Complete the sentences as in the example.

例）朝　　　　　　　→　朝に　なりました。
れい　あさ　　　　　　　あさ

1)　夜　　　　　　　→　... なりました。
　　よる

2)　１０さい　　　　→　... なりました。
　　　じゅっ

3)　はたち　　　　　→　... なりました。

4)　大学生　　　　　→　... なりました。
　　だいがくせい

5)　しゃちょう　　　→　... なりました。

6)　びょうき　　　　→　... なりました。

3 Construct pairs of sentences as in the example.

例）はる、あたたかい
れい
　→ はるに　なりました。
　　あたたかく　なりました。

1)　なつ、あつい

　→ ....

　...

2)　あき、すずしい

　→ ....

　...

3)　ふゆ、さむい

　→ ....

　...

VOCABULARY	はたち	twenty years old	ふゆ	winter
	だいがくせい	university student	すずしい	cool
	びょうき	illness, disease		
118	あき	fall		

II "When" (2)

とき, as you have learned, means "when" when it is used after a modifier. When the modifier is a verb, its form is one of the plain forms you learned in Unit 2, Lesson 4 (p. 52). For example:

General しんぶんを 読む とき、めがねを かけます。
I wear glasses when I read ~~the~~ newspaper.

General みちが わからない とき、ちずを 見ます。 ← 状態、
I look at a map when I am lost.

Future あした パーティーに 行く とき、ワインを もっていきます。
I will bring a bottle of wine when I go to the party tomorrow.

Past きょねん ドイツに 行った とき、ビールを たくさん 飲みました。
I drank a lot of beer when I went to Germany last year.

The meaning of the sentence differs depending on which tense, present or past, you use before とき. Consider these examples:

→ 学校に 行くとき ① パンを 買いました。② お金を 捨いました。

日本に 来る とき、くうこうで ② 買いました。
When I came to Japan (i.e., On my way to Japan), I bought it at the airport (i.e., at an airport outside of Japan).

→ 学校に 行ったとき ① パンを 買いました。② お金を 捨いました。

日本に 来た とき、くうこうで ① 買いました。
When I came to Japan (i.e., Having come to Japan), I bought it at the airport (i.e., an airport in Japan).

When the tense before とき is present, as in the first example, the action in the temporal clause (i.e., the とき clause) has not been completed when the action in the main sentence takes place. On the other hand, if the tense before とき is past, as in the second example, it means that the action in the temporal clause has been completed at the moment the action in the main sentence occurs.

does it imply that deep?

Read the following sentences aloud while considering their meanings.

1) 鈴木さんは よく しんかんせんで 大阪に 行きます。

2) しんかんせんに のる とき、いつも ビールを 買います。

VOCABULARY　　かける (R2)　　put on (glasses)
　　　　　　　　　　みち　　　　　　　road, way

119

3) きのうも　しんかんせんに　<u>のる</u>　とき、<u>ばいてんで</u>
<u>ビールを　買いました</u>。
_か

not completed before getting on the shinkansen.

4) しんかんせんに　<u>のった</u>　とき、ビールを　おとし
ました。

same time?

5) ビールを　ひろって、せきに　すわりました。

6) すぐ　ビールを　飲みたく　なりました。
_の

7) ビールを　あける　とき、すこし　しんぱいでした。

8) ビールを　あけた　とき、……。

9) 鈴木さんは　大阪まで　とても　さむかったです。
_{すず き}　　　　_{おおさか}

10) 大阪に　ついた　とき、かぜを　ひいていました。
_{おおさか}

| VOCABULARY | ばいてん | stall, kiosk |
| | ひろう | pick up |

120

Plain Forms of Adjectives and of Nouns +です

You learned the plain forms of verbs in Unit 2, Lesson 4 (p. 52). Adjectives and nouns + です have plain forms, too. They are as follows:

-I adjectives

	-*desu* form	plain form
present aff.	おいしいです	おいしい
present neg.	おいしくないです	おいしくない
past aff.	おいしかったです	おいしかった
past neg.	おいしくなかったです	おいしくなかった

-Na adjectives

	-*desu* form	plain form
present aff.	便利です	便利だ
present neg.	便利では ありません	便利では ない
past aff.	便利でした	便利だった
past neg.	便利では ありませんでした	便利では なかった

Nouns +です

	-*desu* form	plain form
present aff.	あめです	あめだ
present neg.	あめでは ありません	あめでは ない
past aff.	あめでした	あめだった
past neg.	あめでは ありませんでした	あめでは なかった

Ⅳ Using Direct and Indirect Quotation

You use と言（い）っていました to report what someone said, in both direct and indirect quotation. (In direct quotation, you use 「　」 in place of quotation marks.)

林さんは 「京都に 行きます」と 言っていました。
はやし　　　きょうと　　い　　　　　　　い
Mr. Hayashi said, "I will go to Kyoto."

In indirect quotation, you use plain forms for the part quoted.

林さんは 京都に 行くと 言っていました。
はやし　　きょうと　　い　　　　　い
Mr. Hayashi said he would go to Kyoto.

林さんは 京都に 行ったと 言っていました。
はやし　　きょうと　　い　　　　　　い
Mr. Hayashi said he went to Kyoto.

You use 言（い）いました instead of 言（い）っていました when you want to emphasize the fact that someone said something, rather than the content of what they said.

---

1 Complete the sentences as in the example.

例） マルタン：かんじは おもしろいです。
れい

→ マルタンさんは <u>かんじは おもしろい</u>と 言っていました。
い

1) 鈴木：ゆうべの パーティーは にぎやかでした。
すずき

→ 鈴木さんは _____ と 言っていました。
すずき　　　　　　　　　　　　　　　　　　　　　い

2) 佐々木：きいろい さいふが ほしいです。
ささき

→ 佐々木さんは _____ と 言っていました。
ささき　　　　　　　　　　　　　　　　　　　　い

3) グリーン：毎年 しょうがつは ハワイで すごします。
まいとし

→ グリーンさんは _____ と 言っていました。
い

言（い）ます is not the only verb that you use after と in quotations. You can also use おもいます, "to think," or ききます "to ask," "to hear," for instance.

（私は）林さんは 京都に 行くと おもいます。
わたし　はやし　　きょうと　　い
I think Mr. Hayashi will go to Kyoto.

To say, "I don't think . . ." you use 〜ないと　おもいます.

> （私は）林さんは　京都に　行かないと　おもいます。
> わたし　　はやし　　きょうと
> I don't think Mr. Hayashi will go to Kyoto. (lit., "I think Mr. Hayashi will not go to Kyoto.")

と　おもいます is the phrase to use when expressing your opinion or asking another person theirs. To state what a third person thinks, use と　おもっています (to be studied in Book III).

> 部長は　林さんは　京都に　行くと　思っています。
> ぶちょう　はやし　　きょうと　　い　　おも
> Our department manager thinks Mr. Hayashi will go to Kyoto.

---

2 Complete the answers to the questions as in the example.

例）あたらしい　プロジェクトには　お金が　たくさん　かかりますか。
れい　　　　　　　　　　　　　　かね

　　A：かかると　おもいます。

　　B：かからないと　おもいます。

1) プロジェクトは　今年中に　終わりますか。
　　　　　　　　　ことしじゅう　お

　　A：..............................と　おもいます。 　終わる

　　B：..............................と　おもいます。 　終わらない）

2) プロジェクトには　あたらしい　コンピューターが　ひつようですか。

　　A：..............................と　おもいます。 　必要だ

　　B：..............................と　おもいます。 　必要ではない

3) A社の　コンピューターは　いいですか。
　　しゃ

　　A：..............................と　おもいます。 　いい）

　　B：..............................と　おもいます。 　よくない

4) A社の　コンピューターより　安くて　いい　コンピューターが　ありま
　　しゃ　　　　　　　　　　　やす
　　すか。

　　A：..............................と　おもいます。 　ある

　　B：..............................と　おもいます。 　ない）

VOCABULARY

（おかねが）かかる	cost (money)
ことしじゅう	within the year
ひつよう（な）	necessary
コンピューター	computer

123

PRACTICE 1

WORD POWER

I. Nature:

① 木
　き
② みどり
③ かわ
④ うみ
⑤ いけ
⑥ みずうみ
⑦ 空気
　くうき

⑧ くも
⑨ やま
⑩ もり
⑪ はやし
⑫ はたけ
⑬ たんぼ

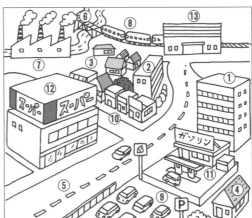

II. Urban life:

① マンション
② アパート
③ じゅうたく
④ いえ
⑤ どうろ／みち
⑥ はし
⑦ こうじょう

⑧ こうつうきかん
⑨ ちゅうしゃじょう
⑩ しょうてんがい
⑪ ガソリンスタンド
⑫ おおがたスーパー
⑬ えきビル

III. Expressions for talking about change:

① できる
② なくなる
③ かわる
④ きれいになる

⑤ きたなくなる
⑥ おおくなる（ふえる）
⑦ すくなくなる（へる）
⑧ 便利になる
　べんり

⑨ ふべんになる
⑩ ひろくなる
⑪ せまくなる

VOCABULARY					
き	tree	たんぼ	rice paddy	えきビル	station building
みどり	green	じゅうたく	housing	できる (R2)	be built
かわ	river	いえ	house	なくなる	disappear
いけ	pond	どうろ	road	かわる	change
くうき	air	はし	bridge	きたない	dirty
くも	cloud	こうつうきかん	means of transportation	ふえる (R2)	increase
もり	forest	しょうてんがい	shopping street	へる	decrease
はやし	grove	ガソリンスタンド	gas station	ふべん (な)	inconvenient
はたけ	field, patch	おおがたスーパー	large supermarket	せまい	cramped

SPEAKING PRACTICE

I. Talking about a change that has come over an area of town:

マルタン：この　あたり、7年前は　はたけでしたよね。

中島：　　ええ。3年前に　えきが　できてから、きゅうに　マンションや
　　　　　じゅうたくが　ふえたんです。

マルタン：あの　白くて　大きい　たてものは　何ですか。

中島：　　コミュニティーセンターですよ。きょねん　できたんです。

Martin: Seven years ago, this area was fields, wasn't it?

Nakajima: Yes. Ever since the station was built three years ago, (the number of) apartment blocks and residences has increased dramatically.

Martin: What is that large, white (lit., "white, large") building over there?

Nakajima: It's the community center. It was built last year.

II. Being relieved to see that a park one once knew is still the same old park:

マルタン：あっ！　この　こうえんは　かわっていませんね。

中島：　　ええ。木も　いけも　むかしの　ままです。

マルタン：よかった！

Martin: Wow! This park hasn't changed, has it?

Nakajima: That's right. The trees and the pond are just as they were back in the old days.

Martin: I'm so glad!

VOCABULARY		
	〜よね	right? (sentence-final particle combination)
	たてもの	building
	きゅうに	suddenly, dramatically
	あっ	wow
	〜も　〜も	both . . . and . . .
	むかし	back in the old days
	〜の　まま	just as it is/was

PRACTICE 2

SPEAKING PRACTICE

Greeting a friend one has not seen in a long time:

前田： ひさしぶりですね。

佐々木：ほんとうに。何年ぶりでしょう。

前田： ２０年ぶりじゃありませんか。

佐々木：むかしと　ぜんぜん　かわりませんね。

前田： 佐々木さんも。

佐々木：今、何を　しているんですか。

前田： のぞみ銀行に　つとめています。

佐々木：ずっと　東京に？

前田： ５年前から　きょねんまで　シンガポールに　行っていました。

Maeda:	Long time no see.
Sasaki:	You can say that again. How many years has it been, I wonder.
Maeda:	It's been (a period of) twenty years, hasn't it?
Sasaki:	You haven't changed a bit since then, have you!
Maeda:	Same goes for you.
Sasaki:	What are you doing these days?
Maeda:	I work for Nozomi Bank.
Sasaki:	And you've been in Tokyo this whole time?
Maeda:	I was in Singapore from five years ago until last year.

まえだ	Maeda (surname)
のぞみぎんこう	Nozomi Bank (fictitious bank)
〜ぶり	after an interval of . . . (suffix)

READING TASK 1

ホームステイの　おもいで

　私は　7年前に　東京で　ホームステイを　しました。ホストファミリーに　会う　とき、とても　ドキドキしました。はじめて　日本の　りょうりを　食べた　とき、あまり　おいしくないと　おもいましたが、だんだんすきに　なりました。ホームステイを　して、日本人の　ともだちも　たくさん　できました。日本を　はなれる　とき、くうこうで　ホストファミリーに　また　来ると　やくそくしました。

Answer the following questions, assuming you are Ms. Martin:

1) いつ　東京で　ホームステイを　しましたか。
2) ホストファミリーに　会う　とき、どんな　きもちでしたか。
3) はじめて　日本の　りょうりを　食べた　とき、どう　おもいましたか。
4) 日本を　はなれる　とき、くうこうで　どんな　やくそくを　しましたか。

VOCABULARY

おもいで	memory
ホストファミリー	host family
ドキドキする	be nervously excited
だんだん	gradually
はなれる (R2)	leave
きもち	feeling

127

READING TASK 2

原宿物語
はらじゅくものがたり

　原宿は、東京の有名なファッションエリアです。メインストリートの表
はらじゅく　　とうきょう　ゆうめい　　　　　　　　　　　　　　　　　　　　　　　　おもて

参道には、世界中のブランドショップがならんでいます。
さんどう　　せかいじゅう

　私は子どものころからずっと原宿に住んでいます。むかし原宿は静かな
わたし　こ　　　　　　　　　　　　　　　はらじゅく　す　　　　　　　はらじゅく　しず

住宅地でした。小さな川が流れていて、近くのうちの庭にはいちご畑もあり
じゅうたくち　　ちい　かわ　なが　　　　　ちか　　　　　　にわ　　　　　　ばたけ

ました。緑が多くて、空気も今よりきれいでした。商店街には魚屋や八百
みどり　おお　　　くうき　いま　　　　　　　　　しょうてんがい　　さかなや　やお

屋があって、近所の主婦が買い物をしていました。でもそのころ表参道には、
や　　　　　　きんじょ　しゅふ　か　もの　　　　　　　　　　おもてさんどう

もう東京でいちばんモダンなアパートがたっていました。同潤会アパート
とうきょう　　　　　　　　　　　　　　　　　　　　どうじゅんかい

です。

　街は少しずつ変わりました。川がなくなって、道になりました。いちご畑
まち　すこ　　　か　　　　　　かわ　　　　　　　みち　　　　　　　　ばたけ

は駐車場になりました。庭が減って、緑が少なくなりました。商店街に
ちゅうしゃじょう　　　　　にわ　へ　　　みどり　すく　　　　　　しょうてんがい

はブティックやアクセサリーの店ができて、魚屋や八百屋がなくなりまし
みせ　　　　　さかなや　やおや

た。レストランやカフェがたくさんできて、東京でいちばんおしゃれな街
とうきょう　　　　　　　　　まち

になりました。

　２００６年２月に表参道ヒルズがオープンしました。同潤会アパートが
ねん　がつ　おもてさんどう　　　　　　　　　　どうじゅんかい

新しいデザインのファッションビルに変わったのです。原宿はむかしも今
あたら　　　　　　　　　　　　　　　　　か　　　　　はらじゅく　　　　いま

も新しい東京を象徴しています。
あたら　とうきょう　しょうちょう

原宿
はらじゅく

VOCABULARY

原宿 はらじゅく	Harajuku (district in Tokyo)	主婦 しゅふ	housewife
物語 ものがたり	story, tale	そのころ	at that time
ファッションエリア	fashionable part of town	モダン（な）	modern
メインストリート	main street	同潤会アパート どうじゅんかい	Dojunkai Apartments (one of the oldest modern apartments in Japan, dating back to 1926 and constructed of reinforced concrete)
表参道 おもてさんどう	Omotesando (street name)		
世界中 せかいじゅう	all over the world	少しずつ すこ	little by little
ブランドショップ	store selling brand-name apparel	ブティック	boutique
		アクセサリー	accessories
ならぶ	line up	おしゃれ（な）	stylish
ころ	time	表参道ヒルズ おもてさんどう	Omotesando Hills (name of a shopping center)
住宅地 じゅうたくち	residential area		
流れる (R2) なが	flow	オープンする	open (of business)
いちご畑 ばたけ	strawberry patch	デザイン	design
いちご	strawberry	ファッションビル	stylish building containing boutiques and other fancy shops
魚屋 さかなや	fish dealer	〜のです	(written/formal style of 〜んです)
八百屋 やおや	fruit and vegetable dealer	象徴する しょうちょう	symbolize
近所 きんじょ	neighborhood		

STYLE NOTE

When you write Japanese, you do not actually leave a space between one word and another; the use of kanji and kana in combination makes it clear where one word ends and another begins. In this textbook, we have been keeping the number of kanji small, so to make the stories and dialogues easier to read, we have written words separately. With this "Story of Harajuku," however, we have followed the original Japanese notation rules. You should feel that the more kanji there are, the less need there is to have spaces between words.

KANJI PRACTICE

東	東 ひがし 東京 とうきょう	二	厂	戸	戸	亘	車	東
east		東	東	東				

京	東京 とうきょう ＊京都 きょうと	丶	亠	产	宁	亨	亨	京
capital		京	京	京				

西	西 にし	二	厂	丌	丙	西	西	西
west		西						

南	南 みなみ	二	十	忄	市	市	南	南
south		南	南	南	南			

北	北 きた ＊北海道 ほっかいどう	二	十	土	北	北	北	北
north								

| 便 | 便利
べんり | ノ | ノ | イ | イ | イ | 伊 | 便 |
| convenient | | 便 | 便 | 便 | 便 | | | |

| | | | | | | | | |

| 利 | 便利
べんり | ノ | 二 | 千 | 禾 | 禾 | 利 | 利 |
| advantage
profit | | 利 | 利 | | | | | |

| | | | | | | | | |

| 言 | 言う
い | 丶 | 二 | 三 | 言 | 言 | 言 | 言 |
| tell | | 言 | 言 | | | | | |

| | | | | | | | | |

| 夕 | 夕日
ゆうひ
夕食
ゆうしょく | ノ | ク | 夕 | 夕 | 夕 | | |
| evening | | | | | | | | |

| | | | | | | | | |

| 空 | 空ら
そら
空気
くうき
空う | 丶 | 丷 | 宀 | 宇 | 空 | 空 | 空 |
| sky, air
empty | | 空 | 空 | 空 | | | | |

| | | | | | | | | |

LESSON 9 · JOINING A CIVIC ORCHESTRA

TARGET DIALOGUE

Ms. Martin is at a local community center, talking to Mr. Yamakawa, who is in charge of a civic orchestra.

マルタン：この　オーケストラは　いつ　できたんですか。

山川：　去年です。この　コミュニティーセンターが　できた　とき、
やまかわ　きょねん

友人と　メンバーを　ぼしゅうして　作ったんです。
ゆうじん　　　　　　　　　　　　　　　　つく

マルタン：みなさん、けいけんの　長い　方ですか。
なが　かた

山川：　長い　方も　いますが、はじめての　方も　いますよ。
なが　かた　　　　　　　　　　　　かた

マルタン：れんしゅうは　いつですか。

山川：　毎週　水曜の　夜です。メンバーは　はたらいている　人が
まいしゅう　すいよう　よる　　　　　　　　→ p. 134　　　　　　　　　ひと

おおいんです。8時からですが、マリーさんは　間にあいま
じ　　　　　　　　　　　　　　　　　　ま

すか。

マルタン：仕事が　終わるのは　7時ごろですから、だいじょうぶだと
しごと　お　→ p. 136　じ

おもいます。

山川：　じゃ、一度　見に　来ませんか。
いちど　み　き

マルタン：来週　うかがっても　よろしいですか。
らいしゅう

山川：　どうぞ　どうぞ。みんなも　よろこぶと　おもいます。

Martin: When was this orchestra founded?

Yamakawa: Last year. When this community center was founded, a friend and I created the orchestra by recruiting members.

Martin: Are all of them very experienced?

Yamakawa: There are some experienced people, but there are some beginners, too.

Martin: When do you practice?

Yamakawa: Every Wednesday night. Most of the members have jobs. We start at eight o'clock; can you make it?

Martin: Work finishes around seven, so I think I can (lit., "I think it will be all right").

Yamakawa: Well, wouldn't you like to come see us?

Martin: Would it be all right to visit next week?

Yamakawa: Please do. I think everyone will be delighted.

VOCABULARY

オーケストラ	orchestra	〜も　いる	there are also those who . . .
山川 やまかわ	Yamakawa (surname)	はたらく	work
友人 ゆうじん	friend	間にあう ま	be on time, make it
メンバー	member	うかがう	visit (humble form; see Note 5 below)
ぼしゅうする	recruit	よろしいですか	would it be all right? (politer form of いいですか)
ぼしゅう	recruitment	よろこぶ	be pleased, be delighted
けいけん	experience		

NOTES

1. コミュニティーセンター
   Community centers are buildings owned by local governments and established to support residents' cultural activities.

2. 友人（ゆうじん）と　メンバーを　ぼしゅうして　作（つく）ったんです。
   The -te form sometimes indicates a cause or means for another action. Here it means "by" rather than "and."

3. けいけんの　長（なが）い　方（かた）
   This is the same as けいけんが　長（なが）い　方（かた）. When the modifying clause is short, の can replace が.

4. だいじょうぶだと　おもいます。
   と　おもう can express either an opinion or a guess. In this case it indicates that Ms. Martin is guessing that the time of the orchestra practice will suit her schedule. You can even use と　おもう when you are actually sure of your opinion but want to avoid sounding too assertive.

5. うかがう
   This is a humble equivalent of 行（い）く, "to go," and たずねる, "to visit." When you use うかがう, you are being humble about your own actions and showing respect toward the other person.

GRAMMAR & PATTERN PRACTICE

I Forming Modifying Clauses

You have already learned how nouns and adjectives modify nouns.

会社の　くるま   the company car
かいしゃ

かわいい　子ども   a cute child
こ

しんせつな　人   a kind person
ひと

The formation of modifying clauses constructed from nouns or adjectives is as follows:

あめの　日   a rainy day
ひ

あめではない　日   a day that isn't rainy
ひ

けいけんが　長い　人   a person with much experience
なが　ひと

けいけんが　長くない　人   a person who doesn't have much experience
なが　　　　ひと

テニスが　じょうずな　人   a person who is good at tennis
ひと

テニスが　じょうずではない　人   a person who isn't good at tennis
ひと

You use the past tense (plain form) to indicate that the noun being modified used to be in some state but is not anymore.

むかし　高かった　ウイスキー   whiskey that was expensive in the old days
たか

子どもの　ころ　すきだった　本   a book I liked as a child
こ　　　　　　　　　　　　　ほん

去年まで　ちゅうしゃじょうだった　ところ
きょねん

the place that was a parking lot until last year

１０年前は　ぜんぜん　ゆうめいじゃなかった　じょゆう
ねんまえ

an actress who was not at all famous ten years ago

Verbs can also modify nouns, in which case their plain forms are used.

あした　パーティーに　来る　人   a person who will come to the party tomorrow
く　ひと

あした　パーティーに　来ない　人   a person who won't come to the party tomorrow
こ　　ひと

きのう　パーティーに　来た　人   a person who came to the party yesterday
き　ひと

きのう　パーティーに　来なかった　人 a person who didn't come to the party yesterday
こ　　　　　ひと

Any noun in a sentence can be modified by a modifying clause.

これは　マリーさんが　かいた　えです。

This is the picture that Marie drew.

私は　マリーさんが　かいた　えを　見ました。
<ruby>私<rt>わたし</rt></ruby>は　マリーさんが　かいた　えを　<ruby>見<rt>み</rt></ruby>ました。

I saw the picture that Marie drew.

マリーさんが　かいた　えは　会議しつに　あります。
マリーさんが　かいた　えは　<ruby>会議<rt>かいぎ</rt></ruby>しつに　あります。

The picture that Marie drew is in the meeting room.

Note that you cannot use the topic particle は inside a modifying clause. So:

ミルズさんは　本を　買いました。
ミルズさんは　<ruby>本<rt>ほん</rt></ruby>を　<ruby>買<rt>か</rt></ruby>いました。

Mr. Mills bought a book.

but これは　ミルズさんが　買った　本です。
これは　ミルズさんが　<ruby>買<rt>か</rt></ruby>った　<ruby>本<rt>ほん</rt></ruby>です。

This is the book that Mr. Mills bought.

Complete the sentences as in the example.

<ruby>例<rt>れい</rt></ruby>) <ruby>私<rt>わたし</rt></ruby>は　きのう　<u>さいふ</u>を　なくしました。
（<ruby>父<rt>ちち</rt></ruby>に　もらいました）
→ <ruby>私<rt>わたし</rt></ruby>は　きのう　<u><ruby>父<rt>ちち</rt></ruby>に　もらった</u>　さいふを　なくしました。

1) <u>ケーキ</u>は　とても　おいしいです。

（<ruby>母<rt>はは</rt></ruby>が　<ruby>作<rt>つく</rt></ruby>りました）

→ ....　ケーキは　とても　おいしいです。

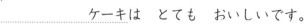

2) <ruby>日曜日<rt>にちようび</rt></ruby>に　<u>デパート</u>で　<ruby>買<rt>か</rt></ruby>いものを　しました。
（<ruby>去年<rt>きょねん</rt></ruby>　できました）

→ <ruby>日曜日<rt>にちようび</rt></ruby>に　......................　デパートで　<ruby>買<rt>か</rt></ruby>いものを　しました。

3) <ruby>私<rt>わたし</rt></ruby>は　<ruby>友<rt>とも</rt></ruby>だちに　<u>ぼうし</u>を　<ruby>見<rt>み</rt></ruby>せました。
（メキシコで　<ruby>買<rt>か</rt></ruby>いました）

→ <ruby>私<rt>わたし</rt></ruby>は　<ruby>友<rt>とも</rt></ruby>だちに　......................　ぼうしを　<ruby>見<rt>み</rt></ruby>せました。

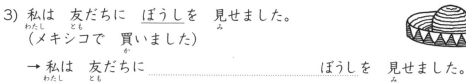

4) <u>ホテル</u>は　あたらしくて　きれいでした。
（<ruby>先月<rt>せんげつ</rt></ruby>　スミスさんが　とまりました）

→ ....　ホテルは　あたらしくて　きれいでした。

VOCABULARY

なくす	lose
メキシコ	Mexico
とまる	stay overnight

135

II Nominalizing Sentences

You can nominalize a sentence (i.e., turn it into a noun clause) by using the particle の.

仕事が　終わるのは　7時ごろです。
し ごと　　お　　　　　　じ

Work ends at around seven. (lit., "As for work's ending, it is around seven o'clock.")

Here の is used to identify the entire phrase 仕事（しごと）が 終（お）わる as the topic of the sentence. の can function to make topics, subjects, or objects out of any sentence segment.

私は　朝　ジョギングを　するのが　すきです。
わたし　あさ

I like jogging in the morning.

私は　ミルズさんが　来るのを　まっています。
わたし　　　　　　　　く

I am waiting for Mr. Mills to get here (lit., "to come")

As these examples show, you use plain forms before の, and the particle が replaces the topic particle は.

Complete the sentences as in the examples.

例1）ひこうきが　つきます。
れい

→ <u>ひこうきが　つく</u>のは　4時です。
じ

1）あしたの　会議に　でます。
かい ぎ

→ ....のは　加藤さんです。
か とう

2）ミルズさんは　しゅっちょうに　行きます。
い

→ ....のは　来週です。
らいしゅう

3）マルタンさんは　日本に　来ました。
に ほん　き

→ ....のは　2か月前です。
げつまえ

4）ABCフーズの　本社が　あります。
ほんしゃ

→ ....のは　サンフランシ

スコです。

例2) スポーツを 見ます。
→ 私は スポーツを 見るのが すきです。

5) えを かきます。
→ マルタンさんは ＿＿＿＿＿＿＿＿＿＿＿＿＿＿ のが すきです。

6) 子どもと あそびます。
→ 加藤さんは ＿＿＿＿＿＿＿＿＿＿＿＿＿＿ のが すきです。

7) おかしを 作ります。
→ 中村さんは ＿＿＿＿＿＿＿＿＿＿＿＿＿＿ のが じょうずです。

8) ヨガを おしえます。
→ シカさんは ＿＿＿＿＿＿＿＿＿＿＿＿＿＿ のが じょうずです。

例3) たまごを 買います。
→ 私は たまごを 買うのを わすれました。

9) お金を はらいます。
→ 私は ＿＿＿＿＿＿＿＿＿＿＿＿＿＿ のを わすれました。

10) メールの へんじを だします。
→ 私は ＿＿＿＿＿＿＿＿＿＿＿＿＿＿ のを わすれました。

11) 会議が 終わります。
→ 加藤さんは ＿＿＿＿＿＿＿＿＿＿＿＿＿＿ のを まっています。

12) にもつが とどきます。
→ ミルズさんは ＿＿＿＿＿＿＿＿＿＿＿＿＿＿ のを まっています。

VOCABULARY		
	たまご	egg
	はらう	pay
	とどく	be delivered

PRACTICE 1

WORD POWER

① ホール   ② じむしつ   ③ しりょうしつ   ④ わしつ   ⑤ きつえんしつ

Explain about the various rooms in a community center by saying the following sentences:

1) ここは　ホールです。コンサートや　こうえん会を　する　ところです。

2) ここは　じむしつです。コミュニティーセンターで　はたらいている　人が　いる　ところです。

3) ここは　しりょうしつです。本や　しりょうが　たくさん　ある　ところです。

4) ここは　わしつです。生け花や　さどうを　ならう　ところです。

5) ここは　きつえんしつです。たばこを　すう　ところです。

1) This is a hall. It's where people give concerts and lectures.
2) This is an office. It's where people working at the community center spend their time.
3) This is a reference room. It's where there are books and lots of other reference materials.
4) This is a Japanese-style room. It's where people take lessons in ikebana and tea ceremony.
5) This is a smoking lounge. It's where people smoke.

VOCABULARY

じむしつ	office	こうえんかい	lecture presentation
しりょうしつ	reference room		
わしつ	Japanese-style room		
きつえんしつ	smoking lounge		

PRACTICE 2

WORD POWER

① おちゃ　　② しゃしん　　③ チャイナ　　④ こうすい　　⑤ かいがら
　　　　　　　　　　　　　　ドレス

Imagine that you are doing "show and tell" with some souvenirs from a recent trip.

1) これは　中国に　行った　とき、買った　おちゃです。でも、まだ　飲んで
　　います。とても　高かったんです。

2) これは｛パリから　ギリシャに　行く　とき、ひこうきから　とった　しゃし
　　ん｝です。きれいな　うみでしょう。

3) これは｛ホンコンに　行った　とき、チャンさんに　もらった　チャイナドレ
　　ス｝です。とても　気に　入っています。

4) これは｛ハワイから　日本に　帰る　とき、ひこうきの　中で　買った　こう
　　すい｝です。あまくて　いい　かおりが　します。

5) これは｛沖縄に　行った　とき、ひろった　かいがら｝です。うみに　しずむ
　　夕日が　ほんとうに　きれいでした。

1) This is tea I bought when I went to China (i.e., while I was in China). I haven't drunk it yet. It was very expensive, you see.
2) This is a photo I took from a plane when I went from Paris to Greece (i.e., on the plane from Paris to Greece). The ocean is beautiful, isn't it?
3) This is a Chinese dress I received from Ms. Chan when I went to Hong Kong. I like it very much.
4) This is perfume I bought in a plane on my way back to Japan from Hawaii. It has a sweet, nice fragrance (lit., "It smells sweet and nice.")
5) These are seashells I picked up when I went to Okinawa (i.e., when I was in Okinawa). The sunset (lit., "the evening sun that sunk into the sea") was truly beautiful.

PRACTICE 3

PHRASE POWER

Describing yourself:

① スポーツを 見る
watch sports

② 人や ものを
かんさつする
observe people and things

③ そとで からだを
うごかす
move around (lit., "move
one's body") outdoors

④ はじめての ことに
ちょうせんする
try new things

⑤ いろいろな 人と
であう
meet new (lit., "various")
people

⑥ あたらしい ぶんかを
しる
know new cultures

⑦ どうぶつの せわを する
take care of animals

⑧ しずかに 時間を すごす
spend time quietly

What type of person are you? Talk about yourself in terms of what you like to do.

1) 私は スポーツを 見るのが すきです。
2) 私は 人や ものを かんさつするのが すきです。
3) 私は そとで からだを うごかすのが すきです。

VOCABULARY					
もの	(concrete) thing	はじめての こと	new things	であう	meet (by chance), encounter
かんさつする	observe	はじめての	first, first-time		
かんさつ	observation	こと	(abstract) thing, matter	ぶんか	culture
そと	outside	ちょうせんする	challenge, test oneself against	どうぶつ	animal
からだ	body	ちょうせん	challenge	せわを する	take care (of)
				せわ	care

READING TASK 1

マルタンさんの　ブログ

Some people use their blogs to describe everyday things that they find curious, things they like or dislike, or things they are fanatical about. Read Ms. Martin's blog.

今日　はじめて　しみんオーケストラの　れんしゅうに　さんかしました。
半年ぶりでしたから、ゆびが　ちゃんと　うごきませんでした。でも、れんしゅうは
たのしかったです。いろいろな　ねんだいの　人が　います。いろいろな　仕事を　もっ
た人が　います。仕事の　後　8時から　れんしゅうするのは　たいへんですけど、何
とか　つづけたいです。

© forca - FOTOLIA

あいようの　チェロと私

私の　プロフィール
　　ニックネーム：マリー・アントワネット
　　ねんれい：２５さい
　　たんじょう日：９月２日
　　けつえきがた：ＡＢがた

VOCABULARY

ブログ	blog	あいよう	my favorite, my beloved
しみん	civic, civil	チェロ	cello
ちゃんと	properly	プロフィール	profile
うごく	move	ニックネーム	nickname
ねんだい	age group	マリー・アントワネット	Marie Antoinette
けど	but . . . (particle; less formal than が)	ねんれい	age
何とか	somehow, one way or another	けつえきがた	blood type

READING TASK 2

アメリカ人かぞくの　ブログ

私たち　かぞくは　5年前に　アメリカから　東京に　来ました。
むすめの　モニカは　13さいに　なりました。
むすこの　ジョナは　11さいに　なりました。
私たちの　東京の　せいかつを　しょうかいします。

これは　おっとの　マーティンが　六本木ヒルズの　うえから　とった　しゃしんです。

マーティンの　しゅみは　カメラです。とくに、とかいの　やけいを　とるのが　すきです。でも、なかなか　しゃしんを　とる　時間が　ないのが　ざんねんだと　言っています。

むすめの　モニカです。

モニカは　おんがくが　すきです。　これは　先日　かぞくで　でかけた　帰りです。iPodで　ちちおやと　いっしょに　おんがくを　きいています。ちちおやに　じぶんの　すきな　きょくを　おしえています。

むすこの　ジョナです。

からだを　うごかすのが　すきです。今年の　4月から　テコンドーを　ならっています。れんしゅうが　大すきです。

私は　パメラです。
わたし

私の　しゅみは　スケートです。インラインスケートで
わたし
東京の　こうえんや　まちを　すべります。東京に
とうきょう　　　　　　　　　　　　　　　　とうきょう
来てから　スケートを　はじめました。スケートは　た
き
のしくて、けんこうに　いいです。

スケートの　おかげで、友だちが　たくさん　できまし
た。日本語を　はなす　きかいも　ふえました。けがを
にほんご
した　ことも　ありますが、やめたいと　おもった　こ
とは　ありません。ほとんど　毎週　すべっています。
まいしゅう
スケートは　私の　ライフスポーツです。
わたし

クリスマスの　ときの　しゃしんです。ス
ケートグループの　みんなと　東京駅から
とうきょうえき
渋谷まで　すべりました。クリックしてく
しぶや
ださい。大きく　なります。私は　前の
おお　　　　　　わたし　　まえ
れつの　みぎから　3ばんめです。

VOCABULARY

モニカ	Monica	じぶん	oneself
ジョナ	Jonah	きょく	song, piece of music
せいかつ	life	テコンドー	tae kwon do
マーティン	Martin	パメラ	Pamela
六本木ヒルズ ろっぽんぎ	Roppongi Hills (name of a shopping center)	スケート	skating
しゅみ	interest, hobby	インラインスケート	in-line skating
とくに	especially	すべる (R2)	skate, glide around
とかい	big city	おかげで	thanks to . . .
やけい	city lights	ライフスポーツ	lifetime sport
なかなか　〜ない	not easily	グループ	group, club
ざんねん（な）	regrettable, unfortunate	クリックする	click
先日 せんじつ	the other day	れつ	line
でかける (R2)	go out, set out	〜ばんめ	(counter for ordinal numbers)
ちちおや	father		

KANJI PRACTICE

去	去年 きょねん	一	十	土	去	去	去	去
go away								

友	友だち とも 友人 ゆうじん	一	ナ	方	友	友	友	
friend								

作	作る つく	ノ	イ	イ	作	作	作	作
		作	作					
make								

長	長い なが 課長 か ちょう	ﾄ	ﾄ	F	F	長	長	長
		長	長	長				
long **chief**								

方	方 かた 作り方 つく かた 夕方 ゆうがた 方 ほう	ﾄ	一	方	方	方	方	
direction **way**								

度	今度 こんど 一度 いちど	丶	亠	广	戸	庐	庐	度
time **degree**		庐	度	度	度			

山	山 やま *富士山 ふ じ さん	丨	屮	山	山	山		
mountain								

川	川 かわ 山川 やまかわ	丿	丿丨	川	川	川		
river								

花	花 はな 花見 はな み 生け花 い　 ばな	一	十	艹	艹	花	花	花
flower		花	花					

田	田んぼ た 田中 た なか 山田 やま だ 土田 つち だ	丨	冂	皿	田	田	田	田
rice field								

I Fill in the blanks with the appropriate particle.

1) 大学（　　　　）そつぎょうする　前に、会社を　作りました。
   だいがく　　　　　　　　　まえ　　　かいしゃ　つく

2) 子ども（　　　　）とき、本が　すきでした。
   こ　　　　　　　　　　ほん

3) 私は　東京（　　　）生まれました。
   わたし　とうきょう　　　う

4) エンジニア（　　　　）なりたいです。

5) スミスさん（　　　　）とまった　ホテルは　あたらしくて　きれいでした。

II Choose the correct word from among the alternatives (1–4) given. The same word cannot be used twice in the same dialogue.

1) A：（　　　）日本語が　じょうずに　なりましたね。
        にほんご
   　　（　　　）べんきょうしているんですか。
   B：毎日　日本語の　CDを　きいています。
     まいにち　にほんご
   1. ほとんど　　　2. ずいぶん　　　3. どうやって　　　4. どのぐらい

2) A：（　　　）ぎんこうに　つとめているんですか。
   B：10年ぐらいです。そつぎょうしてから（　　　）この　ぎんこうに
     ねん
   　　つとめています。
   1. どうやって　　2. どのぐらい　　3. だいぶ　　4. ずっと

3) 日本に　来る　前は　日本について（　　　）しりませんでした。
   にほん　く　まえ　にほん
   1. はじめて　　2. ぜんぜん　　3. だんだん　　4. だいぶ

III Change the form of the word given in parentheses to complete the sentence in a way that makes sense.

1) うちを（　　　　　　　　　）前に　メールを　チェックします。（でます）
   　　　　　　　　　　　　　まえ

2) 先週　かぜを　ひきましたが、もう（　　　　　　　　）なりました。（いいです）
   せんしゅう

3) ここに（　　　　　　　　　）とき、みちで　さいふを　ひろいました。（来ます）
   　　　　　　　　　　　　　　　　　　　　　　　　　　　　　　き

4) マルタンさんは　来月　京都に（　　　　　　　　　）と　言っていました。
   　　　　　　　　らいげつ　きょうと　　　　　　　　　　い
   （行きます）

5) 今朝は　朝ごはんを（　　　　　　　）時間が　ありませんでした。（食べます）
   けさ　あさ　　　　　　　　　　　　じかん　　　　　　　　　　　た

IV Choose the most appropriate word or phrase from among the alternatives (1–4) given.

1) あたらしいえきが （　　　）から、この　あたりは　にぎやかに　なりました。

   1. 生まれて　　　　2. はじめて　　　　3. できて　　　4. 作って

2) フランス語の　しけんを　（　　　）。

   1. とります　　2. うけます　　3. べんきょうします　　4. ならいます

3) ダンスを　ならっています。　毎日　2時間　（　　　）　しています。

   1. れんしゅう　　2. れんらく　　3. けいけん　　4. けいざい

4) 5年前に　（　　　）、べんごしから　がいこうかんに　なりました。

   1. てんしょくして　　2. ひっこして　　3. しゅっちょうして

   4. ざんぎょうして

5) A：なつかしいですね。前に　会ったのは　3年前でしたね。

   B：ええ、ほんとうに　（　　　）。

   1. はじめまして　　2. また　今度　　3. おひさしぶりです

   4. さようなら

V Fill in the blanks with the correct reading of each kanji.

1) 花を　もっている　女の人は　だれですか。

   （　　　）　　　　（　　　　　）

2) 去年　むすこが　小学校に　入りました。

   （　　　）　　　（　　　　）（　　　）

3) 高校の　ちかくに　コンビニが　できて　便利に　なりました。

   （　　　）　　　　　　　　　　　　　（　　　）

4) 学生の　とき、友人と　北海道を　回りました。

   （　　　）　　　（　　　）　　　　　（　　　）

PLANNING A VACATION

Above all else, words are for communicating one's intentions to others. The focus of this unit is on using Japanese to cooperate with other people in accomplishing common goals. Drawing on the example of planning a vacation, the unit presents expressions for negotiating schedules, gathering information, stating preferences, and explaining special circumstances.

TARGET DIALOGUE

It is March. Ms. Martin has come to her section chief, Mr. Kato, to ask for permission to take a vacation the following month.

マルタン：課長、今、ちょっと　よろしいでしょうか。

加藤：　　はい、何ですか。

マルタン：あのう、両親が　日本に　来るので、来月の　初めに　３
　　　　　　日ほど　きゅうかを　いただきたいのですが……。

加藤：　　来月ですか……。東京フードフェアの　じゅんびが　始ま
　　　　　　りますが、６日の　うちあわせには　出られますか。

マルタン：はい、４日に　両親が　帰る　予定なので、５日から　出
　　　　　　社できます。

加藤：　　そうですか。それなら　いいですよ。

マルタン：ありがとうございます。

Martin: Boss, may I bother you for a moment?
Kato:　Yes, what is it?
Martin: Uhh, my parents are coming to Japan, so I'd like to take about three days of vacation at the beginning of next month.
Kato:　Next month . . . Preparations for the Tokyo Food Fair will be starting. Can you attend the planning meeting on the sixth?
Martin: Yes, my parents plan to go home on the fourth, so I'll be able to come to the office from the fifth.
Kato:　I see. If that's the case, fine.
Martin: Thank you very much.

VOCABULARY

課長 か ちょう	section chief
ほど	about (lit., "to the extent of") (particle)
きゅうか	vacation
いただく	receive (humble form)
始まる はじ	begin
うちあわせ	planning meeting
出られる (R2) で	can attend
出社できる (R2) しゅっしゃ	can show up at the office
出社する しゅっしゃ	clock in, show up at the office
できる (R2)	can
それなら	if that is the case, if so

NOTES

1. ちょっと　よろしいでしょうか。

   "May I bother you for a moment?" This is a polite way of getting someone's attention. You use it when you want to ask a superior or stranger a favor or question.

2. ３日 (みっか) ほど　きゅうかを　いただきたいのですが……。

   There are three points to be made about this sentence:

   (1) The のですが serves as a kind of preliminary to a request. It is the same as the んですが you studied in Unit 2, but it is more polite. Here Ms. Martin is speaking to her boss, so のですが is more appropriate. よろしいでしょうか is omitted after のですが because it is too straight-forward and Ms. Martin's boss can understand what she means without her saying it.

   (2) ほど means the same as くらい／ぐらい but is more polite.

   (3) きゅうかを　とる is the usual word for "take a vacation," but here Ms. Martin uses the polite verb いただく, "to receive humbly," instead of とる because she is talking to her boss. いただく is one of a number of special verbs used to express humility.

3. それなら　いいですよ。

   "If that's the case, fine." You use それなら to indicate that what you are about to say—in this case, "okay" to Mr. Martin's request—applies only if the situation just mentioned holds true.

GRAMMAR & PATTERN PRACTICE

I Giving a Reason (1)

Like から, ので indicates a reason for what is stated in the main sentence, although it sounds a bit softer than から. ので is the conjunctive form of のです, which has the same meaning as んです but is more formal. The function of ので is just like that of んです (Unit 2, Lesson 4, p. 55): to explain circumstances. ので is appropriate in cases where you are asking someone to do something for you, or are explaining a situation that is acceptable or understandable to your listener.

両親が　日本に　来るので、　きゅうかを　いただきたいのですが……。
りょうしん　にほん　く

My parents are coming to Japan, so I'd like to take a vacation.

ねつが　あったので、　学校を　休みました。
がっこう　やす

I had a fever, so I stayed home from school.

から, on the other hand, is best used when you are trying to convince someone of something.

この　本は　とても　おもしろいですから、ぜひ　読んでみてください。
ほん　よ

This book is very interesting, so please read it (and see how you like it)

あぶないですから、ここに　入らないでください。
はい

It's dangerous, so please don't come in here.

Plain forms ordinarily come before ので, except that -na adjectives in the present-affirmative tense and nouns + です take な instead of だ. (See p. 121 for plain forms of -na adjectives and nouns + です.)

この　パソコンは　便利なので、人気があります。
べんり　にんき

This computer is convenient, so it is popular.

いい　てんきなので、さんぽに　行きます。
い

It is fine weather, so I will go for a walk.

In polite speech, though, people often use the desu/masu form before ので.

かぶきは　初めてですので、とても　たのしみです。
はじ

It will be the first time I see Kabuki, so I'm very much looking forward to it.

Construct sentences as in the example.

例) あした　テストが　あります。はやく　帰ります。
れい
　　あした　テストが　あるので、はやく　帰ります。
　　　　　　　　　　　　　　　　　　　　　　　かえ

1) お金が　ありません。何も　買いません。
　　かね　　　　　　　なに　　か
　　→ ....

2) 父が　びょうきです。国に　帰りたいです。
　　ちち　　　　　　　くに　かえ
　　→ ....

3) あめでした。　どこにも　出かけませんでした。
　　　　　　　　　　　　で
　　→ ....

4) おんがくが　すきです。よく　コンサートに　行きます。
　　　　　　　　　　　　　　　　　　　　い
　　→ ....

5) あたまが　いたいです。すこし　休んでも　いいですか。
　　　　　　　　　　　　　　　やす
　　→ ....

6) せつめいが　わかりません。もう　一度　ゆっくり　言ってください。
　　　　　　　　　　　　　　　　いちど　　　　　い
　　→ ....

7) おとといは　おっとの　たんじょう日でした。うちで　パーティーを
　　　　　　　　　　　　　　　　　　び
　　しました。
　　→ ....

8) そうべつ会は　6時からです。お先に　しつれいします。
　　　　　かい　　じ　　　　　さき
　　→ ....

VOCABULARY	テスト	test
	ゆっくり	slowly, leisurely
	おとといは	the day before yesterday

II Expressing Potentiality

In Japanese you can express potentiality in the two ways:

(1) By using a noun followed by が できます

　　Q：中国語が　できますか。
　　　　ちゅうごくご
　　A：はい、すこし　できます。

　　Q:　Can you speak/read etc. Chinese?
　　A:　Yes, a little.

(2) By using the potential form of the verb. This form is used to say that someone "can" do something, or that something "is possible."

　　カードで　はらえますか。

　　Can I pay by credit card?

The potential form is constructed as follows:

　Regular I verbs: The final -u sound of the dictionary form is replaced by -eru.

会う	→	会える		はなす	→	はなせる
あ		あ				
meet		*can* meet		speak		*can* speak

　Regular II verbs: The final -ru is replaced by -rareru.

食べる	→	食べられる		見る	→	見られる
た		た		み		み
eat		*can* eat		see		*can* see

　Irregular verbs:

来る	→	来られる		する	→	できる
く		こ				
come		*can* come		do		*can* do

Once a verb changes into the potential form, it becomes a potential verb and conjugates the same as a Regular II verb.

	-*nai* form	-*masu* form	-*te* form	-*ta* form
買える か	買えない か	買えます か	買えて か	買えた か
読める よ	読めない よ	読めます よ	読めて よ	読めた よ
食べられる た	食べられない た	食べられます た	食べられて た	食べられた た
見られる み	見られない み	見られます み	見られて み	見られた み
来られる こ	来られない こ	来られます こ	来られて こ	来られた こ
できる	できない	できます	できて	できた

Examples:

あした　9時に　来られる　人は　だれですか。

Who can come tomorrow at nine?

かんじが　読めないとき、どうしますか。

What do you do when you can't read a kanji?

Those verbs that take を can take either を or が when they have been turned into their potential forms. できる (the potential form of する) takes が almost all the time.

かんじを　読む　→　　かんじが　読める　or　かんじを　読める

read kanji　　　　　　can read kanji

テニスを　する　→　　テニスが　できる

play tennis　　　　　　can play tennis

Change the verbs to their potential forms and create questions.

例）スペイン語を　はなす。　　　→　スペイン語が　はなせますか。

1) ひらがなを　書く。　　　　→ ....

2) パソコンを　つかう。　　　→ ....

3) じゅうどうを　する。　　　→ ....

4) あした　6時に　来る。　　→ ....

5) カードで　はらう。　　　　→ ....

6) 5時に　おきる。　　　　　→ ....

7) ここに　くるまを　とめる。→ ....

8) ひこうきの　中で　ねる。　→ ....

9) じてんしゃに　のる。　　　→ ....

10) 400メートル　およぐ。　→ ....

11) 日本語の　うたを　うたう。→ ....

12) すしを　作る。　　　　　　→ ....

VOCABULARY

スペインご	Spanish
ひらがな	hiragana
メートル	meter

PRACTICE 1

WORD POWER

I. Time frames:

２月
<small>がつ</small>

日	月	火	水	木	金	土
	1	2	3	4	5	6
7	8	9	10	11	12	13
14	15	16	17	18	19	20
21	22	23	24	25	26	27
28						

① 今週
<small>こんしゅう</small>
② 先週
<small>せんしゅう</small>
③ 来週
<small>らいしゅう</small>
④ さ来週
<small>らいしゅう</small>
⑤ 今月
<small>こんげつ</small>
⑥ 先月
<small>せんげつ</small>
⑦ 来月
<small>らいげつ</small>
⑧ 初め
<small>はじ</small>
⑨ 中ごろ
<small>なか</small>
⑩ 終わり
<small>お</small>
⑪ 前半
<small>ぜんはん</small>
⑫ 後半
<small>こうはん</small>
⑬ さいしょ
⑭ さいご
⑮ １週目
<small>いっしゅうめ</small>
⑯ 週末
<small>しゅうまつ</small>
⑰ 月末
<small>げつまつ</small>
⑱ 上じゅん
<small>じょう</small>
⑲ 中じゅん
<small>ちゅう</small>
⑳ 下じゅん
<small>げ</small>

３月
<small>がつ</small>

日	月	火	水	木	金	土
	1	2	3	4	5	6
7	8	9	10	11	12	13
14	15	16	(17)	18	19	20
21	22	23	24	25	26	27
28	29	30	31			

きょう →

４月
<small>がつ</small>

日	月	火	水	木	金	土
				1	2	3
4	5	6	7	8	9	10
11	12	13	14	15	16	17
18	19	20	21	22	23	24
25	26	27	28	29	30	

VOCABULARY	さらいしゅう	the week after next	さいご	the last
	なかごろ	around the middle	いっしゅうめ	the first week of the month
	おわり	the end	げつまつ	the end of the month
	ぜんはん	the first half	じょうじゅん	the first ten days of the month
	こうはん	the latter half	ちゅうじゅん	the middle ten days of the month
	さいしょ	the first	げじゅん	the last ten days of the month

SPEAKING PRACTICE

Look at next month's planning calendar and assuming you are a member of the sales staff, talk about the events planned.

えいぎょう部　4月予定ひょう

1	木	↕ きゅうか	16	金	↓	
2	金	（マルタン）	17	土		
3	土		18	日	↓	
4	日		19	月	午前　けんこうしんだん	
5	月	部長会議	20	火		
6	火	フードフェアうちあわせ	21	水		
7	水		22	木		
8	木		23	金		
9	金	かんげい会	24	土	↑ けんしゅう	
10	土		25	日	↓ （鈴木）	
11	日		26	月		
12	月	フードフェアかいじょうしたみ	27	火		
13	火		28	水	↑ フードフェア（〜5月2日）	
14	水	↑ ペリーさん来日	29	木		
15	木	（加藤）	30	金		

Confirming the schedules of staffs:

加藤：　鈴木くんの　けんしゅうは　来月の　何週目ですか。

鈴木：　4週目の　週末です。

加藤：　マリーさんが　きゅうかを　とるのは　来月の　中ごろですか。

マルタン：いいえ、来月の　初めです。2日間　お休みを　いただきます。

Kato:　　Suzuki, your training program—what week of next month is it?

Suzuki:　It is the weekend of the fourth week.

Kato:　　Marie, you are going to take your vacation around the middle of next month?

Martin:　No, at the beginning of next month. I'll take two days off.

VOCABULARY			
よていひょう	planning calendar	けんしゅう	training session
かいじょう	gathering place	〜くん	(title of courtesy used among friends or toward people who rank beneath you)
したみ	preliminary inspection	きゅうかを　とる	take a vacation
ペリー	Perry (surname)	とる	take, have
らいにち	coming to Japan		
けんしゅう	training session		

PRACTICE 2

WORD POWER

I. Services available at a department store:

① うけつけ　② くるまいす　③ ベビーカー　④ コインロッカー　⑤ きつえんじょ

⑥ おてあらい　⑦ ちゅうしゃじょう　⑧ じゅにゅうしつ　⑨ ATM　⑩ きゅうけいじょ

II. Things one can do at a department store:

① かりる　② かえす　③ あずける　④ 入る(はい)　⑤ かえる

⑥ とめる　⑦ おろす　⑧ ふりこむ　⑨ はらう　⑩ 休む(やす)

VOCABULARY

くるまいす	wheelchair	じゅにゅうしつ	nursing room	かえる (R2)	exchange, change
ベビーカー	baby carriage	きゅうけいじょ	rest area	おろす	withdraw (money)
コインロッカー	coin locker	かえす	give back	ふりこむ	make a direct deposit into a bank account
きつえんじょ	smoking area	あずける (R2)	give to (someone) to look after		

158

SPEAKING PRACTICE

Asking about services available at a department store:

田中：ちゅうしゃじょうに　くるまを　とめたんですが、何時間まで　むりょう
　　　で　とめられますか。

店員：３千円いじょうの　お買いもので、２時間まで　とめられます。

田中：２時間ですね。

店員：はい。でぐちで　ちゅうしゃけんと　レシートを　見せてください。

田中：わかりました。それから、どこか　休める　ところが　ありますか。

店員：エスカレーターの　そばに　ベンチが　ございますので、そちらで　どうぞ。

田中：どうも。

Tanaka: I parked my car in the parking lot, but for how many hours can I park it there for free?

salesperson: For purchases of more than ¥3,000, you can park there for two hours.

Tanaka: Two hours, is it?

salesperson: Yes. At the exit, show your parking ticket and receipts.

Tanaka: Okay. And is there somewhere I can rest?

salesperson: Beside the escalator there is a bench; feel free to use it.

Tanaka: Thank you.

おむつが　かえられる　トイレは　ありますか。
Is there a bathroom where one can change a baby's diaper?

ペットと　入れる　レストランを　さがしているんですが……。
I'm looking for a restaurant where pets are allowed . . .

なまものが　あずけられる　ロッカーは　ありますか。
Is there a locker where perishables can be stored?

VOCABULARY					
むりょう	free	〜の　そばに	beside, by	ペット	pet
〜いじょう	more than . . .	ございます	be, exist (polite form)	なまもの	perishables
ちゅうしゃけん	parking ticket	おむつ	diaper		
レシート	receipt	トイレ	toilet, bathroom		159

READING & WRITING TASK

おさそい

Read the e-mails below and then write a response. Refer to the sales department's April Schedule on p. 157.

テニスの　おさそい

鈴木さま
4月２４日、２５日の週末に　1ぱ
くで　伊豆に　テニスに　行きません
か。メンバーは　システム部の　シカ
さんと　田中さんと　私です。
中村

飲み会の　おさそい

加藤さま
えきまえに　あたらしく　できた　い
ざかやに　行きませんか。4月の３週
目は　いかがですか。ごつごうの　い
い日を　しらせてください。
林

RE：テニスの　おさそい

中村さま
おさそい　ありがとうございます。ざ
んねんですが、その週末は　けんしゅ
うが　あるので、さんかできません。
また　さそってください。
鈴木

RE：飲み会の　おさそい

林さま

....

....

....

....

....

VOCABULARY

（お）さそい	invitation	さそう	invite
1ぱく	stay of one night	えきまえ	in front of the station
〜はく／ぱく	(counter for nights spent at a hotel or an inn)	（ご）つごう	convenience
伊豆	Izu (peninsula southwest of Tokyo)		

READING TASK

かんそう

I. オペラについて

　友だちに　オペラの　チケットを　2まい　もらったので、ひさしぶりに　かないと　見に　行きました。かないは　オペラが　すきなので、とても　よろこびましたが、私は　オペラを　あまり　見た　ことが　ないので、ねむく　なりました。とても　長い　オペラだと　思いました。

II. 日本語学校について

　先週　日本語学校の　ちらしを　もらいました。もうしこむ　前に　見学が　できると　きいたので、きのう　見学に　行きました。

　しょきゅうの　クラスは　せいとが　6人でした。先生は　おしえ方*が　じょうずで、ユーモアの　ある　人でした。じゅぎょうが　終わってから、クラスの　人たちと　すこし　はなしました。とても　気に　入ったので、来週　もうしこみたいと　思っています。

Answer the following questions:

1) この　人が　日本語学校に　行ったのは　いつですか。
2) 何を　しに　行きましたか。
3) 先生の　おしえ方は　どうでしたか。

VOCABULARY

かんそう	impression	しょきゅう	beginning level
オペラ	opera	せいと	student
ちらし	advertising flyer	～方	way of ——ing (suffix)
もうしこむ	apply	ユーモア	humor
見学	visit for educational purposes, field trip		

---

* 方 (かた)　added to the -masu stem of a verb means "how to" or "way of," e.g., おしえ方 (かた), "way of teaching," すしの 作 (つく) り方 (かた), "how to make sushi," かんじの 読 (よ) み方 (かた), "how to read (a) kanji (character)," etc.

KANJI PRACTICE

両	両方 りょう ほう	一	厂	厅	两	両	両	両
both		両						

親	父親 ちちおや 母親 ははおや 両親 りょうしん	㇔	亠	立	立	立	立	辛
parent		辛	亲	亲	新	親	親	親
親	親	親	親					

初	初めて はじ	㇏	ネ	ネ	ネ	ネ	初	初
first		初	初					

始	始める はじ 始まる はじ	㇛	女	女	始	始	始	始
start		始	始	始				

出	出る で 出す だ 出社 しゅっしゃ	丨	屮	屮	出	出	出	出
go/come out **put out**								

予	予定 よ てい	フ	マ	予	予	予	予	
in advance								

定	予定 よ てい	`	`	宀	宁	宇	守	定
fix	定	定	定					

目	目 め 二週目 に しゅう め 二つ目 ふた め	｜	冂	月	月	目	目	目
eye								

末	週末 しゅう まつ 月末 げつ まつ	一	二	丰	末	末	末	末
last part								

思	思う おも	｜	冂	四	田	田	思
think	思	思	思	思			

SELECTING A VACATION PLAN

TARGET DIALOGUE

It is lunchtime. Ms. Martin is looking at travel brochures.

鈴木：　　マリーさん、旅行に　行くんですか。

マルタン：ええ。今度　両親と　旅行を　しようと　思っているんです。
　　　　　　　　　　　　　　　　　　　　→p. 166

鈴木：　　どこに　行くんですか。

マルタン：それが……。行きたい　ところが　多くて、まよっているん
　　　　　　　　　　→p. 168
　　　　　　です。京都も　いいし、神戸にも　行きたいし……。

鈴木：　　よかったら、そうだんに　のりますよ。

マルタン：ほんとうですか。たすかります。

Work has finished, and Mr. Suzuki and Ms. Martin are at a cyber café, looking at the website of a traditional Japanese inn.

鈴木：　　ここは　どうですか。部屋から　さくらが　見えますよ。

マルタン：いいですね。予約できるか　どうか　聞いてみます。
　　　　　　　　　　　→p. 170

Suzuki: Marie, are you going on a trip?
Martin: Yes, I'm thinking of traveling with my parents.
Suzuki: Where are you going?
Martin: That's just it. There are so many places I want to go, I'm at a loss. Kyoto would be nice, but
　　　　　I also want to go to Kobe . . .
Suzuki: If you'd like, I'll give you advice.
Martin: Really? That would be a great help.
. . . . . .
Suzuki: How about this place? You can see cherry blossoms from the rooms.
Martin: Very nice. I'll ask if I can make reservations.

VOCABULARY

しよう	(see p. 166)	たすかる	be a help
まよう	be at a loss	さくら	cherry blossom
〜し 〜し	and moreover . . .	見える (R2)	be visible, can see
よかったら	if you would like	〜か どうか	if/whether (something is the case)
そうだんに のる	give asked-for advice		

NOTES

1. 旅行（りょこう）に 行（い）くんですか。
In this case, Mr. Suzuki's intention is not to find out whether Ms. Martin is going on a trip. Instead, he is guessing that she is going somewhere based on the circumstances, and is using that guess as a way of starting a conversation. You use constructions like this one when you are interested in what someone else is doing and want to find out more. Starting a conversation with んですか demonstrates your interest and lets you begin talking in a friendly manner. (See also Unit 2, Lesson 4, p. 57.)

2. それが……。
This expression indicates that the following sentence is quite different from what would be expected. You use it when beginning a response.

3. 京都（きょうと）も いいし、神戸（こうべ）にも 行（い）きたいし……。
When you link related reasons, excuses, or thoughts, you connect them with し, implying "and besides which" or "and moreover . . ." Sometimes you can use both も and し in the same sentence to imply that you have too many choices and are confused about what to do.

4. よかったら、そうだんに のりますよ。
よかったら, "if you'd like," "if it's all right with you," is a phrase you use at the beginning of an invitation or a suggestion. It shows that you respect your listener's preference.

5. たすかります。
Literally "you save me," たすかります is an expression of gratitude. Use it when someone offers you help that you would be glad to accept.

6. 部屋（へや）から さくらが 見（み）えますよ。
見（み）える and 聞（き）こえる translate literally as "to come into sight" and "to reach one's ear," respectively. They are different from the potential forms 見（み）られる, "to be able to see," and 聞（き）ける, "to be able to hear." 見（み）える indicates that something is visible regardless of the speaker's volition, while 見（み）られる indicates only ability or possibility. Note that the particle you use with 見（み）える and 聞（き）こえる to mark the object of the sentence is が, not を.

まどから うみが 見えます。
I can see the ocean from my window.

だれかが うたっているのが 聞こえます。
I can hear someone singing.

GRAMMAR & PATTERN PRACTICE

❶ Expressing Volition: "I Am Thinking about . . ."

Verbs ending in う／よう (plain form) or ましょう (polite form) are in the volitional form and trans-late as "I'll . . . ," "we'll . . . ," or "let's . . ." This form can be combined with と思（おも）っています to mean "I'm thinking of doing" or "I'm planning to do."

いっしょに　旅行に　行こうと　思っています。
　　　　　　りょこう　　い　　　　おも

I am thinking of going on a trip with them.

To produce the volitional form of a Regular II verb, simply drop る from the dictionary form and add よう. As for Regular I verbs, see the table below and keep in mind the correlation with the *a-i-u-e-o* vowel order.

		-nai form	*-masu* form	dictionary form	conditional form	volitional form
Regular I		会わない	会います	会う	会えば	会おう
		書かない	書きます	書く	書けば	書こう
		およがない	およぎます	およぐ	およげば	およごう
		けさない	けします	けす	けせば	けそう
		またない	まちます	まつ	まてば	まとう
		しなない	しにます	しぬ	しねば	しのう
		よばない	よびます	よぶ	よべば	よぼう
		飲まない	飲みます	飲む	飲めば	飲もう
		帰らない	帰ります	帰る	帰れば	帰ろう
Regular II		食べない	食べます	食べる	食べれば	食べよう
		あけない	あけます	あける	あければ	あけよう
		見ない	見ます	見る	見れば	見よう
		おりない	おります	おりる	おりれば	おりよう
Irregular		来ない	来ます	来る	来れば	来よう
		しない	します	する	すれば	しよう

NOTE: Potential verbs do not have volitional forms.

1 Change the verbs to their volitional forms.

例) 会う　→　<u>会おう</u>

1) 買う　→　.................................
2) うたう　→　.................................
3) ならう　→　.................................
4) 行く　→　.................................
5) あるく　→　.................................
6) はたらく　→　.................................
7) およぐ　→　.................................
8) いそぐ　→　.................................
9) はなす　→　.................................
10) まつ　→　.................................
11) しぬ　→　.................................

12) あそぶ　→　.................................
13) 飲む　→　.................................
14) 休む　→　.................................
15) がんばる　→　.................................
16) 見る　→　.................................
17) おきる　→　.................................
18) ねる　→　.................................
19) 始める　→　.................................
20) 来る　→　.................................
21) する　→　.................................

2 Construct sentences as in the example.

例) 旅行に　行きます。　→　<u>旅行に　行こうと</u>　思っています。

1) 富士山に　のぼります。　→　.................................
2) ピアノを　ならいます。　→　.................................
3) ジョギングを　始めます。　→　.................................
4) つまに　花を　おくります。→　.................................
5) はやく　うちに　帰ります。→　.................................
6) 来年　けっこんします。　→　.................................

VOCABULARY	いそぐ	hurry
	おくる	give

II Giving a Reason (2)

The *-te* form can indicate a reason for or cause of what the main sentence expresses. Used in this way, it is usually followed by an explanation of the speaker's feelings or circumstances and is virtually interchangeable with ので.

行きたい　ところが　多くて、まよっているんです。

There are so many places I want to go, I'm at a loss.

この部屋は　しずかで、気に入っています。

This room is quiet and I'm pleased with it.

時間が　なくて、本が　読めません。

I don't have time, so I can't read the book.

If the main sentence expresses a result you have control over, you cannot use the *-te* form. Instead you have to use から or ので. Compare the following sentences.

お金が　なくて、新しい　くるまが　買えません。

I have no money, so I can't buy a new car.

お金が　ないので、新しい　くるまを　買いません。

I have no money, so I won't buy a new car.

A noun followed by the particle で can also express a reason or cause.

じこで　みちが　こんでいます。

The road is crowded because of an accident.

びょうきで　会社を　休みました。

I was absent from work due to illness.

VOCABULARY　　じこ　　　　　accident

1 Complete the sentences as in the example.

例）このかばんは　かるいです。
れい
　　→ このかばんは　かるくて、気に　入っています。
　　　　　　　　　　　　　　　き　　い

1) この　もんだいは　むずかしいです。
　　→ ....、よく　わかりません。

2) きのうは　あめでした。
　　→ ....、テニスが　できませんでした。

3) そとが　うるさいです。
　　→ ....先生の　こえが　聞こえません。
　　　　　　　　　　　　　　　　　　　　　　せんせい　　　　　　き

4) じしんの　ニュースを　聞きました。
　　　　　　　　　　　　　　　き
　　→ ....、しんぱいに　なりました。

5) 友だちに　会えませんでした。
　　とも　　　あ
　　→ ....、ざんねんでした。

6) 日本に　来た　とき、かんじが　読めませんでした。
　　にほん　き　　　　　　　　　　よ
　　→ ....、こまりました。

2 Complete the sentences as in the example.

例）ねつが　あります。はやく　帰ります。
れい
　　→ ねつが　あるので、はやく　帰ります。
　　　　　　　　　　　　　　　　　かえ

1) うたを　うたうのが　すきです。
　　→ ....、よく　カラオケに　行きます。
　　　　　　　　　　　　　　　　　　　　　　　　　　　い

2) あついです。
　　→ ....、すみませんが、まどを　あけてください。

3) コピーの　つかい方が　わかりません。
　　　　　　かた
　　→ ....、せつめいしてください。

VOCABULARY			
もんだい	question	じしん	earthquake
うるさい	noisy, irritating, annoying	こまる	have a hard time, be troubled
こえ	voice		
きこえる (R2)	be able to hear (lit., "reach one's ear")		169

III Forming Indirect Questions

"I don't know when I will go," "Please tell me whether you will go." Sentences like these, which contain indirect questions, are formed in Japanese as follows:

(1) For yes/no questions, you change the form of the verb or adjective before か to its plain form and replace か with か どうか (often omitting どうか in everyday speech).

予約できるか どうか わかりません。
よやく
I don't know whether I can make a reservation.

高いか どうか わかりません。
たか
I don't know whether it is expensive.

However, if the word before か is a -na adjective in the present-affirmative tense or a noun + です, you leave out だ from the plain form.

便利か どうか わかりません。
べんり
I don't know whether it is useful.

学生か どうか わかりません。
がくせい
I don't know whether he is a student.

(2) In the case of wh-questions, the procedure is the same as (1) above but you leave out どうか.

どこに 行くか おしえてください。
い
Please tell me where you are going.

どのぐらい 大きいか おしえてください。
おお
Please tell me about how big it is.

何が すきか おしえてください。
なに
Please tell me what you like.

どんな くるまか おしえてください。
Please tell me what kind of car it is.

If it is necessary to specify the subject in an indirect question, use が.

私は 田中さん が どこに いるか しりません。
わたし たなか
I don't know where Mr. Tanaka is.

Construct sentences as in the examples.

例1) 予約できますか。わかりません。
　　→ 予約できるか　どうか　わかりません。

例2) いつ　会いますか。　わかりません。
　　→ いつ　会うか　わかりません。

1) 来週　しゅっちょうが　ありますか。課長に　聞いてください。
　→ ....

2) 田中さんは　フランス語が　じょうずですか。しりません。
　→ ....

3) あの　人の　仕事は　コンサルタントですか。わかりません。
　→ ....

4) りょかんに　とまった　ことが　ありますか。ミルズさんに　聞いてみます。
　→ ....

5) あした　何時に　来られますか。おしえてください。
　→ ....

6) どこに　かぎを　入れましたか。わすれました。
　→ ....

7) にくと　さかなと　どちらが　すきですか。山本さんに　聞いてください。
　→ ....

8) いつ　ひっこしますか。　まだ　きめていません。
　→ ....

PRACTICE 1

WORD POWER

Feelings:

① うれしかったです ② くやしかったです ③ おどろきました ④ かなしかったです

⑤ がっかりしました ⑥ こまりました ⑦ たいへんでした ⑧ はずかしかった
　　　　　　　　　　　　　　　　　　　　　　　　　　　　　　　　です

PHRASE POWER

Events:

① しけんに　ごうかくする　　　　　　　　pass an exam
② しけんに　おちる　　　　　　　　　　　fail an exam
③ しあいに　かつ　　　　　　　　　　　　win a match
④ しあいに　まける　　　　　　　　　　　lose a match
⑤ かばんを　わすれる　　　　　　　　　　leave one's bag somewhere
⑥ さいふを　おとす　　　　　　　　　　　lose one's wallet
⑦ でんわばんごうを　まちがえる　　　　　dial the wrong phone number
⑧ ねぼうする　　　　　　　　　　　　　　oversleep
⑨ 会議に　おくれる　　　　　　　　　　　be late for a meeting
　 かいぎ
⑩ エアコンが　こわれる　　　　　　　　　the air conditioner breaks down

VOCABULARY

うれしい	happy, glad	がっかりする	be disappointed	おちる (R2)	fail	ねぼうする	oversleep
くやしい	regrettable	はずかしい	embarrassing	かつ	win	ねぼう	getting up late
おどろく	be surprised	ごうかくする	pass	まける (R2)	lose	おくれる (R2)	be late
かなしい	sad	ごうかく	passing an exam	まちがえる (R2)	mistake	こわれる (R2)	break

SPEAKING PRACTICE

 Mr. Mills and Ms. Martin are talking about their experiences since coming to Japan. Listen to what they say, and then talk about your own experience.

ミルズ

店に　たいせつな　かみぶくろを　わすれて、
たいへんでした。

I left an important paper bag at a store. It was a real headache (lit., "It was great trouble.")

アイスホッケーの　しあいに　まけて、
くやしかったです。

I lost an ice hockey match. It was a bummer.

マリー

前　すんでいた　まちが　かわっていて、
びっくりしました。

The town in which I had lived changed. I couldn't believe it (lit., "I was surprised.")

スピーチで　日本語を　まちがえて、
はずかしかったです。

I goofed up my Japanese in a speech. It was embarrassing.

（私は）……

VOCABULARY		
たいせつ（な）	important	
アイスホッケー	ice hockey	
びっくりする	be surprised	
スピーチ	speech	

PRACTICE 2

READING & SPEAKING PRACTICE

Read the vacation brochures for Shiretoko, Kanazawa, and Okinawa, and summarize their content. How do you get to these places, and how long do the journeys take? How much do the tours cost? And what can you do at these popular destinations?

どこに　行こうか　まよっているんです。

知床２日間
しれとこふつかかん
３５,８００円
えん
釧路から
くしろ
　　　レンタカーつき

世界自然遺産にとまろう！
せかいしぜんいさん

知床
しれとこ

釧路
くしろ

（羽田から１００分）
はねだ　　　ひゃっ　ぶん

うみ・山・たき
やま

そして、野生動物
やせいどうぶつ

VOCABULARY		
せかいしぜんいさん	world natural heritage site	
せかい	the world	
しぜん	nature	
いさん	heritage site	
しれとこ	Shiretoko (peninsula in Hokkaido)	
レンタカー	rental car	
くしろ	Kushiro (city in Hokkaido)	
はねだ	Haneda (location of an airport in Tokyo)	

やせいどうぶつ	wild animals
やせい	the wild

Lynn's Jewelry   John

(805) 642-5500

- Atsuko hasn't been able to wear it.
- She had to stay in Japan to help her dad while he was in the hospital
- She doesn't like the design
- Also she is scared to wear it because the value is way too high.
- What she wants is a smaller diamond on a thin, tapered ring. I can send you pictures of what she wants.
- We also need each a wedding ring, simple
- Atsuko is flying in on 6/21
- Can we make an appointment on 6/28 (sat)?

- Can you give me full value of the ring if we use it to make the new engagement ring and the two wedding rings?

(Week before call)

歴史の町・金沢　古い文化を楽しもう！
れきし　まち　かなざわ　ふる　ぶんか　たの

城
しろ

日本庭園
にほんていえん

温泉
おんせん

伝統文化
でんとうぶんか

グルメ＆おいしい酒
さけ

3日間
みっかかん
25,200〜65,400円
えん

東京―新幹線4時間―金沢
とうきょう　しんかんせん　じかん　かなざわ

飛行機1時間
ひこうき　じかん

ビーチ・リゾート in OKINAWA！！

飛行機とホテルのセット
ひこうき
3・4・5日間 38,000円〜
かかん　えん

羽田発　⇒⇒⇒　那覇着
はねだはつ　なはちゃく
6:45　　　　9:00
10:30　　　13:00

市内観光　日帰りツアー　レンタカー・プランなど
しないかんこう　ひがえ

VOCABULARY			
かなざわ	Kanazawa (city in Ishikawa Prefecture)	なは	Naha (city in Okinawa)
たのしむ	enjoy	〜ちゃく	arriving at . . .
ていえん	garden	しないかんこう	sightseeing within the city
でんとう	tradition	しない	within the city
グルメ	gourmet	かんこう	sightseeing
ビーチ・リゾート	beach resort	ひがえり	day trip
セット	package	レンタカー・プラン	rental car option
〜はつ	departing . . .	〜など	and so on (particle)

WORD POWER

I. Travel:

① 〜発
　　はつ
② 〜着
　　ちゃく
③ 〜つき
④ りょうきん
⑤ 大人、子ども
　　おとな　こ
⑥ おうふく、かたみち
⑦ ぶんか
⑧ めいしょ
⑨ しないかんこう
⑩ 日帰りツアー
　　ひがえ
⑪ 北
　　きた
⑫ 南
　　みなみ
⑬ 西
　　にし
⑭ 東
　　ひがし

PARTICLE REVIEW

Take special note of the particles in these senetences:

１０時に　羽田を　出発する。 じ　　はねだ　　しゅっぱつ	I depart Haneda at ten o'clock.
１１時半に　那覇に　とうちゃくする。 じはん　　なは	I arrive in Naha at 11:30.
りょかんの　りょうきんを　しらべる。	I check out prices of inns.
ホテルに　とまる。	I stay at a hotel.
メニューから　りょうりを　えらぶ。	I select food from a menu.
日本の　れきしに　きょうみが　ある。 にほん	I have an interest in Japanese history.
めいしょを　まわる。	I see sights.
日帰りツアーに　さんかする。 ひがえ	I participate in a one-day tour.

りょうきん	fare	みなみ	south	とうちゃくする	arrive
おうふく	roundtrip	にし	west	とうちゃく	arrival
おとな	adult	ひがし	east	えらぶ	choose
かたみち	one-way	しゅっぱつする	depart	きょうみが　ある	have an interest
めいしょ	place of interest	しゅっぱつ	departure	きょうみ	interest
			north		

SPEAKING PRACTICE

Consulting a colleague about where to go for vacation:

ミルズ： なつ休みに 旅行に 行く 予定なんですが、どこに 行こうか ま
よっているんです。

中村： 金沢は どうですか。れきしの ある まちですよ。ゆうめいな に
わも 見られるし、おんせんにも 入れるし……。

ミルズ： ぼくは おてらや にわを 見るより、しぜんの 中で すごす ほ
うが すきなんです。

中村： それなら、北海道の 知床が いいですよ。せかいいさんに なって
から、人気が あります。友だちが 去年 行ったんですが、ふねか
ら くじらが およいでいるのが 見えたと 言っていました。

ミルズ： えっ、ほんとうですか。

Mills: I plan to go on a trip for summer vacation, but I'm at a loss as to where to go.
Nakamura: How about Kanazawa? It is a city with history. (There) you can see famous gardens, and
             moreover you can bathe in the hot springs.
Mills: I prefer to spend my time amidst nature, rather than (spending it) seeing temples and
             gardens and other such things.
Nakamura: If that's the case, Shiretoko in Hokkaido would be good. Ever since it became a world
             heritage site, it has been popular. A friend went there last year. She said she could see
             whales from the boat (her tour took her on).
Mills: Oh, really?

VOCABULARY	せかいいさん	world heritage site
	ふね	boat
	くじら	whale

KANJI PRACTICE

旅	旅行 りょこう	レ	亠	方	方	方	扩	於
		旅	旅	旅	旅	旅		
trip								

多	多い おお	ク	ク	タ	多	多	多	多
		多						
many								

少	少ない すく 少し すこ	リ	小	小	少	少	少	
few **little**								

屋	部屋 へや 薬屋 くすりや 屋上 おくじょう	⁊	ヨ	尸	尸	居	居	屋
		屋	屋					
house, shop **roof**								

約	予約 よやく 約 やく	く	幺	幺	幺	糸	糸	糹
		約	約					
contract/promise **aproximately**								

聞 listen	聞く き 新聞 しんぶん	l	l⌐	F	月	門	門	門
		門	閅	閅	間	閏	聞	聞

新 new	新しい あたら 新年 しんねん	⌐	ユ	立	立	立	立	辛
		辛	亲	亲	新	新	新	新
新								

| 古 old | 古い ふる | 一 | 十 | 十 | 古 | 古 | | |
| | | | | | | | | |

発 depart	～発 はつ 出発する しゅっぱつ	フ	フ	ヲ	癶	癶	癶	癶
		癶	発					

着 reach wear	着く き っ着る き ～着 ちゃく	ヽ	ヽ	兰	丷	羊	羊	羊
		羊	着	着	着	着		

RESERVING A ROOM AT AN INN

TARGET DIALOGUE

Ms. Martin has phoned the inn where she plans to stay, the Miyako Inn.

TRACK
59

旅館の人：みやこ旅館でございます。

マルタン：予約を　おねがいしたいんですが。

旅館の人：ありがとうございます。

マルタン：4月　1日と　2日、3名なんですが……。ホームページに
　　　　　出ている、一人1泊　18,000円の　部屋は　まだ　空
　　　　　いていますか。

旅館の人：しょうしょう　おまちください。……はい、ご用意できます。

マルタン：では、それで　おねがいします。

旅館の人：お名前と　ごれんらくさきを　いただけますか。

マルタン：マリー・マルタンです。電話番号は　090-1234-
　　　　　56XXです。

旅館の人：駅まで　おむかえに　まいりますが、ごとうちゃくは　何時
　　　　　ごろでしょうか。

マルタン：6時ごろだと　思いますが、少し　おくれるかもしれません。
　　　　　　　　　　　　　　　　　　　　→p. 182
　　　　　駅に　着いたら、電話します。
　　　　　　　　　→p. 184

旅館の人：しょうちしました。それでは　おまちしております。

innkeeper: This is the Miyako Inn.

Martin: I'd like to make a reservation.

innkeeper: Thank you very much.

Martin: April first and second for three people, and are the rooms at ¥18,000 per person, per night, shown on your website still available?

innkeeper: Just a moment, please. Yes, we can have one ready for you.

Martin: Will you do me the favor, then (of booking me a room)?

innkeeper: Could I have your name and contact information?

Martin: Marie Martin. My telephone number is 090-1234-56XX.

innkeeper: We'll come and pick you up at the station. About what time might you be arriving?

Martin: I think it will be around six o'clock, but we may be a little late. I'll call you when we arrive at the station.

Innkeeper: Understood. We'll be waiting for you.

VOCABULARY

みやこ旅館 りょかん	Miyako Inn (fictitious inn)	おむかえに まいります	go to meet (humble form)
～名 めい	(counter for people)	まいります	go, come (humble form)
ホームページ	website	～かもしれません	may, might
出る (R2) で	appear	～たら	when, if
空く あ	open up, become vacant	しょうちする	I understand (polite form)
ご～	(polite prefix)	それでは	well then
用意する ようい	prepare, get (something) ready	おまちしております	I will be waiting (humble form)
れんらくさき	contact information	おります	be, exist (humble form)

NOTES

1. *RYOKAN* CHARGES

   One night per person with supper and breakfast included (いっぱくにしょく) is the most conspicuous formula for *ryokan* charges. It is not common in Western-style hotels, which are more apt to quote room charge only or room charge plus, optionally, breakfast. It is better to confirm whether tax is included (ぜいこみ) or whether a service charge is included (サービスりょうこみ) in the room rate. These days reservations at some *ryokan* can be made online.

2. POLITE LANGUAGE

   People in the service industry often use the following polite expressions.

   (1) おまちください, meaning "please wait" but more formal than まってください;

   (2) ごれんらくさき and ごとうちゃく, where ご before the noun has the same function as お in お名前（なまえ）—i.e., to show respect toward the person spoken to or the persons or things connected with him or her;

   (3) しょうちしました, "I understand and agree to do it."

GRAMMAR & PATTERN PRACTICE

1 Expressing Uncertainty

かもしれません means "may" or "might," literally, "I cannot tell if it is true." You use it when you cannot say something for certain, though you know the possibility definitely exists.

少し おくれるかもしれません。
すこ
I might be a little bit late.

Plain forms come before かもしれません. However, like with indirect questions (Lesson 11, p. 170), if the word is a -na adjective in the present-affirmative tense or a noun + です, you leave out だ from the plain form.

友だちが うちに 来るかもしれません。
とも   く
A friend may come to my house.

あの 本は おもしろいかもしれません。
    ほん
That book may be interesting.

田中さんは スキーが じょうずかもしれません。
た なか
Mr. Tanaka may be good at skiing.

あしたは あめかもしれません。
It might rain tomorrow.

男の子かもしれません。
おとこ こ
It might be a boy.

女の子かもしれません。
おんな こ
It might be a girl.

Construct sentences as in the example.

例) あしたは　あめが　ふります。
れい
　　→ <u>あしたは　あめが　ふるかもしれません。</u>

1) びょうきに　なります。
　　→ ....

2) 時間が　ありません。
じかん
　　→ ....

3) みちが　すいています。

　　→ ....

4) あの　人は　鈴木さんの　いもうとさんです。
ひと　　すずき
　　→ ....

5) タクシーより　ちかてつの　ほうが　はやいです。

　　→ ....

6) いい　てんきなので、富士山が　見えます。
ふじさん　み
　　→ ....

7) 今日は　ひまなので、はやく　うちに　帰れます。
きょう　　　　　　　　　　　　　　　　　かえ
　　→ ....

8) ちゅうしゃじょうが　せまいので、くるまが　とめられません。

　　→ ....

9) げんきに　なったので、サッカーの　しあいに　出られます。
で
　　→ ....

10) あまり　べんきょうしなかったので、しけんに　おちます。

　　→ ....

VOCABULARY

ふる	fall (of rain, snow)
ちゅうしゃじょう	parking space/spot
せまい	narrow

❙❙ Talking about Future Events Coming into Being

The -ta form of a verb followed by ら (hereafter 〜たら) essentially means "upon completion of an action/event." In present-tense sentences, a clause with 〜たら expresses a condition that triggers an action described in the main sentence. The condition may range in likelihood of occurrence from likely to highly unlikely. In this lesson you will learn how to use 〜たら in the sense of "when" to speak about an occurrence that is likely to take place. (You will learn another usage of 〜たら in Unit 5.)

今　9時50分です。10時に　なったら、しけんを　始めます。
It is now 9:50. When it is 10:00, we will begin the exam.

Here you can see that the meaning of 〜たら is that when a certain circumstance (described by the 〜たら clause) holds true, then some action/event will occur.

A：いつ　出かけましょうか。
B：昼ごはんを　食べたら、出かけましょう。
A:　When shall we go out?
B:　When we finish lunch, let's go out.

この　仕事が　終わったら、帰っても　いいですか。
May I go home when this work is finished?

Earlier you learned 〜た とき (Unit 3, Lesson 8, p. 119). The difference between 〜た とき and 〜たら is that 〜たら is used to state a necessary condition for what follows, while 〜た とき is used only to specify a point in time.

今　時間が　ないので　来週　会った　とき　はなしましょう。
I don't have time now, so let's talk when we meet next week.

In this sentence 〜た とき is more appropriate. If the speaker had used 〜たら instead, he would have been saying, "I don't have time now, so let's talk if we meet next week," implying, "If we don't meet next week, we cannot talk." Such a nuance is unnecessary, so he uses 〜た とき.

The reason you often use 〜たら instead of 〜た とき in expressions like 10時（じ）に　なったら (first example above) is that 〜た とき implies "at the moment," focusing on the time rather than the condition.

Complete the sentences as in the example.

例) 7時になる
　→ <u>7時になったら</u>、帰りましょう。

1) 仕事が　終わる
　→ ....、会議しつに　来てください。

2) にもつが　とどく
　→ ....、しらせてください。

3) 大学を　そつぎょうする
　→ ....、国に　帰る　予定です。

4) ミルズさんが　来る
　→ ....、うちあわせを　始めましょう。

5) じゅんびが　できる
　→ ....、よびに　来てください。

6) ホテルに　着く
　→ ....、れんらくします。

7) オーケストラの　れんしゅうが　終わる
　→ ....、夕はんを　食べに　行きましょう。

8) しゅくだいが　すむ
　→ ....、テレビを　見ても　いいですよ。

9) うちに　帰る
　→ ....、電話してください。

10) 少し　休む
　→ ....、おんせんに　入りましょう。

VOCABULARY

ゆうはん	dinner
しゅくだい	homework
すむ	be finished

185

PRACTICE 1

WORD POWER

I. Cooking:

① おゆが
　わく

② おゆを
　わかす

③ にくが
　やける

④ にくを
　やく

⑤ にくが
　にえる

⑥ にくを
　にる

⑦ やさいを
　いためる

⑧ やさいを
　あげる

⑨ やさいを
　きる

⑩ やさいを
　入れる

⑪ さとう

⑫ しお

⑬ しょうゆ

⑭ す

⑮ あぶら・
　オイル

⑯ こしょう

⑰ ぎゅうにく

⑱ とりにく

⑲ ぶたにく

⑳ さかな

NOTE: Japanese, like English, has intransitive and transitive verb pairs. Intransitive verbs do not take a direct object, whereas transitive ones do.

おゆが　わく　(INTRANSITIVE)
the water boils

おゆを　わかす　(TRANSITIVE)
boil the water

VOCABULARY							
おゆ	hot water	にえる (R2)	cook (in liquid) (intr.)	しお	salt	こしょう	(black) pepper
わく	boil (intr.)	にる (R2)	cook (in liquid) (trans.)	しょうゆ	soy sauce	ぎゅうにく	beef
わかす	boil (trans.)	いためる (R2)	stir-fry	す	vinegar	とりにく	chicken (meat)
やける (R2)	roast (intr.)	あげる (R2)	deep-fry	あぶら	oil, fat	ぶたにく	pork
やく	roast (trans.)	きる	cut, chop	オイル	oil		

186

SPEAKING PRACTICE

Helping out at a barbecue party:

加藤： もう　やけましたか。

グリーン： まだ　はやいかもしれません。(*checking the other side*) あっ、まだですね。やけたら　よびますから、どうぞ、ビールを　飲んでいてください。

マルタン： 何か　おてつだいしましょうか。

グリーン： じゃ、すみませんが、おゆが　わいたら、ポットに　入れてください。それから、その　やさいを　きってください。

……………

グリーン： にくが　やけましたよ。

グリーンふじん：みなさん、たくさん　めしあがってください。

マルタン： ああ、いい　においですね。何を　つけて　食べますか。

加藤： ぼくは　しおと　こしょう。マリーさんは？

マルタン： 私は　おしょうゆに　します。

Kato: Is it done yet?

Green: It's probably too early (to take it off the grill). (*checking the other side*) Not yet. I'll call you when it's done, so please help yourself to the beer.

Martin: Is there something I might help you with?

Green: Well, sorry to trouble you, but when the water boils, put it in the thermos jug. Then cut up those vegetables.

‧‧‧‧‧‧

Green: The meat is done.

Green's wife: Please, everyone, help yourself to lots of food.

Martin: What a wonderful smell. What are we supposed to put on it/dip it in?

Kato: I'll take salt and pepper. What about you, Marie?

Martin: I'll take soy sauce.

VOCABULARY			
（お）てつだい	help	におい	smell
おてつだいする	help (humble form)	つける (R2)	put (sauce etc.) on, dip (food) in
ポット	thermos jug	（お）しょうゆ	soy sauce
めしあがってください	please eat (honorific form)		
めしあがる	eat (honorific form)		

PRACTICE 2

LISTENING PRACTICE

 Listen to the tour guide's talk:

今日の　予定について　せつめいいたします。

初めに　東大寺に　行きます。東大寺に　着いたら、まず　みんなで　しゃしんを　とります。その　後　おてらと　だいぶつを　ゆっくり　ごらんください。

つぎに　びじゅつかんに　行きます。1時間半ぐらい　さくひんを　見たら、びじゅつかんの　中に　ある　レストランで　昼食を　とります。昼食の　後で　30分ぐらい　おみやげを　買う　時間が　あります。

2時すぎに　あすか旅館に　むかいます。3時ごろ　旅館に　着く　予定です。旅館に　着いたら、お部屋に　ごあんないします。7時まで　じゆう時間ですので、ゆっくり　おすごしください。4時から　おふろに　入れます。夕食は　7時からです。7時までに　1かいの　しょくどうに　おあつまりください。

それでは　これから　バスに　のりますので、一れつに　おならびください。

Let me explain today's schedule.

To begin with, we will go to Todaiji. Once we arrive at Todaiji, we will take a group picture. After that, feel free to take your time to look at the temple and the large statue of Buddha.

Next, we will go to an art museum. Having seen works of art for about an hour and a half, we will have lunch in the restaurant inside the museum. After lunch there will be about thirty minutes to buy souvenirs.

Just after two o'clock we will head to the Asuka Inn. We are scheduled to arrive at the inn around three o'clock. Once we arrive at the inn, we will show you to your rooms. You will have free time until seven o'clock, so feel free to relax. From four o'clock you can take baths. Dinner is from seven. Please gather in the dining room on the first floor by seven.

Well then, we will board the bus now, so please line up single file.

VOCABULARY			
いたします	do (humble form)	むかう	head to
はじめに	to begin with	じゆう	free, unrestricted
とうだいじ	Todaiji (famous temple)	おすごしください	please spend time (polite form)
まず	first of all	ゆうしょく	dinner
その　あと	after that	しょくどう	dining room, cafeteria
ごらんください	please look (honorific form)	おあつまりください	please gather (polite form)
つぎに	next	あつまる	gather, congregate
さくひん	work of art	いちれつに	one line
ちゅうしょく	lunch	おならびください	please line up (polite form)

SPEAKING PRACTICE

Confirming the details of the day's schedule as described by one's tour guide:

さんかしゃ：よく　聞こえなかったんですが、昼ごはんは　どこで　食べるんで
すか。

ガイド：　　びじゅつかんの　中に　ある　レストランです。

さんかしゃ：食事は　えらべるんですか。

ガイド：　　ええ、おすきなものが　えらべます。

participant:　　I didn't quite hear; where are we going to eat lunch?
tour guide:　　At the restaurant inside the art museum.
participant:　　Can we choose our meals?
tour guide:　　Yes, you can choose a meal you like.

Now explain the schedule in your own words:

9：00	ホテル出発
9：30	東大寺着 → 写真をとる
	お寺と　大仏を　見る。
10：30	東大寺出発
11：00	美術館着
	作品を見る（1時間半）→　昼食
13：30	おみやげ
14：10	美術館出発
15：00	あすか旅館着 →　部屋に案内
	自由時間
19：00	夕食

VOCABULARY　　さんかしゃ　　participant

PRACTICE 3

SPEAKING PRACTICE

I. On the train when one's cell phone rings:

鈴木：　　もしもし……。

山下：　　ああ、鈴木さん？　すみません、今　でんしゃに　のっているので、おりたら　お電話します。

Suzuki:　　Hello . . .

Yamashita: Oh, Mr. Suzuki? I'm sorry, but I'm on a train now. I'll phone when I get off.

II. In a meeting when one's cell phone rings:

鈴木：　　もしもし……。

山下：　　あっ、鈴木さんですか。　何度も　お電話　いただいて、すみません。今　会議中なので……。　会議が　終わったら、こちらから　お電話します。

Suzuki:　　Hello . . .

Yamashita: Oh, is it you, Mr. Suzuki? I'm sorry you've had to call so many times. I am in the middle of a meeting right now, so . . . when the meeting is over, I'll call you.

III. Leaving a message on someone's answering machine:

鈴木：　　　　　もしもし……。

るすばん電話：　ただいま　電話に　出られません。はっしんおんの　後で、メッセージを　ろくおんしてください。

♫♫♫♫♫

鈴木：　　　　　えー、鈴木です。こんばん　うちに　帰ったら、けいたいに　れんらくしてください。まっています。

Suzuki:　　　　　　Hello . . .

answering machine: I cannot come to the phone now. Record your message after the tone.

♫♫♫♫♫

Suzuki:　　　　　　Yes, this is Suzuki. Call me on my cell phone when you come home this evening. I'll be waiting.

VOCABULARY	やました	Yamashita (surname)	はっしんおん	beep (on an answering machine)
	なんども	many times	メッセージ	message
	るすばんでんわ	answering machine	ろくおんする	record
	ただいま	right now (polite form)	ろくおん	recording
190	（でんわに）でる (R2)	answer (the phone)		

READING TASK 1

しんぱいしょうの　人の　話

私は　ねる　前に　ニュースを　見ます。さいきん　くらい　ニュースが　多いので、私は　しんぱいに　なります。

　子どもが　じこに　あうかもしれません。会社が　とうさんするかもしれません。両親が　おもい　びょうきに　なるかもしれません。うちに　どろぼうが　入るかもしれません。こんばん　じしんが　あるかもしれません。

　私は　しんぱいで、夜　ねられません。

VOCABULARY

しんぱいしょう	worrywart
くらい	gloomy
じこに　あう	get into an accident
とうさんする	go under, go bankrupt
とうさん	bankruptcy
おもい	serious
どろぼう	thief, robber

191

READING TASK 2

富士山
ふ じ さん

富士山は、高さ*約３８００メートルで、日本で一番高い山だ。そして、
ふ じ さん　　　たか　やく　　　　　　　　　　　　　　　　　　　に ほん　いちばんたか　やま

日本で一番有名なところかもしれない。ぜひ富士山に登りたいと思っている
に ほん　いちばんゆうめい　　　　　　　　　　　　　　ふ じ さん　　のぼ　　　　　　おも

外国人も多い。もちろん日本人にも人気があり、夏のシーズン中には毎年
がいこくじん　おお　　　　　　　　に ほんじん　　　にん き　　　　　なつ　　　　　　ちゅう　　　　まいとし

１５万人ぐらいが富士登山にチャレンジする。
まんにん　　　　　　ふ じ と ざん

江戸時代には、いろいろな富士山が浮世絵の題材になった。今も大ぜい
え ど じ だい　　　　　　　　　　　　ふ じ さん　うき よ え　だいざい　　　　　　いま　おお

のマニアが、美しい富士山の写真をとろうと思ってシャッターチャンスを
うつく　　ふ じ さん　しゃしん　　　　　　おも

待っている。朝日と富士山、夕日の中の富士山、雪をかぶった富士山、おも
ま　　　　　あさ ひ　ふ じ さん　ゆう ひ　なか　ふ じ さん　ゆき　　　　　　ふ じ さん

しろい雲と富士山など、富士山は美しく変化する。遠くに見える富士山は、
くも　ふ じ さん　　　ふ じ さん　うつく　へん か　　　とお　み　　ふ じ さん

たしかに美しい。
うつく

「富士山をユネスコの世界自然遺産に！」という運動が１９９２年から
ふ じ さん　　　　　　せ かい し ぜんい さん　　　　　　　うんどう　　　　　ねん

始まった。しかし、その願いはまだ実現していない。なぜなら、残念なことに
はじ　　　　　　　　　　ねが　　　　じつげん　　　　　　　　　　ざんねん

富士山はとてもごみの多い山だからだ。
ふ じ さん　　　　　　おお　やま

今人々は、どうしたら本当に美しい富士山を取り戻せるか考えている。富
いまひとびと　　　　　　　ほんとう　うつく　ふ じ さん　と　もど　　かんが　　　　　ふ

士山は、日本の環境問題も象徴している。
じ さん　　に ほん　かんきょうもんだい　しょうちょう

---

* The stem of an adjective followed by さ expresses a condition, nature, or extent. For example:

安（やす）さ　　　cheapness
楽（たの）しさ　　fun
まじめさ　　　　　serious-mindedness

VOCABULARY

高<ruby>さ<rt>たか</rt></ruby>	height
約<ruby><rt>やく</rt></ruby>	approximately
あり	(-*masu* stem of ある, used in place of the -*te* form in writing)
シーズン	season
登山<ruby><rt>と ざん</rt></ruby>	mountain climbing
チャレンジ	challenge
江戸時代<ruby><rt>え ど じ だい</rt></ruby>	Edo period (1603–1867)
時代<ruby><rt>じ だい</rt></ruby>	age, period
題材<ruby><rt>だいざい</rt></ruby>	material, subject matter
大ぜい<ruby><rt>おお</rt></ruby>	many (of people)
マニア	mania
美しい<ruby><rt>うつく</rt></ruby>	beautiful
シャッターチャンス	chance at a perfect photo
朝日<ruby><rt>あさ ひ</rt></ruby>	morning sun
かぶる	cover (with)
変化する<ruby><rt>へん か</rt></ruby>	change

遠くに<ruby><rt>とお</rt></ruby>	far away
たしかに	certainly
ユネスコ	UNESCO
～という	called . . .
運動<ruby><rt>うんどう</rt></ruby>	movement
しかし	however
実現する<ruby><rt>じつげん</rt></ruby>	be realized
なぜなら　～から	the reason why is because . . .
残念なことに<ruby><rt>ざんねん</rt></ruby>	regrettably
ごみ	trash
人々<ruby><rt>ひとびと</rt></ruby>	people
どうしたら　～か	how
取り戻す<ruby><rt>と もど</rt></ruby>	take back
考える<ruby><rt>かんが</rt></ruby> (R2)	think about
環境<ruby><rt>かんきょう</rt></ruby>	environment
問題<ruby><rt>もんだい</rt></ruby>	problem

STYLE NOTE

Up to this point you have seen plain forms used in a variety of sentence structures where they have acted as modifiers. Used in this way, plain forms have no effect on sentence tense or politeness level. Another usage of plain forms is in the sentence-final position. In both spoken and written Japanese, plain forms appear frequently at the ends of sentences, where they indicate tense and, in the case of spoken Japanese, add an air of casualness to what is said. The sentences in the reading task at left, you might have noticed, all end in the plain style. This is typical of written Japanese, which with the exception of letters and essays usually requires plain forms.

KANJI PRACTICE

館	旅館 りょかん	ノ	入	今	今	今	今	食
public building		食	食	食	飮	節	節	館
館	館	館	館					

名	名前 なまえ 何名 なんめい	ノ	ク	タ	名	名	名	名
name		名						

泊	泊まる と 一泊 いっぱく 二泊 にはく	、	ミ	シ	シ	汁	泊	泊
stay overnight		泊	泊	泊				

円	百円 ひゃくえん	丨	冂	冂	円	円	円	
yen								

意	用意 ようい	、	亠	产	立	音	音	音
mind **meaning**		音	音	音	意	意	意	意
意								

電	電気 でん き	一	厂	戸	帀	雨	雨	雨
electricity		雷	雷	霄	雪	雪	電	電
電								

話	話す はな 電話 でん わ	丶	二	三	言	言	言	言
speak **tell**		言	計	訐	話	話	話	話
話								

番	一番 いちばん 何番 なんばん	一	乀	乥	平	平	乎	采
number		釆	番	番	番	番	番	番

号	番号 ばんごう	乚	口	口	弓	号	号	号
number								

駅	駅 えき 駅員 えきいん 駅前 えきまえ	⌐	厂	厈	厈	馬	馬	馬
station		馬	馬	馬	駅	駅	駅	駅
駅	駅							

I Fill in the blanks with the appropriate particle.

1) 子どもが あそんでいるの（　　）見えます。

2) びょうき（　　）学校を 休みました。

3) どこに かぎを おいた（　　）わすれました。

4) じゅんび（　　）できたら、よんでください。

5) 古い たてもの（　　）きょうみが あります。

II Choose the correct word from among the alternatives (1–4) given. The same word cannot be used twice in the same dialogue.

1) 午後の かんこうについて せつめいします。（　　）浅草に 行って おてらを 見ます。（　　）秋葉原に 行って 買いものを します。
   1. つぎに　　2. まだ　　3. では　　4. まず

2) Ａ：あしたの 会議に 出られますか。
   Ｂ：（　　）しゅっちょうで 出られないんです。
   Ａ：（　　）会議は あさってに しましょう。
   1. それから　　2. それなら　　3. それが　　4. たしかに

3) Ａ：富士山に のぼった ことが ありますか。
   Ｂ：いいえ、ないんです。
   Ａ：（　　）今度 いっしょに 行きましょう。
   1. それから　　2. それでは　　3. まず　　4. まだ

III Change the form of the word given in parentheses to complete the sentence in a way that makes sense.

1) マルタンさんは 日本語が（　　　　）か。（話します）

2) 父の たんじょう日に カードを（　　　　）と 思っています。（おくります）

3) そとが（　　　　）、ねられません。（うるさいです）

4) あしたは（　　　　）かもしれません。（あめです）

5) １０時に（　　　　）ら、会議を 始めます。（なります）

IV Choose the most appropriate word or phrase from among the alternatives (1–4) given.

1) おきゃくさんの　名前を　まちがえて　（　　）です。
   1. うれしかった　　2. はずかしかった　　3. むずかしかった　　4. くらかった

2) A：この　せき、（　　）いますか。
   B：ええ、どうぞ。
   1. 空いて　　2. 出て　　3. つかって　　4. すわって

3) この　コートが　買いたいんですが、カードで　（　　）か。
   1. ふりこめます　　2. えらべます　　3. はらえます　　4. もうしこめます

4) A：あ、富士山が　（　　）よ。
   B：ああ、きれいですね。
   1. 見ます　　2. 見られます　　3. 見えます　　4. 見せます

5) A：旅行ですか。よかったら　そうだんに　のりますよ。
   B：（　　）。
   1. ぜひ、のりましょう　　2. ええ、とても　よかったです
   3. ええ、てつだいます　　4. たすかります

V Fill in the blanks with the correct reading of each kanji.

1) ホテルの　部屋を　　予約しました。
   　　　（　　　）（　　　）

2) マリーさんの　ご両親は　　週末に　　初めて　旅館に　泊まりました。
   　　　　　（　　）（　　）（　　）（　　）（　）

3) 用意が　できたら、出かける　予定です。
   　（　　）　　　（　　）（　　）

UNIT 5

SOLVING PROBLEMS

At no time are verbal skills more crucial than when you face some sort of trouble. This unit provides practice in telling someone what is wrong and asking for help, as well as in explaining how to deal with a problem when you are asked for help by others. Taken up are ways of giving instructions on how to use equipment, showing someone how to reach a certain destination, and other expressions necessary to getting around in everyday life.

TALKING ABOUT PRODUCTIVITY

TARGET DIALOGUE

Mr. Suzuki walks by while Mr. Mills and Ms. Martin are looking at a computer screen.

マルタン：すごい！

鈴木：　　何、何？

マルタン：うちの　新しょうひんの　売れ行きを　見ていたんです。

　　　　　(*turning toward Mr. Mills*) すごいですね。

ミルズ：　そうなんです。今月の　売り上げは　先月の　倍ですよ。

鈴木：　　へぇ。きゅうに　のびてきましたね。
　　　　　　　　→ p. 202

ミルズ：　１００万ケース　売れたら、特別ボーナスが　出ると　聞き
　　　　　→ p. 204 まん　　　う　　　　とくべつ　　　　　　　で　　　き
　　　　　ましたよ。

鈴木：　　ほんとうですか。特別ボーナスが　出たら、みんなで　何か
　　　　　　　　　　　　とくべつ　　　　　で　　　　　　　　　　なに
　　　　　おいしい　ものを　食べに　行きましょうよ。
　　　　　　　　　　　　　た　　　い

ミルズ：　それは　いいなあ。ぼくは　まだ　ふぐを　食べた　ことが
　　　　　　　　　　　　　　　　　　　　　　　　た
　　　　　ないんだけど……。

マルタン：私は　りょうていに　行ってみたいなあ。
　　　　　わたし　　　　　　　い

Martin: Fantastic!
Suzuki: What? What?
Martin: We were just looking at the sales trends of our new product. It's fantastic, isn't it?
Mills:　It sure is. This month's sales are twice last month's.
Suzuki: Is that right? Sales have grown dramatically, haven't they?
Mills:　I heard that if one million cases are sold, a special bonus will be issued.

Suzuki: Really? If a special bonus is issued, let's all go out for some sort of delicious meal.

Mills: That would be great. I haven't yet had the experience of eating *fugu*, you know.

Martin: I'd like to go to a *ryotei*.

VOCABULARY

すごい	fantastic, wonderful	売れる (R2)	sell, be sold
うち	us, our company	特別 (な)	special
売れ行き	sales trends	ボーナス	bonus
売り上げ	sales amount	出る (R2)	be issued
倍	times, double	ふぐ	blowfish
のびる (R2)	extend, grow	りょうてい	an elegant and expensive traditional Japanese restaurant
ケース	case	〜なあ	I wish . . . (sentence-final particle)

NOTES

1. すごい！

You use this word to express surprise at something that is exceptional in some way. Repeating すごい, as in すごい！すごい (ですね！) intensifies the emotion. Using すごく before an adjective makes the adjective more intense, so that すごく さむい and すごく とおい are similar to "terribly cold" and "awfully far" in English.

2. 何 (なに)、何 (なに)？

Mr. Suzuki could have said 何 (なに) only once, but by saying it twice he indicates that he is really interested in finding out what Ms. Martin is referring to.

3. うち

うち literally means "inside," and groups—employees of the same company, students of the same university, or members of the same household, for example—use it to refer to themselves or things belonging to them as opposed to outsiders. Thus, a businessperson might speak of うちの 部長 (ぶちょう), "our department manager," while a student might mention うちの 大学 (だいがく), "our university." If someone says うちの いぬ, he or she means "our dog."

4. 行 (い) きましょうよ。

Use this pattern when you are eagerly inviting a friend or close colleague to do something with you. But be careful, because it is considered rude to use it toward someone who ranks above you, such as a supervisor or teacher.

5. MIXING THE *DESU/MASU* AND PLAIN STYLES

The second half of this dialogue contains a mixture of the *desu/masu* and plain styles. This kind of mixture is common in everyday speech, especially in a situation like this, where the speakers are of approximately equal social rank. (For more on mixing of speech styles, see p. 206.)

6. いいなあ／行 (い) ってみたいなあ。

When talking to yourself or expressing a wish or a vague question in a casual setting, you can add なあ

to the end of the sentence to say "I wish" or "I wonder," as in 私 (わたし) も 行 (い) ってみたいなあ, "I wish I could go, too," or だいじょうぶかなあ, "I wonder if it is all right." In form なあ is an utterance to oneself, but you can use it to make your feelings known to those around you in a roundabout way.

7. ぼくは まだ ふぐを 食 (た) べた ことが ないんだけど……。
んだけど is a casual way of saying んですが, example of which you saw in Units 1 and 2. This んだけど makes Mr. Mills's otherwise matter-of-fact statement, "I haven't yet had the experince of eating *fugu*," imply, "I'd like to eat *fugu*." You can use んだけど in this way to subtly make your desires understood.

GRAMMAR & PATTERN PRACTICE

I Describing a Change in State (2)

Earlier you learned 〜てきます (Unit 2, Lesson 6, p. 85). This pattern is also used, in a completely different sense, to express a process of change. You use 〜てきます when you have become aware of a change in some state and want to make a note of it.

(1) To indicate that something has changed over time:

人口が ふえてきました。
じんこう
The population has increased.

人口が へってきました。
じんこう
The population has decreased.

(2) To indicate that something has begun to change:

雨が ふってきました。
あめ
It has begun to rain.

さむく なってきました。
It has gotten cold.

1 Construct sentences as in the example.

例) 人口、へる
れい じんこう
→ 人口が　へってきました。
じんこう

1) マンション、ふえる
→ ....

2) 木、へる
き
→ ....

3) りゅうがくせい、ふえる
→ ....

4) 子どもの　かず、へる
こ
→ ....

5) かいがい旅行を　する人、ふえる
りょこう ひと
→ ....

2 Complete the conversations as in the example.

例) こむ (**NOTE:** This conversation takes place in a train.)
れい
→ A：こんできましたね。
B：ええ、帰りの　時間ですからね。
かえ じ かん

1) すく (**NOTE:** This conversation takes place in a train.)
→ A：...
B：ええ、前の　駅で　学生が　おりましたからね。
まえ えき がくせい

2) 空が　くらくなる
そら
→ A：...
B：ほんとうですね。（雨が）ふるんでしょうか。
あめ

3) はれる
→ A：...
B：よかったですね。

VOCABULARY	りゅうがくせい	foreign student
	かず	number, quantity
	そら	sky
	はれる (R2)	clear up

Ⅱ Making Hypothetical Statements

You can use 〜たら to make if-statements as well as when-statements. The if-clause formed with 〜たら is used to assume a condition that is uncertain or unlikely to occur, and you use it to make comments or ask questions concerning what you or the other party would do, or would like to do, if some event were to occur.

ボーナスが　たくさん　出たら、かいがい旅行に　行きたいです。

If a big bonus was issued, I'd want to go abroad.

You use もし, "if," at the beginning of a 〜たら clause when you want to make it clear that what you are about to say is a supposition.

もし　ＵＦＯを　見たら、しゃしんを　とります。

If I saw a UFO, I'd take a picture of it.

---

1 Complete the sentences as in the example.

例）休みが　１年　ある
　　→ <u>休みが　１年　あったら</u>、何を　しますか。

1) たからくじに　あたる
　　→ .... 、何を　買いますか。

2) 空を　とべる
　　→ .... 、どこに　行きますか。

3) がいこくで　パスポートを　なくす
　　→ .... 、どう　しますか。

4) あした　ストが　ある
　　→ .... 、どうやって　会社に　行きましょうか。

5) かんじが　読めない
　　→ .... 、だれに　聞きますか。

もし	if	パスポート	passport
たからくじ	lottery	スト	(labor) strike
あたる	win		

2 Complete the sentences as in the example.

例）あつい　　　→　あつかったら、クーラーを　つけてください。

ひま（な）　→　ひまだったら、飲みに　行きませんか。

雨　　　　　→　雨だったら、しあいは　ちゅうしです。

1) 部屋が　さむい

→ .... 、言ってください。

2) パーティーが　つまらない

→ .... 、はやく　帰っても　いいですか。

3) あしたが　むり（な）

→ .... 、あさっては　どうですか。

4) るす

→ .... 、また　あとで　電話します。

3 Read the following conversation aloud and practice it thoroughly.

男の　人：あした　ひまだったら、デートを　しませんか。

女の　人：いいですよ。　どこに　行きましょうか。

男の　人：てんきが　よかったら、うみに　行きましょう。

女の　人：ええ。でも　さむいかもしれませんね。

男の　人：さむかったら、うみが　見える　レストランで　食事を　しましょう。さむくなかったら、そとの　テラスで　食事を　しましょう。

女の　人：雨だったら、どうしましょうか。

男の　人：雨だったら、えいがを　見ましょう。

VOCABULARY	クーラー	air conditioning unit	デート	date
	ちゅうし	cancellation, being called off		
	るす	being away from home		
	デートを　する	go on a date		205

USAGE NOTE

In Unit 4, you studied examples of the plain style used in written documents. Here we are going to see examples of it used in conversation.

When speaking with family members or close friends, the plain style is generally used more often than the *desu/masu* style.

The plain style is often used to express intimacy, while the *desu/masu* style tends to create distance between speaker and listener. Yet when speaking with colleagues in the workplace, for example, where you have to consider human relationships in terms of both level of intimacy and relative social position, you may use the *desu/masu* style to show a businesslike attitude while occasionally slipping into the plain style to express closeness to the person you are talking to.

Keigo, or honorific language, is a means of clarifying interpersonal relationships, and we will cover that topic in *Japanese for Busy People III*.

One point worth noting about the plain style is that words and phrases undergo changes in order to make them shorter and easier to say. The commonly occurring changes include:

1. Omissions (for example, particles may be omitted)

2. Abbreviations (leaving *kudasai* off *-te kudasai* or *-naide kudasai*, using *ka mo* instead of *ka mo shiremasen*, etc.)

3. The addition of emotive particles (including *yo* and *naa*)

4. Contractions (such as *-te iru* → *-teru*, *-te iku* → *-teku*, . . . *to itte imashita* →. . . *tte*, or *-nakereba naranai* → *-nakya naranai*.)

5. Substitutions of words (*desu ga* → *da kedo*)

There are many other differences between the *desu/masu* style and the plain style, and one of the best ways to learn them is to develop the habit of listening carefully to conversations among Japanese people. Listen to the following dialogue conducted in the plain style. Can you recognize the casual forms? How would you change the dialogue to the *desu/masu* style? (See p. 205 for answers.)

TRACK
67

男：あした　ひまだったら、デートしない？
おとこ
女：いいわよ。　どこ　行く？
おんな
男：てんきが　よかったら、うみ　行かない？

女：うん、でも　さむいかも。

男：さむかったら、うみが　見える　レストランで　食事を　しようよ。
み
　　さむくなかったら、そとの　テラスで　食事を　しよう。
しょくじ
女：雨だったら、どうする？
あめ
男：雨だったら、えいがを　見ようよ。
あめ　　　　　　　　　　　み

The dialogues at right are ones you have already studied. Here, however, casual language has been added. Study the underlined parts carefully.

I. Unit 3, Lesson 8, Target Dialogue (p. 115):

森田：　　あのう、マリーさんじゃありませんか。

マルタン：えっ、あ、エミちゃん？

森田：　　おひさしぶりです。マリーさん、いつ、こっちに？

マルタン：先月から　東京で　仕事を　してるの。エミちゃん、大きく
　　　　　なったわね。

森田：　　今、中2です。これから　じゅくに　行くんです。

Arriving at the Nakajima home, Marie Martin gets into a conversation with her former host mother.

マルタン：この　あたり、ずいぶん　にぎやかに　なりましたね。

中島：　　そうでしょう。7年前と　くらべて、だいぶ　便利に　なった
　　　　　のよ。

マルタン：ここに　来るとき、おとなりの　エミちゃんに　会いました。
　　　　　じゅくに　行くって　言ってました。日本の　子どもは　た
　　　　　いへんですね。

II. Unit 3, Lesson 8, Practice 2, Speaking Practice (p. 126)—at a class reunion:

前田：　　ひさしぶりだね。

佐々木：ほんとに。何年ぶり？

前田：　　20年ぶりじゃない？

佐々木：むかしと　ぜんぜん　かわらないね。

前田：　　佐々木さんも。

III. Unit 4, Lesson 12, Practice 1, Speaking Practice I (p. 187)—at a barbecue party, assuming Mr.Suzuki and Mr.Mills are friends and are about the same age:

鈴木：　　もう　やけた？

ミルズ：まだ　ちょっと　はやいね。やけたら　よぶよ。ビール　飲んでて。

鈴木：　　何か　てつだおうか。

ミルズ：ありがと。じゃ、わるいけど、おゆが　わいたら、ポットに
　　　　　入れて。それから、その　やさい、きってよ。

VOCABULARY			
こっち	here (informal for こちら)	ほんとに	(abbr. of ほんとうに)
〜の	(sentence-final particle used mainly by women)	ありがと	(abbr. of ありがとう)
〜わね	(sentence-final particle combination used mainly by women)		
〜って	(informal for 〜と)		

PRACTICE 1

WORD POWER

Figures:

～倍 ばい

① 倍／2倍
　ばい　ばい
② 3倍
　　ばい
③ 10倍
　　　ばい
④ 100倍
　　　　ばい

～分の～ ぶん

⑧ 2分の1　（= ½）
　　ぶん
⑨ 3分の2　（= ⅔）
　　ぶん

～パーセント　（%）

⑤ 25%
⑥ 50%
⑦ 100%

PHRASE POWER

Business expressions:

① 売り上げが　のびる 　　う　あ	sales grow
売り上げが　おちこむ 　　う　あ	sales collapse
② 株価が　上がる 　かぶか　あ	stock prices rise
株価が　下がる 　かぶか　さ	stock prices fall
③ 給料が　15パーセント　上がる 　きゅうりょう　　　　　　　あ	salaries increase by 15 percent
給料が　倍に　なる 　きゅうりょう　ばい	salaries double
④ ボーナスが　半分に　なる 　　　　　　はんぶん	bonuses are cut in half (lit., "become half")
ボーナスが　3分の1　へる 　　　　　　ぶん	bonuses decrease by one third
ボーナスが　20パーセント　ふえる	bonuses increase 20 percent
⑤ 業績が　上がる 　ぎょうせき　あ	business productivity increases
業績が　おちこむ 　ぎょうせき	business productivity decreases
⑥ 成績が　上がる 　せいせき　あ	grades increase
成績が　下がる 　せいせき　さ	grades decrease

VOCABULARY	3ばい	triple	あがる	rise, go up	はんぶん	half
	パーセント	percent	さがる	fall, go down	きょうせき	business productivity
	おちこむ	collapse	きゅうりょう	salary	せいせき	grade
208	かぶか	stock prices	ばいに　なる	be doubled		

SPEAKING PRACTICE

I. Speaking to employees about profits and bonuses:

部長：売り上げが　２倍に　なったら、ボーナスも　２倍　出します。
社員：ほ、ほんとうですか。
部長：売り上げが　半分に　なったら、ボーナスは　１００％　カットします。
社員：えー！　そんな……。

department manager: If sales double, we'll issue a double bonus.
employees:　　　　　R-really?
department manager: If profits are half (of the target), we will cut your bonuses 100 percent.
employees:　　　　　What? I can't believe . . .

II. Talking with colleagues at an *izakaya*-style tavern about the performance of one's company:

社員１：のぞみデパートの　仕事が　とれたと　聞きましたよ。よかったですね。
社員２：ええ、おととし　ぎょうせきが　おちこんだ　ときは、しんぱいで　ね
　　　　むれませんでしたが……。
社員１：そうでしたね。
社員２：さいきんは　だんだん　きゅうりょうも　上がってきましたし……。
社員１：よかった、よかった。さあ、今日は　飲みましょう。ま、いっぱい。

employee no. 1: I heard that we got the contract (lit., "were able to get the work") from Nozomi
　　　　　　　　Department Store. That's great, isn't it?
employee no. 2: Yes, the year before last, when we were in a slump (lit., "when productivity had
　　　　　　　　collapsed,") I was so worried, I couldn't sleep, but . . .
employee no. 1: Yes, it was like that, wasn't it?
employee no. 2: Recently our salaries have risen a little, and now . . .
employee no. 1: That's right! Well, today let's drink to that. All right, have one.

CULTURE NOTE

Japanese people usually pour for one another
when they go drinking together.

VOCABULARY		
カットする	cut	
しごとが　とれる	can get work, can get a contract or assignment	
ねむる	sleep	
さあ	well . . .	

ま（あ）	well, in any case
いっぱい	one glass, one cup

PRACTICE 2

PHRASE POWER

Dreams:

① 1年間 休みを とる こと   to take a one-year vacation
　ねんかん　　やす

② ダンスが じょうずに なる こと   to become good at dancing

③ おおがねもちに なる こと   to become super rich

④ 3おく円の たからくじに あたる こと   to win a ¥300 million lottery
　　　えん

⑤ がかに なる こと   to become a painter

⑥ つうやくの しかくを とる こと   to get qualified as an interpreter

⑦ せかい中に 友だちを もつ こと   to have friends all over the world

⑧ いなかで くらす こと   to live in the countryside

⑨ 子どもを 10人 うむ こと   to give birth to ten children
　こ　　　　　にん

⑩ だいとうりょうに なる こと   to become president

USAGE NOTE

こと literally means "thing" or "matter," but when it comes after a verb or an adjective, it functions, like の, as a nominalizer, turning the sentence before it into a noun phrase similar to an infinitive beginning with "to."

　私の ゆめは がいこうかんに なる ことです。
　わたし
　My dream is to become a diplomat.

こと may also, depending on the sentence, translate as the -ing part of a gerund, as in "taking" in the following example.

　私の しゅみは しゃしんを とることです。
　わたし
　My hobby is taking photos.

VOCABULARY				
おおがねもち	the filthy rich	いなか	countryside, rural area
がか	painter	くらす	live (one's life)
つうやく	interpreter	うむ	give birth to
しかくを とる	get qualified	だいとうりょう	president
しかく	certification, qualification	ゆめ	dream

SPEAKING PRACTICE

I. Talking about one's dream of becoming a dancer:

Shall we dance?

ミルズ：ゆめは　何ですか。

愛子：　ダンスが　じょうずに　なる　ことです。

ミルズ：ダンスが　じょうずに　なったら、どうしますか。

愛子：　プロの　ダンサーに　なりたいです。

ミルズ：プロの　ダンサーに　なれなかったら、どうしますか。

愛子：　なれなかったら……。そうですねえ。子どもたちに　ダンスを　おしえます。

Mills:	What is your dream?
Aiko:	To become good at dancing.
Mills:	What would you do if you became good at dancing?
Aiko:	I'd want to become a professional dancer.
Mills:	What would you do if you couldn't become a professional dancer?
Aiko:	If I couldn't . . . That's a good question. I'd give dance lessons to children.

II. Talking about one's dream of becoming a painter:

ミルズ：ゆめは　何ですか。

女の人：がかに　なる　ことです。

ミルズ：がかですか。がかに　なったら、どんな　えを　かきたいですか。

女の人：せかい中の　うつくしい　ふうけいを　かきたいです。せかいいさんを　たずねて　かきたいですね。

ミルズ：そうですか。すばらしい　さくひんを　かいたら　ぜひ　見せてください。

Mills:	What is your dream?
woman:	To become a painter.
Mills:	A painter? What kind of pictures would you want to paint if you became a painter?
woman:	I'd want to paint beautiful landscapes from around the world. I'd want to visit world heritage sites and paint (them).
Mills:	Is that so? When you paint a great work, by all means please show it to me.

VOCABULARY			
プロ	professional	たずねる (R2)	visit
ダンサー	dancer		
そうですね	that is a good question		
ふうけい	landscape		

211

PRACTICE 3

PHRASE POWER

Tragedies that could happen to you:

① おふろに　入っているとき、じしんが　おきた。
はい

An earthquake occurs when you are in the bathtub.

② タクシーだいを　はらうとき、さいふが　ないのに　気づいた。
き

You realize your wallet is missing when you are about to pay the taxi fare.

③ 山の　中で　みちに　まよった。
やま　なか

You get lost in the mountains.

④ がいこくに　すんでいる　とき、ホームシックに　かかった。

You get homesick while living abroad.

⑤ アパートの　となりの　人が　まいばん　うるさい。
ひと

The person in the apartment next to yours is loud night after night.

⑥ ある日　こいびとが　とつぜん　いなくなった。
ひ

One day your sweetheart/darling suddenly disappears.

⑦ いんせきが　とんできて　あした　ちきゅうが　ほろびると　しった。

You find out that a meteorite will come flying (toward Earth) and the world will be obliterated tomorrow.

⑧ ある朝　おきたら、じぶんが　むしに　なっていた。
あさ

You wake up one morning to discover you have turned into a insect.

VOCABULARY					
おきる (R2)	occur	あるひ	one day	いんせき	meteorite
タクシーだい	taxi fare	ある〜	a certain . . .	ちきゅう	Earth
きづく	notice	こいびと	sweetheart, darling	ほろびる (R2)	be destroyed
みちに　まよう	get lost	とつぜん	suddenly	あるあさ	one morning
ホームシックに　かかる	get homesick	いなくなる	disappear (of animate object)	むし	insect

SPEAKING PRACTICE

Talking about what to do in the event of an earthquake . . .

 I. while in one's office:

ミルズ：じむしょに　いる　とき、じしんが　おきたら、どうしますか。

鈴木：　おもい　ファイルが　入っている　キャビネットから　はなれます。

Mills: What would you do if there was an earthquake while you were in your office?

Suzuki: I'd get away from the filing cabinet with the heavy files in it.

 II. while walking:

ミルズ：まちを　あるいている　とき、じしんが　おきたら、どうしますか。

鈴木：　おちてくる　ものに　ちゅういして、ひろい　ところに　行きます。

Mills: What would you do if there was an earthquake while you were walking around town?

Suzuki: I'd be careful about things falling and I'd go to an open space.

 III. on the freeway:

ミルズ：こうそくどうろで　車を　うんてんしている　とき、じしんが　おきたら、どうしますか。

鈴木：　すぐに　車を　とめて、ようすを　見ます。

Mills: What would you do if there was an earthquake while you were driving your car on the freeway?

Suzuki: I'd stop the car right away and gauge the situation.

IV. in an elevator:

ミルズ：エレベーターに　のっている　とき、じしんが　おきたら、どうしますか。

鈴木：非常呼び出しボタンを　おして、まちます。

Mills: What would you do if there was an earthquake while you were riding in an elevator?

Suzuki: I'd press the emergency call button and wait.

VOCABULARY	はなれる (R2)	get away from	うんてんする	drive
	おちる (R2)	fall	うんてん	driving
	ちゅういする	be careful (of)	ようすを　みる (R2)	gauge the situation
	ちゅうい	attention, heed	ようす	appearance, situation
	こうそくどうろ	freeway	ひじょうよびだしボタン	emergency call button
			おす	push, press

213

READING TASK

3おく円　あたったら

さいきん、　たからくじの　さいこうがくが　だんだん　高く　なってきました。　3おく円　あたる　人も　いると　聞きました。あなたは　3おく円　あたったら、どうしますか。

「私は　3おく円　あたったら、まず、車を　買って、それから、うみべに　小さな　マンションを　買います。金曜日に　仕事が　終わったら、すぐ　車で　そのマンションに　行きます。てんきが　よかったら、一日中、かいがんで　すごします。もし　雨が　ふったら、うみが　見える　部屋で　おんがくを　かけて　本を読みます。こんな　週末が　あったら、毎日の　仕事が　もっと　たのしく　なる　かもしれません。」

「私は　3おく円　あたったら、とうしします。1おく円は　あんぜんな　こくさいを　買います。1おく円は　しんらいできる　ファンドマネージャーに　あずけます。1おく円は　インターネットで　ちょっと　リスクの　ある　新しい　ビジネスに　とうしします。もし　かぶかが　上がって　しきんが　ふえたら、もっと　いろいろな　きぎょうに　とうしします。もし　かぶかが　下がって　しきんが　へったら、とうしを　やめます。」

あなただったら、　どうしますか？

VOCABULARY

さいこうがく	largest amount	とうしする	invest	インターネット	the Internet
うみべ	seaside	とうし	investing	リスク	risk
一日中	all day	あんぜん（な）	safe	ビジネス	business
かいがん	seashore	こくさい	national bond	しきん	funds, capital
かける (R2)	put on (music)	しんらいする	trust	きぎょう	enterprise, business
		ファンドマネージャー	fund manager		

KANJI PRACTICE

売	売る 売店 ばいてん	二	十	主	声	声	声	売
sell		売	売					

上	上 うえ 上がる あ 売り上げ う あ	┃	┣	上	上	上		
up								

下	下 した 下がる さ	一	下	下	下	下		
down								

倍	倍 ばい 三倍 さんばい	ノ	イ	イ	仁	位	位	位
double times		倍	倍	倍	倍	倍		

万	一万人 いちまんにん 一千万 いっせんまん	一	フ	万	万	万		
ten thousand								

特 — special

特に
とく

ク	彡	牛	牛	牜	牜	特
特	特	特	特	特		

別 — separate

特別
とくべつ

リ	口	口	另	另	別	別
別	別					

口 — mouth

口
くち
入口
いりぐち
人口
じんこう

�𠃌	冂	口	口	口		

雨 — rain

雨
あめ

一	厂	厅	币	雨	雨	雨
雨	雨	雨				

車 — car

車
くるま
電車
でんしゃ

一	厂	冂	旦	旦	亘	車
車	車					

COMPUTER TROUBLE

TARGET DIALOGUE

Ms. Martin is experiencing computer trouble.

TRACK
79

マルタン：あれっ？

鈴木：　　どうしたんですか。
すずき

マルタン：新しい　ソフトを
　　　　　あたら →p. 219
　　　　　ダウンロードしたら、

　　　　　パソコンが　動かなくなってしまったんです。どうすれば
　　　　　→p. 220　　　　うご
　　　　　いいですか。

佐々木：　少し　待ってみたら　どうですか。時間が　かかっている
ささき　　すこ　ま　　　　　　　　　　　　じかん
　　　　　だけかもしれませんよ。

マルタン：はい。

佐々木：　待ってみて　だめだったら、シカさんに　たのみましょう。
　　　　　ま
　　　　　それより、マリーさん、6時から　のぞみデパートで　打ち
　　　　　　　　　　　　　　　　　じ　　　　　　　　　　　　　　う
　　　　　合わせでしょう。
　　　　　あ

マルタン：あ、たいへん、もう　こんな　時間！　あと　３０分しか
　　　　　　　　　　　　　　　　　じかん　　　　　　さんじゅっぷん
　　　　　ありません！

鈴木：　　だいじょうぶですよ。急げば　間に合いますよ。
　　　　　　　　　　　　　　　　いそ →p. 222　ま　あ

Martin: Huh?
Suzuki: What's wrong?
Martin: When I downloaded some new software, my computer just froze up. What should I do?
Sasaki: How about waiting a little bit? It may just take time.
Martin: Okay.
Sasaki: We'll wait and see what happens, and then if it's still no good, we'll ask Shika to do something about it. And more importantly, aren't you supposed to meet someone at six o'clock at Nozomi Department Store?
Martin: Oh, no! Look at what time it is! I have only thirty minutes left.
Suzuki: It's all right. You'll make it if you hurry.

VOCABULARY

ソフト	software	〜だけ	just, only (particle)
ダウンロードする	download	だめ（な）	no good
動かなく　なる うご	stop working	たのむ	call on (for help)
〜てしまう	(used to indicate completion, regret)	それより	more than that (see Note 4 below)
どうすれば　いいですか	what should I do?	こんな	such . . . as this
急げば いそ	if you hurry	〜しか　〜ない	none except for
〜ば	if		

NOTES

1. あれっ？
This is an expression of surprise that you utter almost without thinking when you encounter something completely unexpected. Female speakers may use a variant form: あらっ.

2. どうすれば　いいですか。
"What should I do?" We use this expression to ask for advice or suggestions as to the best course of action in a given situation.

3. 〜たら　どうですか。
We use this form to express a suggestion. Literally it means "What about ——ing?" or "Why don't you . . . ?" ほうが　いいです (Unit 2, Lesson 6) also expresses a suggestion, but it is much stronger.

4. それより
You use this expression to change the subject to something that seems more important or urgent than what you are currently talking about.

5. 時間（じかん）が　かかっているだけかもしれませんよ。
だけ means "just" or "only," as in 今日（きょう）だけ, "today only," or 少（すこ）しだけ, "just a little bit." We use だけ after nouns, adverbs, adjectives, or even sentences ending in the plain form. For example:

かぜじゃありません。くしゃみが　出ただけです。
で

I don't have a cold. I just sneezed, that's all.

6. あと　３０分（ぷん）しか　ありません！
しか always occurs with negative predicates. Xしか with a negative means "only" or "merely," emphasizing that besides X there is nothing else. The choice between しか　〜ない and だけ depends on the speaker's attitude. For example, ３０分（ぷん）しか　ありません emphasizes the feeling of not having enough time, whereas ３０分（ぷん）だけ　あります means "I have time, but it is only 30 minutes." Equally, ３０分（ぷん）しか　ありません emphasizes that besides 30 minutes, there is no time (i.e., 30 minutes is short for the speaker), while ３０分（ぷん）だけ　です implies that it takes time, but only 30 minutes.

GRAMMAR & PATTERN PRACTICE

I Stating the Result of an Action or Event

When the tense of a sentence containing a 〜たら clause is past, the sentence usually indicates that the speaker has noticed something new or unusual.

うちに 帰ったら、母から にもつが とどいていました。
When I got home, the package from my mother had arrived.

はこを あけたら、あかい マフラーが 入っていました。
When I opened up the box, there was a red scarf inside.

---

1 Read the following pairs of sentences aloud while considering their meanings.

1) サッカーの れんしゅうを したら、ひざが いたく なりました。
   マッサージを したら、よく なりました。

2) 東京を 出る とき、雨が ふっていましたが、箱根に 着いたら、
   はれてきました。
   ホテルの 屋上に 上がったら、みずうみと 富士山が 見えました。

3) 朝食を ようしょくから わしょくに かえたら、1か月で 2キロ
   やせました。
   新しい スーツを 着て デートに 出かけたら、かのじょが とても
   よろこびました。

2 Costruct sentences as in the example.

例) スポーツクラブに 行きました。学生の ころの 友だちに 会いました。
   → スポーツクラブに 行ったら、学生の ころの 友だちに 会いました。

1) 朝 おきました。雪が ふっていました。
   → _____

2) うちの ちかくの すし屋に 行きました。しまっていました。
   → _____

VOCABULARY					
にもつ	package	ようしょく	Western-style food	しまる	close
マッサージ	massage	わしょく	Japanese-style food		
おくじょう	roof garden	やせる (R2)	get slim		
ちょうしょく	breakfast	かのじょ	she/her, my girlfriend		219

3) 薬を　飲みました。ねつが　下がりました。
くすり　の　　　　　　　　　　　さ

→ ....

4) １０時間　パソコンで　仕事を　しました。目が　つかれました。
じかん　　　　　　　しごと　　　　　　　　　め

→ ....

5) 日光まで　車で　行きました。じゅうたいで　8時間　かかりました。
にっこう　くるま　い　　　　　　　　　　　　　じかん

→ ....

II Indicating That an Action or Event Has Been Completed

A verb in the -te form followed by しまいます indicates that an action or event has been completed. It often expresses the speaker's regret, reluctance, or resignation.

きのう、レポートを　ぜんぶ　書いてしまいました。
か

Yesterday I wrote the entire report.

時間が　ありませんから、はやく　食事を　してしまいましょう。
じかん　　　　　　　　　　　　しょくじ

We don't have time, so let's quickly have a meal and be done with it.

会議に　おくれてしまいました。　　　　　　　　　　　(IMPLIES REGRET)
かいぎ

I ended up being late for the meeting.

しりょうを　わすれてしまいました。　　　　　　　　　(IMPLIES REGRET)

I had to go and forget the documents.

In colloquial Japanese, 〜てしまう／でしまう (plain style) is often contracted to 〜ちゃう／じゃう, i.e., 食(た)べちゃう, 飲(の)んじゃう.

---

1 Read the following conversations aloud and practice them thoroughly.

1) 鈴木：　　マリーさんの　パリの　おみやげの　ココアは　どこですか。
すずき
　　マルタン：きのう、みんなで　ぜんぶ　飲んでしまいました。
の

2) ミルズ：　鈴木さん、ここに　のぞみデパートに　おくる　サンプルを
すずき
　　　　　　おいたんですが...。

　　鈴木：　　今朝、もう　おくってしまいましたよ。いけませんでしたか。
すずき　　けさ

3) 鈴木： 　　ミルズさん、もう　おそいですよ。はやく　帰りましょう。

　　ミルズ： 　今日中に　レポートを　書いてしまいたいので、どうぞ　お先に。

4) ミルズ： 　鈴木さん、お昼を　食べに　行きませんか。

　　鈴木： 　　あれ、まだ　だったんですか。もう　マリーさんと　食べてきてしまいましたよ。

2 Construct sentences as in the example.

例） かぎを　なくした

　　→ かぎを　なくしてしまいました。

1) けがを　した

　　→ ....

2) けいたいを　うちに　おいてきた

　　→ ....

3) １０キロ　ふとった

　　→ ....

4) パソコンの　データが　きえた

　　→ ....

5) しょるいが　なくなった

　　→ ....

VOCABULARY			
ココア	hot chocolate	おいてくる	leave (something somewhere)
おく	put (something somewhere)	ふとる	gain weight
いけない	it is no good, it is forbidden, it will not do	きえる (R2)	vanish
おひる	lunch		

III Making Conditional Statements

２時に　会社を　出れば、間に合います。

じ　　かいしゃ　　で　　　　　ま　あ

If we leave the office at two o'clock, we will make it (on time).

〜たら is one of two forms you can use to make if-statements. 〜ば is the other. A clause formed with 〜ば express a straightforward if-then condition that is required for an event or a state to occur or come into being. Examples of the conditional (〜ば) form are shown in the following table.

	word	aff.	neg.
verb	思う おも	思えば おも	思わなければ おも
	出る (R2) で	出れば で	出なければ で
	来る く	来れば く	来なければ こ
	する	すれば	しなければ
-i adj.	はやい	はやければ	はやくなければ
	いい／よい	よ ければ	よくなければ
-na adj.	便利な べんり	(便利で　あれば) べんり 便利なら（ば） べんり	便利でなければ べんり 便利じゃなければ べんり
noun	雨 あめ	(雨で　あれば) あめ 雨なら（ば） あめ	雨でなければ あめ 雨じゃなければ あめ

NOTE: You use なら for the conditional form of a -na adjective or noun. であれば and ならば are found mostly in written Japanese or in very formal speech.

1 Change each word to its conditional form.

例）行く　　　　→　行けば

れい　　い　　　　　　い

1) たのむ　　　→　...
2) おりる　　　→　...
3) しらせる　　→　...
4) もってくる　→　...
5) さむい　　　→　...
6) おもしろくない →　...
7) つごうが　いい →　...
8) 会いたい　　→　...

あ
9) げんきな　　→　...
10) 日曜日　　　→　...

にちようび

2 Complete the dialogues as in the example.

例) やせる
<ruby>例<rt>れい</rt></ruby>)
　　　　A：<ruby>着<rt>き</rt></ruby>られるでしょうか。
　　→ B：<u>やせれば</u>、<ruby>着<rt>き</rt></ruby>られます。

1) <ruby>毎日<rt>まいにち</rt></ruby>　しゅくだいを　する
　　　　A：かんじを　ぜんぶ　おぼえられるでしょうか。
　　→ B：…………………………………………………… 、おぼえられます。

2) <ruby>古<rt>ふる</rt></ruby>い　しりょうを　すてる
　　　　A：この<ruby>部屋<rt>へや</rt></ruby>は　きれいに　なるでしょうか。
　　→ B：…………………………………………………… 、きれいに　なります。

3) どうろが　こんでいない
　　　　A：ひこうきに　<ruby>間<rt>ま</rt></ruby>に<ruby>合<rt>あ</rt></ruby>うでしょうか。
　　→ B：…………………………………………………… 、<ruby>間<rt>ま</rt></ruby>に<ruby>合<rt>あ</rt></ruby>います。

4) かいひが　<ruby>安<rt>やす</rt></ruby>い
　　　　A：のぞみスポーツクラブに　<ruby>入<rt>はい</rt></ruby>りませんか。
　　→ B：…………………………………………………… 、<ruby>入<rt>はい</rt></ruby>っても　いいですよ。
　　せつびが　いい
　　→ C：…………………………………………………… 、<ruby>入<rt>はい</rt></ruby>っても　いいですよ。

5) おしえ<ruby>方<rt>かた</rt></ruby>が　じょうずだ
　　　　A：お<ruby>子<rt>こ</rt></ruby>さんを　やきゅうチームに　<ruby>入<rt>い</rt></ruby>れませんか。<ruby>新<rt>あたら</rt></ruby>しい　コーチは
　　　　　　おしえ<ruby>方<rt>かた</rt></ruby>が　じょうずですよ。
　　→ B：…………………………………………………… 、<ruby>入<rt>い</rt></ruby>れても　いいですよ。

VOCABULARY			
おぼえる (R2)	learn, memorize	せつび	facilities
すてる (R2)	throw away	やきゅうチーム	baseball team
かいひ	membership dues	コーチ	coach
のぞみスポーツクラブ	Nozomi Exercise Club (fictitious business)		

PRACTICE 1

PHRASE POWER

Using computers:

①	パソコンを 起動する	start up the computer
②	パソコンを 再起動する	reboot the computer
③	パソコンを 終了する	shut down the computer
④	インターネットに 接続する	connect to the Internet
⑤	ウェブサイトに アクセスする	go to a website
⑥	メールを 受信する	receive e-mail
⑦	メールを 送信する	send e-mail
⑧	メールを 保存する	save e-mail
⑨	メールを 削除する	delete e-mail
⑩	メールを 印刷する	print e-mail
⑪	メールに ファイルを 添付する	attach a file to an e-mail
⑫	ソフトを インストールする	install software
⑬	ソフトを ダウンロードする	download software
⑭	データを 入力する	input data
⑮	書式を 設定する	select a format
⑯	ファイルを 開く／開ける	open a file
⑰	ウィルスに 感染する	get a virus
⑱	文字化けする	be garbled
⑲	フリーズする	freeze

VOCABULARY			
きどうする	start up (a computer)	てんぷする	attach (a file)
さいきどうする	reboot	インストールする	install
しゅうりょうする	shut down	にゅうりょくする	input
せつぞくする	connect (to)	しょしき	format
ウェブサイト	website	せっていする	set
アクセスする	access	せってい	setting(s)
じゅしんする	receive (electronically)	ひらく／あける	open (a file)
そうしんする	send (electronically)	ウィルス	virus
ほぞんする	save (a file)	かんせんする	get (a virus)
さくじょする	delete	もじばけする	become garbled
いんさつする	print	フリーズする	freeze (of computer)

SPEAKING PRACTICE

I.   Consulting a colleague about a sketchy e-mail one has received:

鈴木：　　　あやしい　メールが　来たんですが、どうすれば　いいでしょう。
　すずき　　　　　　　　　　　　　き
チャンドラ：すぐ　さくじょすれば　だいじょうぶです。

鈴木：　　　てんぷファイルも　ついていますが、だいじょうぶですか。

チャンドラ：あけなければ　だいじょうぶです。

Suzuki: A sketchy e-mail has arrived. I wonder what should I do . . .
Chandra: If you delete it immediately, it will be all right.
Suzuki: There's an attachment in it, too. (Are you sure) it will be all right?
Chandra: It will be all right as long as you don't open it.

II. Consulting a colleague about a printing problem and a garbled e-mail:

鈴木：　　　たびたび　すみません。いんさつできないんですが、どうしたんで
　すずき
　　　　　　しょう。

チャンドラ：(checking out the printer) ええと。ああ、ようしが　ないんです。入れ
　　　　　　　　　　　　　　　　　　　　　　　　　　　　　　　　　い
　　　　　　れば　すぐ　できますよ。

．．．．．．．．．．．．．．．．．

鈴木：　　　入れたんですが、まだ　できないんです。
　　　　　　い

チャンドラ：できませんか。おかしいですね。ああ　せっていが　ちがうんです
　　　　　　よ。せっていを　かえれば　すぐ　できます。私が　しましょう。
　　　　　　　　　　　　　　　　　　　　　　　　　わたし

鈴木：　　　いつも　すみません。

Suzuki: I'm sorry for asking so many questions. I can't print. What happened?
Chandra: Let's see. Oh, there's no paper. If you put (some) in, you'll be able to (print) imme-
             diately.
. . . . . .
Suzuki: I put (some paper) in, but I still can't (print).
Chandra: You can't? That's strange. Oh, the settings are wrong. If you change the settings,
             you'll be able to (print) immediately. I'll do it.
Suzuki: I'm sorry to always bother you.

VOCABULARY		
あやしい	suspicious, sketchy
てんぷファイル	attached file
たびたび	repeatedly, often
ようし	paper
おかしい	odd, strange

PRACTICE 2

SPEAKING PRACTICE

I. Locked out of one's office:

マルタン：　　ドアを　しめたら、うちがわから　かぎが　かかってしまった
んです。カードキーは　部屋の　中に　あるんですが、どうす
れば　いいですか。

そうじの　人：かんり人が　スペアキーを　もっているので、1かいの　かんり
人しつで　聞いてみてください。

Martin: When I closed the door, it locked from the inside. My card key is in the room. What should
I do?

janitor: The building manager has a spare key, so please ask at the building manager's office on
the first floor and see what they say.

II. Having received a notice in one's mailbox that one cannot read:

ミルズ：きのう　ゆうびんうけを　あけたら、この　かみが　入っていたんです。
かんじが　読めないんですが、何の　かみですか。

鈴木：　ああ、たくはいびんの　ふざいつうちですね。にもつが　とどいた
とき、ミルズさんが　るすだったんですよ。

ミルズ：どうすれば　いいですか。

鈴木：　この電話番号に　電話すれば、ミルズさんの　つごうの　いい　ときに
また　もってきますよ。

Mills: When I opened my mailbox yesterday, this paper was in it. I can't read kanji. What is it?

Suzuki: Ahh, it's a notice of attempted delivery for an express package. When the package
arrived, you were not at home.

Mills: What should I do?

Suzuki: If you call this telephone number, they will bring it to you again at a time that is convenient for you.

VOCABULARY			
うちがわ	the inside	スペアキー	spare key
うち	the inside	かんりにんしつ	building manager's office
がわ	side	ゆうびんうけ	home mailbox, mail slot
かかる	lock (intr.)	ふざいつうち	notice of attempted delivery
カードキー	key card		

III. Ordering at a conveyor-belt sushi restaurant:

ミルズ：かいてんずしは　初めてなんです。どうすれば　いいんですか。

鈴木：　食べたい　すしが　来たら、とれば　いいんですよ。

ミルズ：食べたい　すしが　来なかったら、どうすれば　いいですか。

鈴木：　何も　とらなければ　いいんです。何か　食べたい　すしが　あるんですか。

ミルズ：ええ、大トロが　食べたいんです。

鈴木：　その　ばあいは、「大トロ　ください」と　店の　人に　言えば　いいんですよ。

ミルズ：わかりました。(turning to a cook)「すみません。大トロ、おねがいします！」

Mills:　This is my first time at a conveyor-belt sushi restaurant. How does it work?
Suzuki: When a piece of sushi that you want to eat comes around, just grab it.
Mills:　What should I do if a piece that I want to eat doesn't come around?
Suzuki: You don't have to take any pieces (that you don't want to eat). Is there a kind of sushi you'd like to eat?
Mills:　Yes, I'd like to eat fatty tuna.
Suzuki: In that case, just say to the restaurant staff, "Fatty tuna, please."
Mills:　I understand. Excuse me. Fatty tuna, please!

IV. Consulting a colleague about the troubles one has sleeping at night:

社員１：さいきん　あまり　よく　ねむれないんです。

社員２：何か　しんぱいごとが　あるんですか。

社員１：特に　ないんですが、仕事が　いそがしくて。

社員２：ストレスじゃありませんか。気分てんかんに　旅行すれば、よく　なりますよ。私も　前に　ねむれなかった　ことが　ありますが、沖縄に　行って　ダイビングを　したら、よく　なりましたよ。

社員１：休みが　とれれば、もんだいは　ないんです。

社員２：……。

employee 1: Recently I haven't been able to sleep very well.
employee 2: Is there something that's been bothering you?
employee 1: Nothing in particular; I've just been busy with work.
employee 2: It's stress, isn't it? It would get better if you went on vacation for a change. Previously I, too, hadn't been able to sleep, but when I went to Okinawa and did some scuba diving, it got better.
employee 1: It would be great (lit., "There would be no problem") if I could take a vacation.
employee 2: . . .

VOCABULARY			
かいてんずし	conveyor-belt sushi restaurant	とくに　ない	no(thing) in particular
おおトロ	fatty tuna	ストレス	stress
その　ばあい	in that case	きぶんてんかんに	for a change of mood
ばあい	case, instance		
しんぱいごと	concern		

227

V. Consulting a colleague about how to become good at dancing:

社員：ダンスが　じょうずに　なりたいんですが、からだが　すごく　かたいん
しゃいん
　　　　です。どうすれば　いいでしょう。

中村：ヨガを　してみたら　どうですか。
なかむら

社員：ヨガを　する　人は　みんな　からだが　やわらかいと　聞きましたが、
ひと　　　　　　　　　　　　　　　　　　　　　　き
　　　　だいじょうぶでしょうか。

中村：私も　初めは　かたかったんですが、だんだん　やわらかく　なってきま
わたし　はじ
　　　　した。つづければ　少しずつ　やわらかく　なりますよ。
すこ

社員：じゃあ、今度　ヨガクラスに　出てみます。
こんど　　　　　　　　で

employee: I want to get good at dancing, but my body is terribly stiff. I wonder what should I do . . .
Nakamura: How about trying yoga?
employee: I've heard that people who do yoga are flexible, but would it be okay (for someone like me, who is inflexible, to try yoga)?
Nakamura: I, too, was inflexible at first, but gradually I became flexible. If you keep up with it, little by little you will become flexible.
employee: Well then, the next opportunity I have, I will try a yoga class.

VOCABULARY		
かたい	stiff
やわらかい	flexible

PRACTICE 3

SPEAKING PRACTICE

I. A snowy morning at a train station on one's way to work:

ミルズ：　　　すみません、何が　あったんですか。
じょうきゃく：雪で　電車が　とまっているんです。
ミルズ：　　　ええ？　いつごろ　動くんですか。
じょうきゃく：さあ、私も　わからないんです。

Mills: Excuse me, what happened?
passenger: The trains have stopped due to the snow.
Mills: What? When, approximately, will they start moving (again)?
passenger: Well, I don't know (the answer to that question) either.

II. Asking a station employee for information:

ミルズ：　　あのう、電車は　何時に　動きますか。
駅員：　　　私たちも　いつ　動くか　わからないんです。
ミルズ：　　こまったなあ。タクシーのりばは　どこですか。
駅員：　　　南口に　あります。ここは　北口ですから、はんたいがわに
　　　　　　回ってください。

Mills: Umm . . . what time will the trains start moving (again)?
station employee: We, too, don't know when (the trains) will start moving (again).
Mills: This is troubling. Where is the taxi stand?
station employee: At the south exit. This is the north exit, so you'll have to go over to the other platform.

III. Running into a colleage at a taxi stand:

ミルズ：加藤さん！　おはようございます。
加藤：　ああ、ミルズさん。ちょうど　よかった。いっしょに　行きましょう。
ミルズ：加藤さんに　会えて　よかったです。

Mills: Mr. Kato! Good morning.
Kato: Oh, Mr. Mills. Good timing. Let's go (to the office in a taxi) together.
Mills: It's a good thing I was able to run into you, Mr. Kato.

VOCABULARY			
じょうきゃく	passenger	ちょうど　いい	be just right
とまる	stop		
はんたいがわ	opposite side		
はんたい	opposite		

IV. Riding in a taxi:

ミルズ：おきたら 雪が ふっていて、びっくりしましたよ。

加藤： 4月に 雪が ふるのは へんですね。 さいきんは せかい中 ど
こでも 天気が おかしいですね。

ミルズ：そうですね。 それに、駅に 着いたら 電車が とまっていたし、タ
クシーのりばまで 来たら すごい れつだったので、もう 会議に
間に合わないと 思いました。

加藤： この 雪ですから、しかたが ないですよ。今日は ちこくですね。

Mills: When I woke up, it was snowing, so I was surprised.
Kato: The snowfall in April is odd, isn't it? Recently, the weather everywhere around the world has been odd, hasn't it?
Mills: That's right. Moreover, when I arrived at the station, the trains had stopped moving. And when I got to the taxi stand, there was a long line, so I knew I wouldn't be on time for the meeting.
Kato: Because of this snow, it can't be helped. Today we'll be late.

へん（な）	strange, odd
それに	in addition
しかたが ない	there is nothing you can do about it, it cannot be helped
ちこく	being late

READING TASK

ミルズさんの　にっき

4月6日　雪

　朝　おきて　カーテンを　あけたら、雪が　ふっていた。　雪で　電車が　おくれるかもしれないので、いつもより　少し　はやく　うちを　出た。　今日は　午前中に　たいせつな　会議が　あったが、30分　はやく　出れば　間に合うと　思った。

　駅に　着いたら　おおぜいの　人が　電車を　待っていた。電車は　動いていなかった。　駅の　人に　聞いたら、いつ　動くか　わからないと　言った。急いで　タクシーのりばに　行ったら、れつの　中に　加藤さんが　いた。

　加藤さんと　いっしょに　タクシーで　会社に　行った。　雪が　たくさん　ふっていたので、　タクシーは　いつもより　ゆっくり　はしっていた。　会議に　間に合うか　どうか　しんぱいに　なった。

　会社に　着いたら　10時半だった。会議しつの　ドアを　あけたら　会議は　もう　始まっていた。　「すみません。電車が　とまっていたので、おくれてしまったんです」と　あやまって、会議しつに　入った。

　おくれたのは　ぼくと　加藤さんだけだった。　はずかしかった。後で　聞いたら、　システム部の　田中さんは　いつもより　2時間　はやく　うちを　出て、　あるいて　会社に　来たと　言っていた。　おどろいた。

VOCABULARY

にっき	diary	はしる	run (of car)
カーテン	curtain	あやまる	apologize
急いで	in a hurry		

231

KANJI PRACTICE

動	動く 自動ドア	↜	⇁	⇊	⇇	↱	⇥	車
move		重	重	動	動	動	動	

自	自動 自分	⸜	⇂	宀	白	自	自	自
self		自						

待	待つ	⸝	⼻	彳	彳	待	待	待
wait		待	待	待	待			

打	打ち合わせ	⼆	⼿	⼿	扩	打	打	打
strike								

合	打ち合わせ 間に合う	⼑	𠆢	合	合	合	合	合
combine		合						

急	急ぐ いそ 急に きゅう	ノ	⺈	⺈	刍	刍	刍	急
hurry **quickly**		急	急	急	急			

内	内 うち *市内 し ない	｜	冂	内	内	内	内	
innner **inside**								

外	外 そと 外国 がいこく 外食 がいしょく	ノ	⺈	ク	タ	外	外	外	外
out **outer**									

雪	雪 ゆき	一	厂	冖	帀	雨	雨	雨
		雪	雪	雪	雪	雪	雪	
snow								

天	天気 てん き	一	二	𠂉	天	天	天	
weather								

GIVING DIRECTIONS

TARGET DIALOGUE

The project team has finally achieved its sales targets. A celebration has begun, but Mr. Suzuki has not yet arrived.

みんな： かんぱい！

マルタン：(cell phone rings) あ、鈴木さんからです。鈴木さん？　今

どちらですか。

鈴木： のぞみビルに　着いたんですが、レストランに　行く

エレベーターが　見つからないんです。

マルタン：レストランは　専用の　エレベーターが　あるんですよ。

<u>エスカレーターで　2階に　上がると、右側に　あります。</u>
→p. 236

鈴木： えっ、2階の　どっち側ですか。よく　聞こえないんですが。

マルタン：右。右側です。

鈴木： 右側ですね。すぐ　行きます。

The official party ends, and everyone heads to a karaoke bar.

鈴木： ミルズさんも　行きますよね、カラオケ。

ミルズ： あのう、今日は　これで　失礼します。

鈴木： ええっ、もう　帰るんですか。まだ　9時ですよ。あしたは

休みですし。

ミルズ： <u>あした　日本語の　しけんが　あって　6時に　おきなけれ</u>
→p. 238
<u>ば　ならないんです。</u>

鈴木： ざんねんですねえ。ミルズさんの　うた　聞きたかったなあ。

Everyone: Cheers!

Martin: Oh, it's from Mr. Suzuki. Mr. Suzuki? Where are you?

Suzuki: I've arrived at the Nozomi Building, but I can't find the elevator that goes to the restaurant.

Martin: The restaurant has its own elevator. When you take the escalator up to the second floor, it's on the right.

Suzuki: Huh, which way do I go on the second floor? I can't hear well.

Martin: Right. The right side.

Suzuki: The right side? I'll be right there.

. . . . . .

Suzuki: You're going, too, aren't you, Mr. Mills? To karaoke?

Mills: Umm, I'm going to take my leave here.

Suzuki: Huh? You're going home already? It's only nine o'clock. And besides, we have the day off tomorrow.

Mills: I have a Japanese exam tomorrow, so I have to get up at six o'clock.

Suzuki: That's too bad. I wanted to hear you sing.

VOCABULARY

かんぱい	cheers!	〜と	when
のぞみビル	Nozomi Building (fictitious building)	どっち	which
専用 せんよう	exclusive use	ええっ	huh? what?
右側 みぎがわ	right side	〜なければ　ならない	must

NOTES

1. あ、鈴木（すずき）さんからです。
   あ indicates that Marie has noticed something.

2. えっ、2階（かい）の　どっち側（がわ）ですか。
   えっ, はい?, and すみません are all ways to indicate that you have not heard what the other person has said. どっち is a casual abbreviation of どちら, "which of the two."

3. ミルズさんも　行（い）きますよね、カラオケ。
   This means the same as ミルズさんも　カラオケに　行（い）きますよね. You add the particle よ to ね to mean "I assert that . . . but don't you agree?" In this case, Mr. Suzuki is strongly encouraging Mr. Mills to go to karaoke by using よね.

4. 聞（き）きたかったなあ。
   You use the past tense of the -tai form to talk about something you were hoping for or you wish you could have done. For example:

   見せたかった！
   み
   I wanted to show it to you. (i.e., I wish you could have seen it.)

GRAMMAR & PATTERN PRACTICE

I Speaking of Natural or Habitual Results

You use the particle と after a verb in the dictionary form to express the idea that when something happens, another thing occurs as a natural or habitual result. You often use this pattern to explain how one can get somewhere, how machines work, and so on.

まっすぐ　行くと、駅が　あります。

If you go straight, there will be a station.

この　ボタンを　おすと、ドアが　あきます。

If you press this button, the door will open. / When you press this button, the door opens.

Note that you cannot use と clauses when making a request or suggestion.

この　ドアを　あけると、外に　出られます。　　　(NATURAL RESULT)

When you open this door, you can go outside.

but　この　ドアを　あけて、外に　出てください。　　　(REQUEST)

Please open this door and go outside.

---

1 Read the following passages aloud while considering their meanings.

1) **みちあんない**

駅を　出ると、こうさてんが　あります。その　こうさてんを　わたって
ください。100メートルぐらい　あるくと、右側に　白い　アパートが
あります。私の　いえは　その　アパートの　2階です。

2) **カップめんの　おいしい　食べ方**

ふたを　あけると、中に　めんと　スープが　入っています。あつい　お
ゆを　せんまで　入れて、ふたを　しめてください。3分　待つと、おい
しい　ラーメンが　できます。

---

2 Construct sentences as in the example.

例) まっすぐ　行きます。左側に　ポストが　あります。
れい
　→　まっすぐ　行くと、左側に　ポストが　あります。
　　　　　　い　　　　ひだりがわ

1) 右に　まがります。あかい　やねが　見えます。
みぎ　　　　　　　　　　　　　　　み
　→ ....

2) かいさつ口を　出ます。目の　前に　こうばんが　あります。
ぐち　　で　　め　まえ
　→ ....

3) レバーを　ひきます。水が　出ます。
みず　　で
　→ ....

4) ドアを　しめます。電気が　きえます。
でんき
　→ ....

5) パスワードを　にゅうりょくします。がめんが　かわります。
　→ ....

VOCABULARY				
ポスト	mailbox	ひく	pull	
やね	roof	パスワード	password	
めの　まえ	right in front of one	がめん	screen	
レバー	lever			237

❚ Expressing Necessity

〜なければ なりません expresses duty or obligation and, by extension, necessity. 〜なければ is the conditional form of a negative verb. You use 〜なければ なりません to suggest that an action must be taken due to circumstances beyond your own control or someone else's. For example:

今日 中に　お金を　はらわなければ　なりません。
<small>きょう じゅう　　　かね</small>
I/you must pay the money today.

In addition, you often use 〜なければ なりません to make excuses for when you cannot do something, in which case it is common to add んです or ので.

１０時までに　学校に　子どもを　むかえに　行かなければ　ならないんです。
<small>じ　　　　　がっこう　　こ　　　　　　　　　　い</small>
I must go to the school to pick up (lit., "to meet") the children by ten o'clock.

子どもを　むかえに　行かなければ　ならないので　お先に　失礼します。
<small>こ　　　　　　　　　い　　　　　　　　　　　　　さき　　　しつれい</small>
I must go to pick up the children, so I'll be off before you.

〜なきゃ なりません, 〜なきゃ ならない, and 〜なきゃ are, in descending order of formality, the contracted forms of 〜なければ なりません. They are used a lot in colloquial Japanese.

---

1 Complete the sentences as in the example.

例）帰る
<small>れい　かえ</small>
　　→ 8時までに　いえに　<u>帰らなければ　なりません</u>。
<small>　　　　じ　　　　　　　　　かえ</small>

1) ひっこす

　　→ アパートが　学校から　とおいので、..
<small>　　　　　　　がっこう</small>

2) けんしゅうを　うける

　　→ 仕事を　始める前に、半年間 ....
<small>　　しごと　　はじ　　まえ　　はんとしかん</small>

3) かりる

　　→ お金が　足りなければ、ぎんこうで ....
<small>　　かね　　た</small>

4) わたす

　　→ たいせつな　てがみなので、ちょくせつ ....

5) 電話を　かける
<small>でん わ</small>
　　→ 駅に　着いたら、旅館に ....
<small>　　えき　　つ　　　　りょかん</small>

VOCABULARY

たりる (R2)	be sufficient
わたす	hand over
ちょくせつ	directly

2 Complete the dialogues as in the examples.

例1) ６時の　しんかんせんで　大阪に　行く
　　　A：もう　帰るんですか。
→　B：<u>６時の　しんかんせんで　大阪に　行かなければ　ならないんです。</u>

1) トラブルが　あって、とりひきさきの　会社に　行く
　　　A：急いでいるんですか。
→　B：..

2) あした　けんこうしんだんを　うける
　　A：食べないんですか。おいしいですよ。
→　B：..

3) あしたまでに　てがみの　へんじを　書く
　　　A：まだ　帰らないんですか。もう　９時ですよ。
→　B：..

例2) あしたの　朝　はやく　おきる
→　A：<u>あしたの　朝　はやく　おきなければならないので、もう　ねます。</u>
　　　B：じゃあ、おやすみなさい。

4) 今日中に　この仕事を　すませる
→　A：..、どうぞ　お先に。
　　　B：じゃあ、お先に　失礼します。

5) あしたの　しけんの　べんきょうをする
→　A：..、うちに　帰ります。
　　　B：じゃあ、がんばってください。

VOCABULARY
トラブル　　　trouble
とりひきさき　client, person/company with whom one does business
すませる (R2)　finish, complete

239

PRACTICE 1

WORD POWER

I. Features of a building:

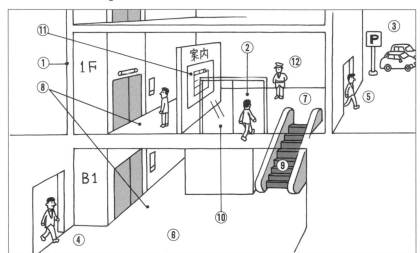

① 建物 たてもの	⑤ 出口 でぐち	⑨ エスカレーター
② 正面玄関 しょうめんげんかん	⑥ 地下 ちか	⑩ 自動ドア じどう
③ 駐車場 ちゅうしゃじょう	⑦ ロビー	⑪ 案内板 あんないばん
④ 入口 いりぐち	⑧ エレベーターホール	⑫ ガードマン

II. Features of an urban landscape:

① 信号 しんごう	③ 歩道橋 ほどうきょう	⑤ 交差点 こうさてん	⑦ 道 みち
② 横断歩道 おうだんほどう	④ 踏み切り ふ　き	⑥ 通り とお	⑧ 坂 さか

VOCABULARY					
しょうめんげんかん	front entrance	じどう〜	automatic	ふみきり	railroad crossing
しょうめん	front	あんないばん	building directory	とおり	avenue
げんかん	entrance	ガードマン	security guard	さか	slope, hill
エレベーターホール	elevator corridor	おうだんほどう	crosswalk		
じどうドア	automatic door	ほどうきょう	pedestrian bridge		

PHRASE POWER

Moving around town:

① 道を　渡る　　　　　　　　　cross the street
　　みち　　わた
② 坂を　上る　　　　　　　　　go up the hill
　　さか　　のぼ
③ 坂を　下る　　　　　　　　　go down the hill
　　さか　　くだ
④ 踏み切りを　通る　　　　　　go over the railroad crossing
　　ふ　き　　　　とお
⑤ 銀行を　通り過ぎる　　　　　go past the bank
　　ぎんこう　とお　す

SPEAKING PRACTICE

Talking on a cell phone while parked in one's car:

のぞみデパートの社員：今、ビルの　前です。
　　　　　　しゃいん　　　　　いま
ミルズ：　　　　　しょうめんげんかんの　右に　ちゅうしゃじょうの　入
　　　　　　　　　　　　　　　　　　　みぎ　　　　　　　　　　　いり
　　　　　　　　　口が　ありますが、見えますか。
　　　　　　　　　ぐち　　　　　　　み
のぞみデパートの社員：はい、見えます。
　　　　　　　　　　　　　　み
ミルズ：　　　　　そこから　入って　ちか2階に　おりると、らいきゃく
　　　　　　　　　　　　　　はい　　　　かい
　　　　　　　　　用の　ちゅうしゃじょうが　あります。どこでも
　　　　　　　　　よう
　　　　　　　　　空いている　ところに　とめて　ください。
　　　　　　　　　あ
のぞみデパートの社員：わかりました。
ミルズ：　　　　　1階で　エレベーターを　おりると、右側に　コーヒー
　　　　　　　　　いっかい　　　　　　　　　　　　　　みぎがわ
　　　　　　　　　ショップが　あります。入って　すぐの　せきに　います。
のぞみデパートの社員：わかりました。では　のちほど。
　　　　　　　　　　　　　　　　　　　　　　はい

Nozomi Department Store employee: I'm in front of the building now.
Mills:　The entrance to the parking garage is to the right of the front entrance. Can you see it?
Nozomi Department Store employee: Yes, I see it.
Mills:　Enter from there, and when you get down to the second basement floor there will be park-
　　　　ing spots for guests. Park in any space that is open.
Nozomi Department Store employee: Okay.
Mills:　When you get off the elevator at the first floor, there will be a coffee shop on your right
　　　　side. I'll be sitting right as you come in.
Nozomi Department Store employee: I see. Well, I'll see you in just a moment.

VOCABULARY			
くだる	go down	どこでも	anywhere
とおる	pass, go over	コーヒーショップ	coffee shop
とおりすぎる (R2)	go past, go by	すぐ	right there (close to one)
そこ	there	のちほど	later on
らいきゃく	having a visitor		

PRACTICE 2

PHRASE POWER

I. Intransitive verbs:

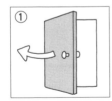 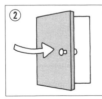   

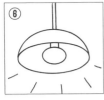 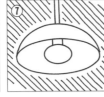   

① ドアが　開く　the door opens
② ドアが　閉まる　the door closes
③ 水が　出る　water comes out
④ 車が　動く　the car moves
⑤ 車が　止まる　the car stops

⑥ 電気が　つく　the lights come on
⑦ 電気が　消える　the lights go out
⑧ 信号が　変わる　the traffic light changes
⑨ 病気が　治る　the illness gets better
⑩ 会議が　始まる　the meeting begins

II. Transitive verbs:

① ドアを　開ける　open the door
② ドアを　閉める　close the door

③ 水を　出す　let out water
④ 車を　動かす　move the car
⑤ 車を　止める　stop the car

VOCABULARY	あく	open		だす	let out
	つく	come on (of electricity)			
	きえる (R2)	go out (of electricity)			
242	なおる	get better (of injury, disease)			

⑥ 電気を　つける　　　turn on the lights　　　⑨ 病気を　治す　　　cure the disease
　　でん き

⑦ 電気を　消す　　　　turn off the lights　　　⑩ 会議を　始める　　begin the meeting
　　でん き　　け　　　　　　　　　　　　　　　　　　かい ぎ　　はじ

⑧ 色を　変える　　　　change the color
　　いろ　　か

Choose the appropriate verb from among the options in parentheses.

1) 前に　立つと、ドアが　（　あきます　　あけます　）
　　まえ　　た

2) 中に　入ると、ドアが　（　しめます　　しまります　）
　　なか　　はい

3) お金を　入れると、ジュースが　（　出ます　　出します　）
　　かね　　い　　　　　　　　　　　　　　　で　　　　だ

4) 人が　のると、エスカレーターが　（　動かします　　動きます　）
　　ひと　　　　　　　　　　　　　　　　　うご　　　　　うご

5) 人が　おりると、エスカレーターが　（　とまります　　とめます　）
　　ひと

6) くらく　なると、電気が　（　つけます　　つきます　）
　　　　　　　　　でん き

7) あかるく　なると、電気が　（　きえます　　けします　）
　　　　　　　　　　でん き

8) おんどが　上がると、いろが　（　かわります　　かえます　）
　　　　　　　あ

9) 薬を　飲むと、びょうきが　（　なおします　　なおります　）
　　くすり　の

10) ７時になると、ニュースが　（　始まります　　始めます　）
　　　じ　　　　　　　　　　　　　はじ　　　　　　はじ

Now study the following sentences.

1) これは　ぼうはんライトです。ちかくで
　　何かが　動くと、電気が　つきます。
　　なに　　うご　　でん き

2) これは　あんぜんファンヒーターです。
　　じしんで　ゆれると、火が　きえます。
　　　　　　　　　　　　ひ

3) これは　自動すいはんきです。セットした
　　　　　　じ どう
　　時間に　なると、スイッチが　入ります。
　　じ かん　　　　　　　　　　　　　はい

1) This is a security light. If something moves in the vicinity (of it), it turns on.
2) This is a "safe" fan heater. In the event of an earthquake (lit., "When things shake due to an earth-quake"), the flame goes out.
3) This is an automatic rice cooker. The (cook) switch activates at the time you set it for.

VOCABULARY	かえる (R2)	change	ライト	light	セットする	set (a timer)
	なおす	fix, cure	ファンヒーター	fan heater	スイッチ	switch
	おんど	temperature	ゆれる (R2)	sway, shake		
	ぼうはんライト	security light	ひ	flame		
	ぼうはん	crime prevention	すいはんき	rice cooker		243

PRACTICE 3

SPEAKING PRACTICE

I. Leaving work early because one's child has a fever:

社員：　あのう、すみません。
佐々木：はい、何でしょうか。
社員：　今日、ちょっと　はやく　帰っても　よろしいでしょうか。
佐々木：どうしたんですか。
社員：　子どもが　ねつを　出したので、びょういんに　つれて行かなければ　ならないんです。
佐々木：それは　たいへんですね。すぐに　帰った　ほうが　いいですよ。
社員：　ありがとうございます。じゃ、お先に　失礼します。

employee: Umm . . . excuse me.
Sasaki:　　Yes, what is it?
employee: May I go home a little early today?
Sasaki:　　What's wrong?
employee: My child has a fever, so I must take him to the hospital, you see.
Sasaki:　　I'm sorry to hear that. You should go home right away.
employee: Thank you very much. Well, I'll take my leave now.

II. Leaving work early to greet one's parents at the airport:

社員：　　あれ、今日は　はやいですね。
マルタン：ええ、両親が　成田に　着くので、むかえに　行かなければ　ならないんです。
社員：　　ああ、そうなんですか。じゃ、気を　つけて。
マルタン：ありがとう。

employee:　Oh, you're (leaving) early today.
Martin:　　Yes, my parents are going to arrive in Narita, so I must go and get them.
employee:　Oh, is that so? Well, take care.
Martin:　　Thank you.

| **VOCABULARY** | ねつを　だす | develop a fever |
| | つれていく | take (someone) somewhere |

READING TASK 1

けいたいメール

I. Mr. Suzuki is having a get-together with friends from college. Mr. Sato is one of those friends.

①

```
📶                        🔋
5／15  18：47

３０分おくれる
さんじゅっぷん
・・・・・・・・・・・・・・・・・・・・・
今、ちかてつの　銀座駅。会
　　　　　　　　ぎんざえき　かい
議が　のびたので　おくれる。
ぎ
先に　始めて。
さき　はじ
鈴木
すずき
```

②

```
📶                        🔋
5／15  18：55

Re：３０分おくれる
　　　　さんじゅっぷん
・・・・・・・・・・・・・・・・・・・・・
わかった。店、わかる？　出口
　　　　　　みせ　　　　　　でぐち
5を出ると、右側にＡＢＣビル。
　で　　　みぎがわ
そのかどを　まがって　3げん
目の　ビルの　2階。1階は
め　　　　　　かい　いっかい
ケーキ屋。
　や
佐藤
さとう
```

③

```
📶                        🔋
5／15  18：58

Re：３０分おくれる
　　　　さんじゅっぷん
・・・・・・・・・・・・・・・・・・・・・
ＯＫ。了解。すぐ　行く。
オーケー　りょうかい　　　い
鈴木
すずき
```

VOCABULARY

のびる (R2)	be prolonged
ＡＢＣビル	ABC Building (fictitious building)
～けん（げん）目 め	(counter for buildings)
ケーキ屋 や	cake shop
了解 りょうかい	I understand

II. Mayumi Nakamura has planned a get-together with some friends this evening, but just as she is about to leave work to meet them, she is delayed. She e-mails her friend Hiro to let her know that she will be late.

①

5／18　16：00

今日少しおくれるかも
m(＿ ＿)m
....

パソコントラブルで　仕事が
終わらない。また、ようす　し
らせるね。

まゆみ

②

5／18　16：50

Re：今日少しおくれるかも
m(＿ ＿)m
....

どう？（＊-＊）
さっちゃんも　いそがしくて、
おくれるって。来週 にしよう
か？

ヒロ

③

5／18　16：55

トラブル解消（＾-＾）V
....

こちらは　だいじょうぶ。
来週 は　しゅっちょうも　あ
るので、できれば、今日が　い
いかな。

まゆみ

④

5／18　17：02

Re：トラブル解消（＾-＾）V
....

じゃ、予定どおり。6時半に、
レストランで。

ヒロ

VOCABULARY

さっちゃん	Sat-chan (nickname)
ヒロ	Hiro (nickname)
解消	doing away with, clearing up
できれば	if possible
～かな（あ）	I wonder . . . (sentence-final particle combination)
予定どおり	as planned, as scheduled
～どおり	just as . . .

READING TASK 2

私の　すんでいる　まちの　ごみの　出し方
わたし　　　　　　　　　　　　　　　　　　だ　かた

　初めに　リサイクルできる　ごみと　できない　ごみに　分けなければ
はじ　　　　　　　　　　　　　　　　　　　　　　　　　　　　　　　　　わ
なりません。スーパーに　行くと、リサイクルできる　ごみを　あつめる
　　　　　　　　　　　　い
ところが　あります。ペットボトル、ぎゅうにゅうパック、かん、びん　な
どに　分けて　すててください。
　　　わ

　つぎに　リサイクルできない　ごみは　もえる　ごみと　もえない　ごみ
に　分けて　すてなければなりせん。ごみは　市や　区の　車が　あつめに
　　わ　　　　　　　　　　　　　　　　　　　　　し　　く　　くるま
来ますが、ごみの　しゅるいによって　出せる　日が　きまっています。
き　　　　　　　　　　　　　　　　　　　　だ　　　ひ

　ごみの　分け方は　すんでいる　ところによって　ちがいます。あなたが
　　　　　わ　かた
すんでいる　町では　どうやって　ごみを　出していますか。
　　　　　　まち　　　　　　　　　　　　　　だ

Answer the following questions:

1) リサイクルできる　ごみには　どんなものが　ありますか。
2) どこに　行くと、リサイクルできる　ごみを　あつめる　ところが　ありますか。
　　　　　　い
3) リサイクルできない　ごみは　どうやって　すてますか。
4) ごみは　いつでも　出せますか。
　　　　　　　　　　　だ

VOCABULARY

出す だ	put out	びん	bottle
リサイクル	recycling	もえる (R2)	burnable, can be burned
分ける わ	divide, separate	市 し	city
あつめる (R2)	gather, collect	区 く	ward of a city
ペットボトル	plastic bottle	しゅるい	type, kind
ぎゅうにゅう	milk	〜によって	depending on, due to, according to
パック	carton	きまる	be decided, be determined
かん	can	いつでも	anytime

KANJI PRACTICE

専	専用 せんよう	一	厂	甘	冐	冐	車	専
exclusive		専	専	専	専			

階	二階 にかい 何階 なんかい なんがい	了	了	阝	阝	阡	阧	阰
floor		阰	陛	階	階	階	階	階

右	右 みぎ	ノ	ナ	大	右	右	右	右
right								

左	左 ひだり	一	ナ	左	左	左	左	左
left								

側	右側 みぎがわ 左側 ひだりがわ 内側 うちがわ	亻	亻	仴	仴	但	但	但
side		側	側	側	側	側	側	

失	失礼 しつれい	ク	�ヒ	三	失	失	失	失
lose								

礼	お礼 れい	�ゝ	�ヲ	ネ	ネ	礼	礼	礼
etiquette								

手	手て 右手みぎて	ー	三	三	手	手	手	
hand								

足	足あし 左足 ひだりあし 足りる た	�ٮ	⼝	口	足	足	足	足
leg **suffice**		足	足					

立	立つ た	⋎	十	十	立	立	立	立
stand								

I Fill in the blanks with the appropriate particle.

1) 一日中　パソコンで　仕事を　したら、目（　　）　つかれました。
   いちにちじゅう　　　　　しごと　　　　　　　　め

2) エレベーター（　　）　のっている　とき、じしんが　おきたら、どうしますか。

3) メールに　ファイル（　　）　てんぷして　おくります。

4) 友だちが　成田に　着くので、むかえ（　　）　行かなければなりません。
   とも　　　　なりた　　つ　　　　　　　　　　　い

5) お金を　入れて　ボタンを　おすと、コーヒー（　　）　出ます。
   かね　　い　　　　　　　　　　　　　　　　　　　　　で

II Choose the correct word from among the alternatives (1–4) given. The same word cannot be used twice in the same dialogue.

1) A：（　　）　1おく円　もらったら　どうしますか。
   　　　　　　　　　えん

   B：（　　）　会社を　やめて　せかい中を　旅行します。
   　　　　　　　かいしゃ　　　　　　　じゅう　　りょこう

   1. たびたび　　　2. すぐ　　　3. もし　　　4. まだ

2) A：（　　）　すみません。また、ちょっと　聞いても　いいですか。
   　　　　　　　　　　　　　　　　　　　き

   B：はい、どうぞ。（　　）　わかると　思います。
   　　　　　　　　　　　　　　　　　おも

   1. どこでも　　　2. 特に　　　3. たぶん　　　4. たびたび
   　　　　　　　　　とく

3) A：もしもし、今　……に　いるんですが……。
   　　　　　　いま

   B：（　　）、どこですか。よく　聞こえなかったんですが。
   　　　　　　　　　　　　　　　き

   A：駅です。駅に　いるんです。
   　　えき　　えき

   1. さあ　　　2. ええ　　　3. えっ　　　4. じゃあ

III Change the form of the word given in parentheses to complete the sentence in a way that makes sense.

1) 子どもの　かずが　（　　　）　きました。（へります）
   こ

2) けいたいを　（　　　）　しまいました。（なくします）

3) （　　　）　ば、買います。（安いです）
   　　　　　か　　　　やす

4) ドアを　（　　　）　と、電気が　つきます。（あけます）
   　　　か　　　　　　でんき

5) 今日中に　しりょうを　（　　　）　なければ　なりません。（作ります）
   きょうじゅう　　　　　　　　　　　　　　　　　　つく

IV Choose the most appropriate word or phrase from among the alternatives (1–4) given.

1) たからくじで　１００万円（まんえん）（　　）ので、旅行（りょこう）を　しました。

   1. 買（か）った　　2. あたった　　3. まけた　　4. うけた

2) きゅうりょうが（　　）、もっと　いい　うちに　ひっこします。

   1. ふえたら　　2. 売（う）れたら　　3. のびたら　　4. かわったら

3) もえるごみと　もえないごみに（　　）すてなければ　なりません。

   1. 出（だ）して　　2. 出（で）て　　3. 分（わ）けて　　4. わかって

4) 雪（ゆき）で　電車（でんしゃ）が（　　）います。

   1. とめて　　2. とまって　　3. 動（うご）いて　　4. 動（うご）かして

5) 売（う）り上（あ）げが　急（きゅう）に　のびてきました。今月（こんげつ）は　先月（せんげつ）の（　　）です。

   1. ３まい　　2. ３回（かい）　　3. ３度（ど）　　4. ３倍（ばい）

V Fill in the blanks with the correct reading of each kanji.

1) 二階に　上がると、左側に　専用エレベーターが　あります。
  （　　）（　　）　　（　　　）（　　　）

2) 打ち合わせが　あるので、お先に　失礼します。
  （　　　　）　　　　　（　）（　　）

3) 天気が　よかったら、ビルの　外で　待っています。
  （　　　）　　　　　　　（　）（　）

Supplement to the Text

TRANSLATIONS OF READING TASKS

Lesson 1

The Rice Ball Project

John Mills is an employee of ABC Foods. Mr. Mills likes Japanese food very much, *o-nigiri* most of all. Overseas, sushi is more famous than *o-nigiri*. ABC Foods has begun (lit., "created") a project to develop *o-nigiri* geared toward overseas (markets). Mr. Mills is the chief of the project.

Lesson 2

Mr. Mills's New Computer

Mr. Mills went to Akihabara last week and bought a new personal computer. The computer has a large screen, but it is lighter than his old computer. Mr. Mills watched DVDs on his computer over the weekend. The colors on the computer's screen were more beautiful than those on a TV. Mr. Mills went to a (DVD) rental shop and rented a lot of DVDs.

Lesson 3

Items Left Behind in a Conference Room

Yesterday at five o'clock, Mr. Mills had a meeting with Mr. Takahashi of Nozomi Department Store concerning PR for a new product. The meeting ended at six thirty. Mr. Mills went to the first floor lobby to see his visitor off, leaving his glasses and memo book on the table in the meeting room. This morning, he went to the meeting room to get them, but they were not there. The frames of Mr. Mills's glasses are black, lightweight plastic. His memo book is a brown leather system notebook.

UNIT 2

Lesson 5

A Balloon Tour

I have ridden in a hot-air balloon. The summer before last, I went to Turkey with my girlfriend. In Cappadocia we participated in a balloon tour. At first it was a bit frightening. However, the views were really spectacular. I definitely want to ride (in a balloon) again somewhere.

Lesson 6

Consultation

Mr. Oki:

This is Tsuchida from the sales department.
I, too, will be working in the Düsseldorf office starting next April.
I'm looking forward to it (lit., "It is a delight"), but I'm a bit worried.

Now I'll be preparing to move. Please tell me the various things (I should know).

Thanks in advance.

Tsuchida

RE: Consultation

Ms. Tsuchida:

Düsseldorf is a very nice place.

Getting ready to move is tough, isn't it?

There aren't many clothes or shoes in small sizes here, so you should bring them from Japan. You should bring medicine, too, because the medicine here is a little bit strong.

It's best to rent furniture here. There are also furnished apartments.

In addition, you should study German a bit in Japan. In the beginning, I didn't understand anything at all, so it was tough.

I'm looking forward to next April.

Oki

UNIT 3

Lesson 7

Ms. Sasaki's Personal History

Ms. Keiko Sasaki was born in Sapporo. When she was ten years old, she moved to Tokyo. She entered a university in Tokyo and studied economics. She graduated from the university and joined ABC Foods.

When she was thirty-two, she got married. Two years later, she had a child. She took a half year off both before and after her child was born, but she has otherwise continued to work the whole time (i.e., since joining the company). Ms. Sasaki is now manager of the sales department. She is the first female department manager at ABC Foods.

Lesson 8

Reading Task 1

Reminiscences of a Homestay

I did a homestay in Tokyo seven years ago. I was nervously excited when I met my host family. The first time I ate Japanese food, I thought it wasn't very tasty, but I gradually came to like it. Doing the homestay, I made a lot of Japanese friends. When I left Japan, I promised my host family at the airport that I would come again.

Reading Task 2

The Story of Harajuku

Harajuku is a famous fashion district of Tokyo. Its main street, Omotesando, is lined with brand-name designer shops from all over the world

I have been living in Harajuku ever since I was a child. In the old days, Harajuku was a quiet residential area. A small river flowed through it, and there was a strawberry patch in the garden of a nearby house. There was plenty of greenery, and the air was cleaner than it is now. There were fish dealers and fruit and vegetable dealers in the shopping area, and the neighborhood housewives shopped there. Yet at that time, the most modern apartments in Tokyo already stood on Omotesando: the Dojunkai Apartments.

The area changed little by little. The river disappeared and became a street. The strawberry patches became parking lots. The (number of) gardens decreased, and there came to be less greenery. Boutiques and accessory shops appeared in the shopping area, and the fish dealers and fruit and vegetable dealers disappeared. Many restaurants and cafés appeared, and Harajuku became the fanciest neighborhood in Tokyo.

Omotesando Hills opened in February 2006. The Dojunkai Apartments turned into a stylish building with a new design. Today, just as it did in the old days (lit. "Both in the old days and now"), Harajuku symbolizes the new Tokyo.

Lesson 9

Reading Task 1

Ms. Martin's Blog

Today I participated in a civic orchestra for the first time. It's been half a year (since I last practiced), so my fingers didn't move properly. But the practice was fun. People of all age groups and professions belong to the orchestra. It is tough practicing from eight o'clock, after work, but one way or another I want to continue with it.

My profile:
    nickname: Marie Antoinette
    age: 25 years old
    birthday: September 2
    blood type: AB

Reading Task 2

The Blog of an American Family

Our family came to Tokyo from the United States five years ago. Our daughter Monica has turned thirteen. Our son Jonah has turned eleven. I will describe our life in Tokyo.

This is a photograph that my husband, Martin, took from the top of Roppongi Hills.

Cameras are Martin's hobby. He especially likes to take nighttime views of the city. He says he regrets that he doesn't have a lot of time to take pictures.

This is our daughter Monica.

Monica likes music. This is our family coming back from after having gone out the other day. Monica and her father are listening to music together on Monica's iPod. Monica is having her father listen to her favorite song.

This is our son Jonah.

Jonah likes to be active. He has been taking lessons in tae kwon do since April of this year. He loves to practice.

I'm Pamela.

My hobby is skating. I glide through the parks and neighborhoods of Tokyo on my inline skates. I began skating after coming to Tokyo. Skating is fun and healthy. I've made a lot of friends thanks to skating. My opportunities to speak Japanese have increased, too. I've injured myself, but I've never thought of quitting. I skate nearly every week. Skating has become my lifetime sport.

This is a photo taken at Christmas time. I skated with my skating club from Tokyo Station to Shibuya. Click on the image. It will become large. I am the third from the right in the front line.

Lesson 10

Reading & Writing Task

Invitations

Invitation to play Tennis

Mr. Suzuki:

Won't you go with us on an overnight trip to play tennis in Izu on the weekend of April 24 and 25? Our group will include Shika and Mr. Tanaka from the systems department, and myself.

Nakamura

RE: Invitation to play tennis

Ms. Nakamura:

Thank you for the invitation. Unfortunately, I have a training session that weekend, so I can't participate. Ask me some other time.

Suzuki

Invitation to go out drinking

Mr. Kato:

Would you like to go to the new *izakaya* in front of the station? How would the third week in April be? Please let me know what day would be convenient for you.

Hayashi

RE: Invitation to go out drinking

Mr. Hayashi:

Reading Task

Impressions

I. About Opera
I received two opera tickets from a friend, so I went with my wife for the first time in a long time. My wife likes opera, so she was very pleased, but as for myself, since I haven't seen much opera, I became sleepy. I thought it was a very long opera.

II. About Japanese Language School
Last week I received an advertising flyer from a Japanese language school. I heard that one could visit before applying, so I went to visit yesterday.

There were six students in the beginning class. The teacher had a skillful way of teaching and a sense of humor. After the lesson was over, I talked a little with the people in the class. I really liked the school, so I'm thinking I'd like to apply next week.

Lesson 12

Reading Task 1

Words from a Worrywart

I watch the news before I go to bed. Recently there has been a lot of gloomy news, so I worry.

My child might get into an accident. My company might go under. My parents might become seriously ill. A robber might come into our house. There might be an earthquake this evening.

I am worried and cannot sleep.

Reading Task 2

Mt. Fuji

Mt. Fuji is about 3,800 meters high and is the highest mountain in Japan. It may be the most famous place in Japan. There are many foreigners who eagerly want to climb Mt. Fuji. Of course, Mt. Fuji is also popular with Japanese people, and every year during the summer season about 150,000 people set themselves the challenge of climbing it.

During the Edo Period, Mt. Fuji (lit., "various views of Mt. Fuji") became the subject of many wood-block prints. Even now, many enthusiasts try to photograph beautiful Mt. Fuji, waiting for their opportunity for a perfect picture. Mt. Fuji changes in beautiful ways, such as Mt. Fuji in the morning sun, Mt. Fuji in the setting sun, Mt. Fuji covered with snow, and Mt. Fuji with interesting clouds. Mt. Fuji viewed from a distance is certainly beautiful.

A movement started up in 1992 to make Mt. Fuji a UNESCO World Natural Heritage Site. However, that wish has not been realized yet. The reason is, regrettably, that Mt. Fuji is covered with trash.

Now people are thinking about how to take back a truly beautiful Mt. Fuji. Mt. Fuji symbolizes Japan's environmental problems (as well as other things).

UNIT 5

Lesson 13

If I Won 300 Million Yen

Recently the highest jackpot amounts have gotten higher and higher. I have heard that some people have won as much as 300 million yen. What would you do if you won 300 million yen?

"If I won 300 million yen, I would first buy a car and then a small condominium by the seaside. When work ended on Fridays, I would go to the condominium in my car right away. If the weather was nice, I would spend the whole day on the seashore. If it rained, I would put on music in my ocean-view room and read a book. If I had weekends like that, my everyday work might become more enjoyable."

"If I won 300 million yen, I would invest it. With 100 million yen, I would buy safe national bonds. I would entrust 100 million yen to a reliable fund manager. I would invest 100 million yen in a slightly risky new business on the Internet. If stock prices rose and my capital increased, I would invest in more enterprises of various sorts. If stock prices fell and my capital decreased, I would stop investing."

If it were you, what would you do?

Lesson 14

Mr. Mills's Diary

April 6, snow

When I woke up in the morning and opened the curtains, it was snowing. Since I knew the trains might be late due to the snow, I left the house a little earlier than usual. Today there was an important meeting in the morning, but I thought I would be on time if I left thirty minutes early.

When I arrived at the station, lots of people were waiting for the trains. The trains were not moving. When I asked a station staff (lit., "a person at the station"), he said he didn't know when they would move. When I hurried to the taxi stand, Mr. Kato was in line.

I went to the office in a taxi with Mr. Kato. Since a lot of snow had fallen, the taxi went more slowly than usual. I became worried about whether I would make it on time for the meeting.

When I arrived at the office, it was 10:30. When I opened the door of the conference room, the meeting had already started. I apologized, saying, "I'm sorry. I'm late because the trains stopped running." Then I entered the conference room.

The only ones late were Mr. Kato and myself. It was embarrassing. Afterwards, when I asked Mr. Tanaka of the systems department (how he had managed to get to work on time), he said that he had left two hours earlier than usual and walked to the office. I was surprised.

Lesson 15

Reading Task 1

Text Messaging

I.

①
5/15 18:47
I'll be 30 minutes late

I'm at the Ginza subway station right now. The meeting ran over, so I'll be late. Please start without me.
Suzuki

②
5/15 18:55
Re: I'll be 30 minutes late

Okay. Know where the restaurant is? When you come out of Exit 5, the ABC Building will be on your right. Turn the corner. It is the second floor of the third building. The first floor is a cake shop.
Sato

③
5/15 18:58
Re: I'll be 30 minutes late

OK. I understand. I'll be right there.
Suzuki

II.

①
5/18 16:00
I might be a little late (sorry!)

I can't get out of work (lit., "Work won't end") due to computer trouble. I'll be in touch. (lit., "I'll inform you of developments")
Mayumi

②
5/18 16:50
Re: I might be a little late (sorry!)

How are things going? Satchan also said she's busy and will be late. Shall we make it next week (instead)?
Hiro

③
5/18 16:55
Problem solved

Everything's fine here. Next week I have a business trip, so today would be better.
Mayumi

④
5/18 17:02
Re: Problem solved

Okay then. 6:00 at the restaurant, as planned.
Hiro

Reading Task 2

How to Put Out the Trash in the Town I Live in

To begin with, you must separate the trash into recyclable trash and non-recyclable trash. If you go to a supermarket, there are places where recyclable trash is collected. Sort the trash into categories such as clear plastic bottles, milk cartons, cans, and bottles, and discard it.

Next you must divide non-recyclable trash into burnable trash and unburnable trash and discard it. Trucks from the city or ward come to collect the trash, but the day you put it out depends on what type of trash it is.

How you divide the trash differs from town to town. How do you put out the trash in the town you live in?

ANSWERS TO EXERCISES AND QUIZZES

Lesson 1

Grammar & Pattern Practice

I.   1) どこか　2) 何<small>なに</small>か　3) いつか　4) だれか

II. **1** 1) にほんごの　レッスンは　なんようびが　いいですか。

      2) なつやすみの　りょこうは　どこが　いいですか。

   2 1) たなかさんの　たんじょうびの　プレゼントは　何が　いいでしょうか。

      2) プロジェクトの　チーフは　だれが　いいでしょうか。

III. **1** 1) Q：こうちゃと　ジュースと　どちらが　やすいですか。

        A：こうちゃの　ほうが　やすいです。

      2) Q：アイスクリームと　ケーキと　どちらが　高いですか。

        A：ケーキの　ほうが　たかいです。

   2 1) Q：カナダと　ブラジルと　どちらが　おおきいですか。

        A：カナダの　ほうが　おおきいです。

      2) Q：ちゅうごくと　オーストラリアと　どちらが　おおきいですか。

        A：ちゅうごくの　ほうが　おおきいです。

   3 1) Q：スペイン人<small>じん</small>と　ポルトガル人<small>じん</small>と　どちらが　たくさん　ワインを　のみますか。

        A：ポルトガル人<small>じん</small>の　ほうが　たくさん　のみます。

      2) Q：アルゼンチン人<small>じん</small>と　ルーマニア人<small>じん</small>と　どちらが　たくさん　ワインを　のみますか。

        A：アルゼンチン人<small>じん</small>の　ほうが　たくさん　ワインを　のみます。

IV. **1** 1) だれ　2) 何<small>なに</small>　3) どれ

   2 1) Q：1年<small>ねん</small>の　なかで　何<small>なん</small>がつが　いちばん　さむい　ですか。

        A：1がつが　いちばん　さむいです。

      2) Q：1年<small>ねん</small>の　なかで　何<small>なん</small>がつが　いちばん　あめが　おおい　ですか。

        A：9がつが　いちばん　あめが　おおいです。

      3) Q：1年<small>ねん</small>の　なかで　何<small>なん</small>がつが　いちばん　あめが　すくない　ですか。

        A：12がつが　いちばん　あめが　すくないです。

V.   1) くつを　はいてみます

      2) コートを　きてみます

Reading Task (translation on p. 255)

    1) おにぎりが　いちばん　すきです。

    2) おすしの　ほうが　ゆうめいです。

    3) かいがいむけの　おにぎりの　かいはつプロジェクトを　つくりました。

    4) ミルズさんです。

Lesson 2

Grammar & Pattern Practice

I.   1) おんせんに　行きたいんですが、どこが　いいでしょうか。

      2) プロジェクトの　かいぎを　したいんですが、いつが　いいでしょうか。

      3) くうこうに　行きたいんですが、でんしゃと　タクシーと　どちらが　はやいでしょうか。

      4) あたらしい　けいたいを　かいたいんですが、Aしゃと　Bしゃと　どちらが　べんりでしょうか。

II. **1** 1) いもうとは　私より　ゴルフが　じょうずです。

      2) いもうとは　私より　よく　べんきょうします。

      3) いもうとは　私より　ともだちが　おおいです。

      4) いもうとは　私より　たくさん　ほんを　よみます。

  2 1) Aホテルは　Bホテルより　しずかです。

      2) Aホテルは　Bホテルより　へやが　ひろいです。

      3) Aホテルは　Bホテルより　サービスが　いいです。

      4) Aホテルは　Bホテルより　えきから　ちかいです。

      5) Aホテルは　Bホテルより　チェックインが　かんたんです。

  3 1) Aホテルは　とうきょうで　いちばん　あたらしいです。

      2) Aホテルは　とうきょうで　いちばん　人気が　あります。

      3) Aホテルは　とうきょうで　いちばん　がいこくじんの　おきゃくさんが　おおいです。

      4) Aホテルは　とうきょうで　いちばん　べんりな　ところに　あります。

III.   1) Q：おくさんの　おみやげは　何に　しましたか。

        A：ネックレスに　しました。

      2) Q：かいぎの　ひは　なんようびに　しましたか。

        A：げつようびに　しました。

Reading Task (translation on p. 255)

    1) あきはばらで　かいました。

    2) パソコンで　DVDを　みました。

3) パソコンの　スクリーンの　ほうが　いろが　きれいでした。

4) ＤＶＤを　（たくさん）　かりました。

Lesson 3

Grammar & Pattern Practice

I. **1** 1) さとうさんは　べんごしで、ミルズさんの　ともだちです。

2) これは　いちばん　大きい　サイズで、いちばん　高いです。

3) アナさんは　スイス人で、ミルズさんは　カナダ人です。

4) こちらは　ちゅうごくの　おかしで、そちらは　にほんの　おかしです。

2 1) あたらしくて　きれいです。

2) べんりで　安いです。

3) きれいですが、人気が　ありません。

II. 1) ネクタイが　入っています。

2) お金が　入っています。

3) しょるいが　入っています。

4) 何も　入っていません。

5) なふだが　ついています。

6) ポケットが　ついています。

7) フライドポテトが　ついています。

8) バルコニーが　ついています。

III. **1** 1) えいがを　みに　行きます。

2) ビールを　のみに　行きます。

3) おべんとうを　かいに　行きます。

2 1) Shall we go and eat something?

2) Next time come over to our house to visit (lit., "to play").

3) I will go to the post office to buy stamps.

4) I will go to the post office to pick up a package.

5) I will go home to get something I left behind.

Reading Task (translation on p. 255)

1) のぞみデパートの　たかはしさんと　しんしょうひんの　ＰＲについて　かいぎを　しました。

2) めがねと　てちょうを　わすれました。

3) おきゃくさん　（たかはしさん）を　おくりに　行きました。

4) フレームが　くろくて　かるい　プラスチックの　めがねです。

5) ちゃいろの　かわの　システムてちょうです。

QUIZ 1

I.   1) が   2) で   3) より   4) に   5) に

II.   1) 4   2) 3   3) 2   4) 1   5) 1

III.   1) 小さくて   2) 入って   3) はいて   4) よくて   5) み
         ちい   はい

IV.   1) 1   2) 2   3) 4   4) 2   5) 4

V.   1) おお   ひと   ひゃく
         2) ことし   しろ   にんき
         3) ごご   ちち   ごにん   き

Lesson 4

Grammar & Pattern Practice

I.   1) 行く   行かない
         い   い
         2) きく   きかない
         3) ぬぐ   ぬがない
         4) はなす   はなさない
         5) もつ   もたない
         6) あそぶ   あそばない
         7) よむ   よまない
         8) ある   ない
         9) のる   のらない
         10) わかる   わからない
         11) かう   かわない
         12) ならう   ならわない
         13) いる   いない
         14) きる   きない
         15) あびる   あびない
         16) でる   でない
         17) しらべる   しらべない
         18) とどける   とどけない
         19) みせる   みせない
         20) おしえる   おしえない
         21) わすれる   わすれない
         22) 来る   来ない
         く   こ
         23) する   しない

II.　　1) これから　にほんごの　レッスンが　あるんです。
　　　　2) これから　ニューヨークししゃと　テレビかいぎを　するんです。
　　　　3) これから　しごとの　前に　スポーツクラブで　およぐんです。
　　　　4) これから　おきゃくさまを　いちばに　あんないするんです。
　　　　5) これから　くうこうに　おきゃくさまを　むかえに　行くんです。
　　　　6) 毎日　かいしゃで　朝ごはんを　たべるんです。
　　　　7) 毎朝　にほんごを　ならっているんです。
　　　　8) この　時間は　ちかてつが　すいているんです。

III.　　1) 週／1週間に　2回
　　　　2) 週／1週間に　1回
　　　　3) 週／1週間に　3回

Lesson 5

Grammar & Pattern Practice

I.　　1) 行った　行かなかった
　　　　2) あるいた　あるかなかった
　　　　3) ぬいだ　ぬがなかった
　　　　4) もった　もたなかった
　　　　5) かった　かわなかった
　　　　6) ならった　ならわなかった
　　　　7) あった　なかった
　　　　8) のぼった　のぼらなかった
　　　　9) のった　のらなかった
　　　　10) あそんだ　あそばなかった
　　　　11) よんだ　よまなかった
　　　　12) けした　けさなかった
　　　　13) いた　いなかった
　　　　14) きた　きなかった
　　　　15) あびた　あびなかった
　　　　16) かりた　かりなかった
　　　　17) おきた　おきなかった
　　　　18) ねた　ねなかった
　　　　19) でた　でなかった
　　　　20) しらべた　しらべなかった
　　　　21) はじめた　はじめなかった
　　　　22) 来た　来なかった
　　　　23) した　しなかった

II.　　1) のんだことが　あります。

　　　　2) 行ったことが　あります。

　　　　3) のぼったことが　あります。

　　　　4) のったことが　あります。

Lesson 6

Grammar & Pattern Practice

I.　**1** 1) 大きく　2) 小さく　3) 安く　4) しずかに　5) しんせつに　6) にぎやかに

　　2 1) たのしく　食事を　します。

　　　　2) きれいに　そうじを　します。

　　　　3) おそく　おきます。

　　　　4) じょうずに　うたいます。

II.　**1** 1) 書いてきます　2) さがしてきます　3) とどけてきます　4) とってきます

　　　　5) 食べてきます　6) 飲んできます

　　2 1) カタログを　もらってきて、せつめいします。

　　　　2) 本を　かりてきて、読みます。

　　　　3) としょかんで　しらべてきて、みんなに　おしえます。

III.　　1) すぐ　こうばんに　行った　ほうが　いいですよ。

　　　　2) すぐ　カードがいしゃに　でんわした　ほうが　いいですよ。

　　　　3) すこし　休んだ　ほうが　いいですよ。

　　　　4) たばこを　すわない　ほうが　いいですよ。

　　　　5) おさけを　飲まない　ほうが　いいですよ。

IV.　**1** 1) もう　飲みました。／まだ　飲んでいません。

　　　　2) もう　ききました。／まだ　きいていません。

　　　　3) もう　来ました。／まだ　来ていません。

　　　　4) もう　食べました。／まだ　食べていません。

　　　　5) もう　はなしました。／まだ　はなしていません。

　　2 1) まだ　メールの　へんじを　だしていないんです。

　　　　2) まだ　しりょうを　読んでいないんです。

　　　　3) まだ　データを　おくっていないんです。

　　　　4) まだ　会議の　じゅんびが　できていないんです。

QUIZ 2

I.　　1) に　2) に　3) に　4) が　5) を

II.　　1) 2　2) 3, 4　3) 1, 2

III.　　1) もってくる　2) 帰った　3) 行った　4) しない　5) 買って
　　　　　　　　　　かえ　　　　　　い　　　　　　　　　　　　か

IV.　　1) 2　2) 4　3) 1　4) 2, 3

V.　　1) いちにち　さんかい　くすり　の
　　　2) ひるやす　かいぎ　か
　　　3) ちゅうごく　ほん　よ

Lesson 7

Grammar & Pattern Practice

I.　　1) 仕事を　はじめる
　　　　　しごと
　　　2) パリに　行く
　　　　　　　　い
　　　3) 大学を　そつぎょうする
　　　　　だいがく
　　　4) 会社に　入る
　　　　　かいしゃ　はい
　　　5) 国に　帰る
　　　　　くに　　かえ

II.　**1**　1) 仕事が　終わって
　　　　　　　しごと　お
　　　　2) パリに　行って
　　　　　　　　　い
　　　　3) 大学を　そつぎょうして
　　　　　　だいがく
　　　　4) 会社に　入って
　　　　　　かいしゃ　はい
　　　　5) 会社に　入って
　　　　　　かいしゃ　はい
　　　　6) 中学を　そつぎょうして
　　　　　　ちゅうがく
　　　　7) 中学に　入って
　　　　　　ちゅうがく　はい
　　2　1) 食べてから
　　　　　　た
　　　　2) ついてから
　　　　3) ついてから
　　　　4) でる　前に
　　　　　　　　まえ

III.　　1) 子どもの　とき
　　　　　こ
　　　2) 6さいの　とき
　　　3) あつい　とき
　　　4) げんきな　とき
　　　5) あたまが　いたい　とき

Reading Task (translation on p. 256)

　　　1) 10さいの　とき　ひっこししました。
　　　　　じゅっ
　　　2) さっぽろに　すんでいました。
　　　3) けいざいの　べんきょうを　しました。
　　　4) 半年ずつ　休みました。
　　　　　はんとし　　やす

Lesson 8

Grammar & Pattern Practice

I. **1** 1) おいしく 2) いそがしく 3) くらく 4) きれいに

　　　　5) ゆうめいに 6) げんきに 7) きらいに

　　2 1) 夜に 2) 10さいに 3) はたちに 4) 大学生に

　　　　　　よる　　　　　じゅっ　　　　　　　　　だいがくせい

　　　　5) しゃちょうに 6) びょうきに

　　3 1) なつに　なりました。あつく　なりました。

　　　　2) あきに　なりました。すずしく　なりました。

　　　　3) ふゆに　なりました。さむく　なりました。

II. 　　1) Mr. Suzuki often goes to Osaka by Shinkansen.
　　　　2) He always buys beer when he rides the Shinkansen.
　　　　3) Even yesterday he bought a beer at a kiosk before he got on the Shinkansen.
　　　　4) He dropped his beer as he boarded the Shinkansen.
　　　　5) He picked up his beer and sat in his seat.
　　　　6) He soon became thirsty for his beer.
　　　　7) He was a little worried as he opened his beer.
　　　　8) When he opened his beer . . .
　　　　9) He was very cold all the way to Osaka.
　　　10) He had caught a cold by the time he arrived in Osaka.

IV. **1** 1) ゆうべの　パーティーは　にぎやかだった

　　　　2) きいろい　さいふが　ほしい

　　　　3) 毎年　しょうがつは　ハワイで　すごす

　　　　　　まいとし

　　2 1) A：終わる　B：終わらない

　　　　　　　　お　　　　　　お

　　　　2) A：ひつようだ　B：ひつようではない

　　　　3) A：いい　B：よくない

　　　　4) A：ある　B：ない

Reading Task 1 (translation on p. 256)

　　　　1) 7年前に　しました。

　　　　　　ねんまえ

　　　　2) とても　ドキドキしました。

　　　　3) あまり　おいしくないと　おもいました。

　　　　4) また　来ると　やくそくしました。

　　　　　　　　く

Lesson 9

Grammar & Pattern Practice

I. 　　1) 母が　作った

　　　　　はは　つく

　　　　2) 去年　できた

　　　　　きょねん

　　　　3) メキシコで　買った

　　　　　　　　　　か

　　　　4) 先月　スミスさんが　とまった

　　　　　せんげつ

II.　　1) あしたの　会議に　でる
　　　2) ミルズさんが　しゅっちょうに　行く
　　　3) マルタンさんが　日本に　来た
　　　4) ＡＢＣフーズの　本社が　ある
　　　5) えを　かく
　　　6) 子どもと　あそぶ
　　　7) おかしを　作る
　　　8) ヨガを　おしえる
　　　9) お金を　はらう
　　　10) メールの　へんじを　だす
　　　11) 会議が　終わる
　　　12) にもつが　とどく

QUIZ 3

I.　　1) を　2) の　3) で　4) に　5) が／の

II.　　1) 2, 3　2) 2, 4　3) 2

III.　　1) でる　2) よく　3) 来る　4) 行く　5) 食べる

IV.　　1) 3　2) 2　3) 1　4) 1　5) 3

V.　　1) はな　おんな (の) ひと
　　　2) きょねん　しょうがっこう　はい
　　　3) こうこう　べんり
　　　4) がくせい　ゆうじん　まわ

UNIT 4

Lesson 10

Grammar & Pattern Practice

I.　　1) お金が　ないので、何も　買いません。
　　　2) 父が　びょうきなので、国に　帰りたいです。
　　　3) あめだったので、どこにも　出かけませんでした。
　　　4) おんがくが　すきなので、よく　コンサートに　行きます。
　　　5) あたまが　いたいので、すこし　休んでも　いいですか。
　　　6) せつめいが　わからないので、もう一度　ゆっくり　言ってください。
　　　7) おとといは　おっとの　たんじょう日だったので、うちで　パーティーを
　　　　　しました。
　　　8) うちあわせは　6時からなので、お先に　しつれいします。

II.　　1) ひらがなが／を　書けますか。

　　　2) パソコンが／を　つかえますか。

　　　3) じゅうどうが　できますか。

　　　4) あした　6時に　来られますか。

　　　5) カードで　はらえますか。

　　　6) 5時に　おきられますか。

　　　7) ここに　くるまが／を　とめられますか。

　　　8) ひこうきの　中で　ねられますか。

　　　9) じてんしゃに　のれますか。

　　　10) 400メートル　およげますか。

　　　11) 日本語の　うたが／を　うたえますか。

　　　12) すしが／を　作れますか。

Reading & Writing Task (translation on p. 258)

sample answer:

　　　おさそい　ありがとうございます。4月の3週目は　ペリーさんが　日本に
　　　来るので、すこし　いそがしいです。13日の　火曜日は　だいじょうぶです。
　　　加藤

Reading Task (translation on p. 258)

　　　1) きのうです。

　　　2) (じゅぎょうの)　見学に　行きました。

　　　3) じょうずでした。

Lesson 11

Grammar & Pattern Practice

I.　**1**　1) 買おう　2) うたおう　3) ならおう　4) 行こう　5) あるこう

　　　　6) はたらこう 7) およごう　8) いそごう　9) はなそう　10) まとう

　　　　11) しのう　12) あそぼう 13) 飲もう　14) 休もう　15) がんばろう

　　　　16) 見よう　17) おきよう 18) ねよう　19) 始めよう 20) 来よう

　　　　21) しよう

　　2　1) ふじさんに　のぼろうと　思っています。

　　　　2) ピアノを　ならおうと　思っています。

　　　　3) ジョギングを　始めようと　思っています。

　　　　4) つまに　花を　おくろうと　思っています。

　　　　5) はやく　うちに　帰ろうと　思っています。

　　　　6) 来年　けっこんしようと　思っています。

II. **1** 1) この　もんだいは　むずかしくて

2) きのうは　あめで

3) そとが　うるさくて

4) じしんの　ニュースを　聞いて

5) 友だちに　会えなくて

6) 日本に　来た　とき、かんじが　読めなくて

2 1) うたを　うたうのが　すきなので

2) あついので、すみませんが

3) コピーの　つかい方が　わからないので

III. 1) 来週　しゅっちょうが　あるか　どうか　部長に　聞いてください。

2) たなかさんが　フランス語が　じょうずか　どうか　しりません。

3) あの　人の　仕事が　コンサルタントか　どうか　わかりません。

4) りょかんに　とまった　ことが　あるか　どうか　ミルズさんに　聞いてみます。

5) あした　何時に　来られるか　おしえてください。

6) どこに　かぎを　入れたか　わすれました。

7) にくと　さかなと　どちらが　すきか　やまもとさんに　聞いてください。

8) いつ　ひっこすか　まだ　きめていません。

Lesson 12

Grammar & Pattern Practice

I. 1) びょうきに　なるかもしれません。

2) 時間が　ないかもしれません。

3) みちが　すいているかもしれません。

4) あの　人は　すずきさんの　いもうとさんかもしれません。

5) タクシーより　ちかてつの　ほうが　はやいかもしれません。

6) いい　てんきなので、ふじさんが　見えるかもしれません。

7) 今日は　ひまなので、はやく　うちに　帰れるかもしれません。

8) ちゅうしゃじょうが　せまいので、くるまが　とめられないかもしれません。

9) げんきに　なったので、サッカーの　しあいに　出られるかもしれません。

10) あまり　べんきょうしなかったので、しけんに　おちるかもしれません。

II. 1) 仕事が　終わったら

2) にもつが　とどいたら

3) 大学を　そつぎょうしたら

4) ミルズさんが　来たら

5) じゅんびが　できたら

6) ホテルに　着いたら

7) オーケストラの　れんしゅうが　終わったら
8) しゅくだいが　すんだら
9) うちに　帰ったら
10) 少し　休んだら

QUIZ 4

I.   1) が　2) で　3) か　4) が　5) に

II.   1) 4, 1　2) 3, 2　3) 2

III.   1) 話せます　2) おくろう　3) うるさくて　4) あめ　5) なった

IV.   1) 2　2) 1　3) 3　4) 3　5) 4

V.   1) へや　よやく
       2) りょうしん　しゅうまつ　はじ　りょかん　と
       3) ようい　で　よてい

UNIT 5

Lesson 13

Grammar & Pattern Practice

I. **1** 1) マンションが　ふえてきました。
        2) 木が　へってきました。
        3) りゅうがくせいが　ふえてきました。
        4) 子どもの　かずが　へってきました。
        5) かいがい旅行を　する　人が　ふえてきました。
  2 1) すいてきましたね。
        2) 空が　くらくなってきましたね。
        3) はれてきましたね。

II. **1** 1) たからくじに　あたったら
        2) 空を　とべたら
        3) がいこくで　パスポートを　なくしたら
        4) あした　ストが　あったら
        5) かんじが　読めなかったら
  2 1) 部屋が　さむかったら
        2) パーティーが　つまらなかったら
        3) あしたが　むりだったら
        4) るすだったら

3 man: If you are free tomorrow, how about going on a date?

woman: Okay. Where shall we go?

man: If the weather is good, let's go to the beach (lit., "the ocean").

woman: Okay. But it might be cold.

man: If it's cold, let's have a meal at a restaurant by the sea (lit., "a restaurant where you can see the ocean"). If it isn't cold, let's have a meal on an outdoor terrace.

woman: What should we do if it rains?

man: If it rains, let's see a movie.

Lesson 14

Grammar & Pattern Practice

I. **1** 1) When I practiced soccer, my knees began to hurt.

When I massaged them, they got better.

2) When I left Tokyo it was raining, but by the time I arrived in Hakone it had become sunny.

When I went up to the hotel's roof garden, I could see a lake and Mt. Fuji.

3) When I changed from a Western-style breakfast to a Japanese-style one, I lost two kilos in one month.

When I put on a new suit and went out on a date (with my girlfriend), my girlfriend was overjoyed.

2 1) 朝 おきたら、雪が ふっていました。

2) うちの ちかくの すし屋に 行ったら、しまっていました。

3) 薬を 飲んだら、ねつが 下がりました。

4) １０時間 パソコンで 仕事を したら、目が つかれました。

5) にっこうまで 車で 行ったら、じゅうたいで ８時間 かかりました。

II. **1** 1) Suzuki: Marie, where is the hot chocolate—your gift (to us) from Paris?

Martin: We drank it all yesterday.

2) Mills: Mr. Suzuki, I put the samples we were going to send to Nozomi Department Store here, but . . .

Suzuki: I'm afraid I sent them this morning. Should I not have?

3) Suzuki: Mr. Mills, it's late. Let's go home now.

Mills: I want to finish writing the report today, so feel free to leave ahead of me.

4) Mills: Ms. Suzuki, how about going out for lunch?

Suzuki: Huh? You haven't eaten yet? I already ate lunch—with Mary.

2 1) けがを してしまいました。

2) けいたいを うちに おいてきてしまいました。

3) １０キロ ふとってしまいました。

4) パソコンの データが きえてしまいました。

5) しょるいが なくなってしまいました。

III. **1** 1) たのめば 2) おりれば 3) しらせれば 4) もってくれば

5) さむければ 6) おもしろくなければ 7) つごうが よければ

8) 会いたければ 9) げんきなら（ば） 10) にちようびなら（ば）

2 1) 毎日 しゅくだいを すれば
まいにち

2) 古い しりょうを すてれば
ふる

3) どうろが こんでいなければ

4) かいひが 安ければ
やす

せつびが よければ

5) おしえ方が じょうずなら（ば）
かた

Lesson 15

Grammar & Pattern Practice

I. **1** 1) Giving Directions

When you get out of the station, there will be an intersection. Cross that intersection. Walk for about a hundred meters and there will be a white apartment building on your right. My home is in that building on the second floor.

2) The Delicious Way to Eat Instant Noodles

When you open the lid there will be (dry) noodles and a soup mix inside. Pour hot water up to the line (near the lid) and close the lid. Wait three minutes and the delicious ramen noodles will be done.

2 1) 右に まがると、あかい やねが 見えます。
みぎ　　　　　　　　　　　　　み

2) かいさつ口を 出ると、目の 前に こうばんが あります。
ぐち　で　め　まえ

3) レバーを ひくと、水が 出ます。
みず　で

4) ドアを しめると、電気が きえます。
でん　き

5) パスワードを にゅうりょくすると、がめんが かわります。

II. **1** 1) ひっこさなければ なりません。

2) けんしゅうを うけなければ なりません。

3) かりなければ なりません。

4) わたさなければ なりません。

5) 電話を かけなければ なりません。
でん　わ

2 1) トラブルが あって、とりひきさきの 会社に 行かなければ ならないんです。
かいしゃ　い

2) あした けんこうしんだんを うけなければ ならないんです。

3) あしたまでに てがみの へんじを 書かなければ ならないんです。
か

4) 今日中に この 仕事を すませなければ ならないので、
きょうじゅう　　　し　ごと

5) あしたの しけんの べんきょうを しなければ ならないので、

Practice 2 (Exercise)

1) あきます

2) しまります

3) 出ます
で

4) 動きます
うご

5) とまります

　　6) 着きます
　　　　っ

　　7) きえます

　　8) かわります

　　9) なおります

10) 始まります
　　　はじ

Reading Task 2 (translation on p. 260)

　　1) ペットボトル、ぎゅうにゅうパック、かん、びん　などが　あります。

　　2) スーパーに　行くと、リサイクルできる　ごみを　あつめる　ところが
　　　　　　　　　　　い
　　　あります。

　　3) もえる　ごみと　もえない　ごみに　分けて　すてます。

　　4) いいえ、ごみの　しゅるいによって　出せる　日が　きまっています。
　　　　　　　　　　　　　　　　　　わ　　　　だ　　　ひ

QUIZ 5

I.　　　1) が　2) に　3) を　4) に　5) が

II.　　　1) 3, 2　2) 4, 3　3) 3

III.　　1) へって　2) なくして　3) 安けれ　4) あける　5) 作ら
　　　　　　　　　　　　　　　　　　やす　　　　　　　　　　つく

IV.　　　1) 2　2) 1　3) 3　4) 2　5) 4

V.　　　1) にかい　あ　ひだりがわ　せんよう
　　　　2) う（ち）あ（わせ）　さき　しつれい
　　　　3) てんき　そと　ま

Japanese-English Glossary

Note: This list contains nearly all of the vocabulary introduced in the text, with page numbers given for first appearances. Omitted are words introduced in Book I (which can be found in the glossary of that text), idiomatic phrases, and certain particles and proper nouns.

The following abbreviations are used as necessary:

trans.	transitive (verb)	R2	Regular II verb
intr.	intransitive (verb)	suff.	suffix
pref.	prefix		

ああ: oh, I see, 19

アイスホッケー: ice hockey, 173

あいよう: my favorite, my beloved, 141

あか: red, 12

あがる／上がる: rise, go up, 208

あかるい: cheerful, 41

あかんぼう: baby, 106

あき: fall, 118

あく: (intr.) open, 242

あく／空く: (intr.) open up, become vacant, 181

アクセサリー: accessories, 129

アクセスする: access, 224

あくび: yawn, 89

あける: (trans., R2) open, 224

あげる: (R2) deep-fry, 186

あさひ／朝日: morning sun, 193

アシスタント: assistant, 26

あずける: (trans., R2) give to (someone) to look after, 158

あそぶ: play, visit, 38

あたり: general area, 33

あたる: win, 204

あっ: wow, 125

あつい: thick, 24

あつまる: (intr.) gather, 188; おあつまりください: (polite form) please gather, 188

あつめる: (R2) gather, collect 247

あと: later, afterward, 76

あとで／後で: later, 3

アドレスちょう: address book, 10

あのう: uh, hmm . . . , 19

アパート: apartment (usually smaller and cheaper than a マンション, or "luxury apartment"), 37

あびる: (R2) take (a shower), 54

あぶない: dangerous, 152

あぶら: oil, fat, 196

あめ／雨: rain, 9

あめが おおい／雨が 多い: it rains a lot, 9

あめが すくない／雨が 少ない: it does not rain much, 9

あやしい: suspicious, sketchy, 225

あやまる: apologize, 231

あらう: wash, 60

ある〜: a certain . . . , 212; あるあさ／ある朝: one morning, 212; あるひ／ある日: one day, 212

アルゼンチン: Argentina, 7

あれっ: what?, 63

アレルギー: allergy, 89

あんぜん（な）: safe, 214

あんない: guidance, 56; あんないする: show (someone) around, guide, 56; あんないばん: building directory, 240

いいでしょうか: would (it) be good?, 3

いいです: never mind, 25; no thank you, I am fine, 63

いえ: house, 124

いえじゅう: the entire house, throughout the house, 106

いがく: medical science, 110

いくつか: some, a number of, several, 33

いけ: pond, 124

いけない: it is no good, it is forbidden, it will not do, 221

いざかや: tavern, 60

いさん: heritage site, 174

〜いじょう: more than . . . , 159

いじわる（な）: mean, 41

いそいで／急いで: in a hurry, 231

いそぐ／急ぐ: hurry, 167

いたします: (humble form) do, 188

いただく: (humble form) receive, 151

いためる: (R2) stir-fry, 186

いちご: strawberry, 129

いちごばたけ: strawberry patch, 129

いちにちじゅう／一日中: all day, 214

いちば: market, 56

いちばん: number one, 8

いちれつ／一れつ: one line, 188

いつか: sometime, 4

いっしゅうめ／1週目: the first week of the month, 156

いつでも: anytime, 247

いっぱい: one glass, one cup, 209

いっぱく／1泊: stay of one night, 160

いつも: always, 58

いなか: countryside, rural area, 210

いなくなる: disappear (of animate object), 212

いまから／今から: from now, right away, 33

いろいろ: in various ways, 12; いろいろ（な）: various, all sorts, 140

いんさつする: print, 224

インストールする: install, 224

いんせき: meteorite, 212

インターネット: the Internet, 214

インフルエンザ: the flu, 89

インラインスケート: in-line skating, 143

ウィルス: virus, 224

ウール: wool, 39

ウエイトトレーニング: weight training, 66

ウエスト: waist, 41

ウェブサイト: website, 224

うかがう: (humble form) visit, 133

うける: (R2) receive, 107

うごかす／動かす: (trans.) move, 140

うごく／動く: (intr., R2) move, 141; うごかなく なる／動かなく なる: (R2) stop working, 218

うすい: thin (of cloth, paper, etc.), 24

うた: song, 60

うたう: sing, 60

うち: we/us, our company, 201; うち／内: the inside, 226

うちあわせ／打ち合わせ: planning meeting, 151

うちがわ／内側: the inside, 226

うつくしい: beautiful, 193

うで: arm, 41

うでどけい: wristwatch, 39

うまれる／生まれる: be born, 107

うみべ: seaside, 214

うむ／生む: give birth to, 210

うりあげ／売り上げ: sales amount, profits, 201

うりきれ: sold out, 25

うるさい: noisy, irritating, annoying, 168

うれしい: happy, glad, 172

うれゆき／売れ行き: sales trends, 201

うれる／売れる: (intr., R2) sell, be sold, 201

うわあ: wow, 28

うんてん: driving, 213; うんてん する: drive, 213

うんどう: exercise, 65; movement, 193; うんどうを する: exercise, 65

えいかいわ: English conversation, 104

えいぎょう: sales and marketing, 110

ええっ: huh?, what?, 235

ええと: hmm . . . , uh . . . , 42

えきビル／駅ビル: station building (with shops and restaurants), 124

えきまえ／駅前: in front of the station, 160

えっ: really?, 42

Mサイズ: medium (size) , 25

えらぶ: choose, 176

エレベーターホール: elevator corridor, 240

おい: (one's own) nephew, 26

おいごさん: (someone else's) nephew, 26

おいてくる: leave (something somewhere), 221

オイル: oil, 186

おうだんほどう: crosswalk, 240

おうふく: roundtrip, 176

おおい／多い: a lot, many, 9

おおがたスーパー: large supermarket, 124

おおがねもち: the filthy rich, 210

オーケストラ: orchestra, 133

おおぜい／大ぜい: many (of people), 193

おおトロ: fatty tuna, 227

オープンする: open (of business), 129

おかげさまで: thanks (lit., "thanks to you"), 90

おかげで: thanks to . . . , 143

おかしい: odd, strange, 225

おきゃくさま: (polite form) customer, visitor, 56

おきる: (R2) get up, 60; occur, 212

おく: put (something somewhere), 221

おくじょう／屋上: roof garden, 219

おくりに いく／おくりに 行く: see (someone) off, 43

おくる: send, 43; give (flowers), 167

おくれる: (R2) be late, 172

おけしょう → けしょう

おけしょうを する → けしょう

おこのみやき: floury omelet containing vegetables and meat or seafood, 74

おさきに／お先に: (polite form) ahead (of), 83

おさそい → さそい

おさら → さら

おじ: (one's own) uncle, 26; おじさん: (someone else's) uncle, 26

おじいさん: (someone else's) grandfather, 26

おしはらい → しはらい

おしゃべり: talking, chatting, 61; おしゃべりを する: talk, chat, 61

おしゃれ（な）: stylish, 129

おしょうゆ → しょうゆ

おしろ → しろ

おす: push, press, 213

おすし → すし

おだいじに／お大事に: take care of yourself, 83

おちこむ: collapse, 208

おちる: (R2) fail, 172; fall, 213

おつかれさま: good-bye, 70

おてつだい → てつだい

おてつだいする: (humble form) help, 187

おとす: drop, lose, 86

おととい: the day before yesterday, 152

おととし: the year before last, 79

おとな: adult, 176

おとなしい: mild-mannered, 41

おどろく: be surprised, 172

おなじ: same, 25

おにぎり: rice ball, 13

おねがいする: ask a favor of, 92

おば: (one's own) aunt, 26; おばさん: (someone else's) aunt, 26

おばあさん: (someone else's) grandmother, 26

おひる／お昼: lunch, 221

おふろ → ふろ

オペラ: opera, 161

おべんとう → べんとう

おぼえる: (R2) learn, memorize, 223

おまちしております／お待ちしております: (humble form) I will be waiting, 181

おむつ: diaper, 159

おめでとうございます: congratulations, 108

おもい: heavy, 24; serious, 191

おもいで／思い出: memory, 127

おもう: think, 122

おゆ → ゆ

およぐ: swim, 53

おりたたみ: fold-up, folding, 40

おります: (humble form) be, 181

おろす／下ろす: withdraw (money), 158

おわり／終わり: the end, 156

おわる／終わる: (intr.) end, finish, 43

おんど: temperature, 243

か／課: section, 70
ガーデニング: gardening, 27
カーテン: curtain, 231
カードがいしゃ／カード会社: credit card company, 86
カードキー: key card, 226
ガードマン: security guard, 240
ガールフレンド: girlfriend, 79
〜かい／〜回: (counter) time(s), 51
かいがい: overseas, 13
かいがら: seashell, 139
かいがん: seashore, 214
がいこうかん: diplomat, 110
がいこく／外国: foreign country, 22; がいこくじん／外国人: foreigner, 22
かいしゃの ひと／会社の 人: people at the office, 11
かいしょう: doing away with, clearing up, 246
かいじょう: gathering place, 157
がいしょく／外食: eating out, 62
かいてんずし: conveyor-belt sushi restaurant, 227
ガイドブック: guidebook, 103
かいはつ: development, 13
かいひ: membership dues, 223
かいもの: shopping, 12
かいわ: conversation, 104
かえす: give back, 158
かえり／帰り: going home, 70
かえる: (R2) exchange, change, 158; (trans.) change, 243
かお: face, 60
かおいろ: complexion, 83
かおり: smell, fragrance, 139; かおりが する: smell, be fragrant, 139
がか: painter, 210
かぎが かかる: (intr.) lock, 226
かく: draw, paint, 64
かぐつきの: furnished, 93
がくぶ／学部: department (in a university), 111
かける: (R2) put on (glasses), 119; put on (music), 214; でんわを かける／電話を かける: make a phone call, 238
かず: number, quantity, 203
かぜ: cold, 83

ガソリンスタンド: gas station, 124
かた／方: (polite form) person, 19
〜かた／〜方: (suff.) way of ——ing, 161
かたい: hard, 24; stiff, 228
かたづける: (R2) tidy up, 61
かたみち: one-way, 176
かちょう／課長: section chief, 151
かつ: win, 172
がっかりする: be disappointed, 172
カットする: cut, 209
カッパドキア: Cappadocia, 79
カップめん: instant noodles, 236
〜か どうか: if/whether (something is the case), 165
〜かな（あ）: (part.) I wonder . . . , 246
かなしい: sad, 172
カナダ: Canada, 3
かのじょ: she/her, my girlfriend, 219
カフェ: café, 60
かぶか: stock prices, 208
かぶる: put on (a hat), 36; cover (with), 193
かふんしょう: hay fever, 89
かみ: paper, 33; かみぶくろ: paper bag, 33
かみ（のけ）: hair, 41
がめん: screen, 237
〜かもしれません: may, might 181
〜から: (part.) after . . . , 101
カラオケ: karaoke, 60
からだ: body, 140
からて／空手: karate, 64
かりる: (R2) borrow, rent, 29
かるい: light, lightweight, 24
かれ: he/him, my boyfriend, 108
カレンダー: calendar, 10
かわ: leather, 39
かわ／川: river, 124
〜がわ／〜側: side, 226
かわいい: cute, 24
かわる: (intr.) change, 124
かん: can, 247
かんがえる: think about, 193
かんきょう: environment, 193
かんげいかい／かんげい会: welcome party, 91

がんこ（な）: stubborn, 41
かんこう: sightseeing, 175
かんごし: nurse, 110
かんさつ: observation, 140; かんさつする: observe, 140
かんせんする: get (a virus), 224
かんそう: impression, 161
かんたん（な）: simple, 22
かんぱい: cheers! 235
がんばる: do one's best, 51
かんりにん／かんり人: building manager, 26; かんりにんしつ／かんり人しつ: building manager's office, 226

き／木: tree, 124
キーホルダー: key holder, 10
きいろい: yellow, 122
きえる: (R2) vanish, 221; go out (of electricity), 242
きかい: opportunity, chance, 70
きがえる: (R2) change (clothes), 60
きかく: planning, 110
ききゅう: hot-air balloon, 79
きぎょう: enterprise, business, 214
きこえる／聞こえる: (intr., R2) be able to hear, 169
きしゃ: reporter, 108
きた／北: north, 176
きたない: dirty, 124
きつえんしつ: smoking lounge, 138
きつえんじょ: smoking area, 158
きづく／気づく: notice, 212
きどうする: start up (a computer), 224
きに いる／気に 入る: (R1) like, care for, 139
きびしい: strict, 41
きぶんてんかんに／気分てんかんに: for a change of mood, 227
きまる: be decided, be determined, 247
きめる: (R2) decide (on), 91
きもち: feeling, 127
きもの: kimono, 21
キャビネット: cabinet, 37
きゅうか: vacation, 151; きゅうかを とる: take a vacation, 157

きゅうけいじょ: rest area, 158

きゅうに／急に: suddenly, dramatically, 125

ぎゅうにく: beef, 186

ぎゅうにゅう: milk, 247

きゅうりょう: salary, 208

きょうし: teacher, 110

ぎょうせき: business productivity, 208

きょうだい: siblings, brothers and sisters, 26

きょうみ: interest, 176; きょうみ が ある: have an interest, 176

きょく: song, piece of music, 143

きらい（な）: dislike, be sick of, 117

ギリシャ: Greece, 139

きる／着る: (R2) put on (clothes), 9

きる: cut, chop, 186

きんこ: safe, 37

きんじょ: neighborhood, 129

きんむ: job assignment, duties, 101; 〜きんむ: on duty (in), 101

く: ward (of a city), 247

くうき／空気: air, 124

クーラー: air conditioning unit, 205

くしゃみ: sneeze, 89

くじら: whale, 177

くだる／下る: go down, 241

くち／口: mouth, 41

くつ: shoe, 9

クッキー: cookie, 11

くび: neck, 41

くも: cloud, 124

くやしい: regrettable, 172

くらい: dark, 117; gloomy, 191

くらす: live (one's life), 210

グラス: glass, 37

くらべる: (trans., R2) compare, 116; 〜と くらべて: compared to . . . , 116

クリスマスパーティー: Christmas party, 91

クリックする: click, 143

グループ: group, club, 143

くるまいす: wheelchair, 158

グルメ: gourmet, 175

クレジットカード: credit card, 25

〜くん: (suff.) (title of courtesy used among friends or toward people who rank beneath you), 157

けいえい: management, 110

けいかん: police officer, 110

けいけん: experience, 133

けいざい: economics, 110

けいたいケース: cell phone case, 10

けいり: accounting, 110

けいれき: personal history, 112

ケーキや／ケーキ屋: cake shop, 245

ケース: case, 201

けが: injury, 89; けがを する: get injured, 89

けさ: this morning, 40

げじゅん／下じゅん: the last ten days of the month, 156

けしょう: make-up, 105; けしょうを する: make up (one's face), 105

けつえきがた: blood type, 141

けっこんする: get married, 107

げつまつ／月末: the end of the month, 156

けど: (part.) but . . . , 141

けんがく／見学: visit for educational purposes, field trip, 161

げんき（な）: energetic, 41

けんきゅうしゃ: researcher, 110

げんきん: cash, 25

けんこう: health, 86; けんこうしんだん: health checkup, 86

けんしゅう: training session, 157

けんちくか: architect, 110

〜けん（げん）め／〜けん（げん）目: (counter for buildings), 245

〜ご／〜後: later, 112; にねんご／2年後: two years later, 112

こいびと: sweetheart, darling, 212

コインロッカー: coin locker, 158

こうえんかい／こうえん会: lecture presentation, 138

こうがい: suburbs, 27

ごうかく: passing an exam, 172; ごうかくする: pass (an exam), 172

こうこう／高校: senior high school, 105

こうすい: perfume, 139

こうそくどうろ: freeway, 213

こうつうきかん: means of transportation, 124

こうはん／後半: the latter half, 156

けいえい: management, 110

こうほう: public relations, 110

こうむいん: civil servant, 110

こえ: voice, 169

コーチ: coach, 223

コーヒーショップ: coffee shop, 241

コーラ: cola, 12

ごかぞく: (someone else's) family, 8

ごきょうだい: (someone else's) siblings, 26

こくさい: national bond, 214

こくさいかんけい: international relations, 110

ココア: hot chocolate, 221

ごこんやく → こんやく

ございます: (polite form) be, exist, 159; ございません: (humble form) it is not there, 40

こしょう: (black) pepper, 186

ごぜんちゅう／午前中: during the morning, 77

ごそうだん → そうだん

こちら: here (where I am), 12; (polite) this, this one (here), 19

ごつごう → つごう

こと: (abstract) thing, matter, 140

ことしじゅう／今年中: within the year, 123

こどもが うまれる／子どもが 生まれる: (R2) have a child, 107

こどもが できる／子どもが できる: (R2) become pregnant, 107

このぐらい: about like this, 19

ごぶさたしています: I have not been staying in touch, 101

ゴホゴホッ: (sound of coughing), 83

こまる: have a hard time, be troubled, 169

ごみ: trash, 193

コミュニティーセンター: community center, 66

こむ: become crowded, 12

ごらんください: (honorific form) please look, 188

ごりょうしん／ご両親: (someone else's) parents, 26

これから: starting now, 51

ころ: time (in a broad sense), 129

こわい: frightening, 79

こわれる: (intr., R2) break, 172

コンサルタント: consultant, 110
コンサルティング: consulting, 111
こんど／今度: next time, 38
こんな: such . . . as this, 218
コンピューターサイエンス: computer science, 110
こんやく: engagement, 107; こんやくする: get engaged, 107

さあ: well . . . , 209
サービス: service, 22
～さい: years old, 106
さいきどうする: reboot, 224
さいきん: recently, 3
サイクリング: cycling, 64
さいご: the last, 156
さいこうがく: largest amount, 214
さいしょ: the first, 156
サイズ: size, 19
さか: slope, hill, 240
さがす: look for, search for, 40
さかなや／さかな屋: fish dealer, 129
さがる／下がる: fall, go down, 208
さき／先: ahead, 83
さくじょする: delete, 224
さくひん: work of art, 188
さくら: cherry blossoms, 165
さそい: 160 invitation,160
さそう: invite, 160
サッカーせんしゅ: soccer player, 42
さっき: just now, only a moment ago, 40
さどう: tea ceremony, 64
さら: dish, 10
さらいしゅう／さ来週: the week after next, 156
さんか: participation, 79; さんかする: participate, 79
さんかしゃ: participant, 189
ざんぎょう: overtime work, 63; ざんぎょうを する: do overtime work, 63
ざんねん（な）: regrettable, unfortunate, 143; ざんねんなことに: regrettably, 193
さんばい／3倍: triple, 208

し: city, 247
シーズン: season, 193
しお: salt, 186

しかく: certification, qualification, 210; しかくを とる: get qualified, 210
しかし: however, 193
しかたが ない: there is nothing you can do about it, it cannot be helped, 230
～しか ～ない: none except for, 218
しき: the four seasons, 28
しきん: funds, capital, 214
しけん: exam, test, 107; しけんをうける: take an exam, 107
じこ: accident, 168
しごとが とれる／仕事が とれる: (R2) can get work, can get a contract, 209
じこに あう: get into an accident, 191
じさぼけ: jet lag, 89
～し ～し: and moreover . . . , 165
じしん: earthquake, 169
システムてちょう: system notebook, 43
システムぶ／システム部: systems department, 51
しずむ: sink, 139
しぜん: nature, 174
じだい: age (in history), period, 193
したみ: preliminary inspection, 157
しちゃくしつ: fitting room, 25
じつげんする: be realized, 193
じつは: actually, 83
じてんしゃ: bicycle, 65
じどう～／自動～: automatic, 243; じどうドア／自動ドア: automatic door, 240
しない: within the city, 175; しないかんこう: sightseeing within the city, 175
しぬ: die, 53
しはらい: payment, 25
じぶん／自分: oneself, 143
しまる: (intr.) close, 219
じみ（な）: plain, subdued, 24
しみん: civic, civil, 141
じむしつ: office, 138
じむしょ: office, 93
～しゃ／～社: company, 20
じゃあ: well then, in that case, 86
じゃ ありませんか: is it not . . . ?, are you not . . . ?, 116

しゃいん／社員: company employee, 13
シャツ: shirt, 37
シャッターチャンス: chance at a perfect photo, 193
シャトルバス: shuttle bus, 75
しゃぶしゃぶ: shabu-shabu, 63
シャワー: shower, 60
しゅう／週: week, 51; しゅうに／週に: per week, 51
じゆう: free, unrestricted, 188
～じゅう／～中: (suff.) throughout, 106
しゅうしょく: getting a job, 107; しゅうしょくする: get a job, 107
じゅうたい: traffic jam, 220
じゅうたく: housing, 124; じゅうたくち: residential area, 129
しゅうりょうする: shut down, 224
じゅく: cram school, 116
しゅくだい: homework, 185
じゅけん: taking entrance exams, 109; じゅけんべんきょう studying for entrance exams, 109
じゅしんする: receive (electronically), 224
しゅっしゃする／出社する: clock in, show up at the office, 151
しゅっぱつ／出発: departure, 176; しゅっぱつする／出発する: departure, 176
じゅにゅうしつ: nursing room, 158
しゅふ: housewife, 129
しゅみ: interest, hobby, 143
しゅるい: type, kind, 247
じゅんび: preparation, 56; じゅんびを する do preparations, 56
～しょうかい: that presents . . . , 28
しょうがつ: New Year, 122
しょうがっこう／小学校: elementary/primary school, 106
じょうきゃく: passenger, 229
じょうし: superior, 26
しょうしゃ: trading company, 111
じょうじゅん／上じゅん: the first ten days of the month, 156
しょうしょう: (polite form) a little, 40
しょうちする: (polite form) I understand, 181

しょうちゅう: shochu (clear liquor distilled most commonly from sweet potatoes, rice, or buckwheat), 74
しょうちょうする: symbolize, 129
しょうてんがい: shopping street, 124
しょうひんかんり: merchandise management, 110
しょうめんげんかん: front entrance, 240
しょうゆ: soy sauce, 186
しょきゅう: beginning level, 161
しょくじかい／食事会: dinner party, 91
しょくどう: dining room, cafeteria, 188
しょしき: format, 224
じょせい: female, woman, 112
じょゆう: actress, 108
しょるい: document, 37; しょるいぶくろ: document envelope, 39
しらせる: inform, 91
しらべる: (R2) investigate, look into, 54
しりあう: get to know, 108
しりょうしつ: reference room, 138
しろ／白: (n.) white, 12
しろ: castle, 74
しん〜／新〜: (pref.) new, 33
シンガポール: Singapore, 62
じんこう／人口: population, 202
じんじ／人事: human resources, 110
しんしょうひん: new product, 33
しんだん: checkup, 86
しんねんかい／新年会: New Year party, 91
しんぱい（な）: worried, 93; しんぱいごと: concern, 227; しんぱいしょう: worrywart, 191
シンプル（な）: simple, 24
しんらいする: trust, 214

す: vinegar, 186
スイッチ: switch, 243
すいはんき: rice cooker, 243
ずいぶん: considerably, 116
すうがく: mathematics, 110
スーツ: suit, 60
スーツケース: suitcase, 37
スープ: soup (also refers to the mix used to make instant noodles), 236
〜すぎ: past (the hour), 76
すぎる: (R2) pass, 76
すく／空く: become empty, 56
すぐ: right there (close to one), 241
すぐに: right away, 213
すくない／少ない: few, not many, little, not much, 9
スクリーン: screen, 29
スケート: skating, 143
すごい: fantastic, wonderful, 201
すこし／少し: a little, a bit, 79
すこしずつ／少しずつ: little by little, 129
すごす: pass, spend (time), 140; おすごしください: (polite form) please spend time, 188
すし: sushi, 13
すずしい: cool, 118
〜ずつ: each, 11
ずっと: the whole time, ever (since), 104
すてる: (R2) throw away, 223
スト: labor strike, 204
ストレス: stress, 227
スノーボード: snowboarding, 64
すばらしい: fabulous, fantastic, spectacular, 79
スピーチ: speech, 173
スペアキー: spare key, 226
スペイン: Spain, 7; スペインご／スペイン語: Spanish, 155
すべる: skate, glide around, 143
すませる: finish, complete, 239
すむ: be finished, 185
スモークサーモン: smoked salmon, 11
する，（ネクタイを）: put on (a necktie), 36
すわる: sit, 36

せ: height, stature, 19
せいかつ: life, 143
せいせき: grade, 208
せいと: student, 161
せがたかい／せが 高い: tall (of person), 19
せかい: the world, 174
せかいいさん: world heritage site, 177; せかいしぜんいさん: world natural heritage site, 174

せかいじゅう／せかい中: all over the world, 129
せき: seat, 40; cough, 89
せつぞくする: connect (to), 224
せってい: setting(s), 224; せっていする: set, 224
セット: combo, 92; package, 175; セットする: set (a timer), 243
せつび: facilities, 223
せつめい: explanation, 85; せつめいする: explain, 85
せまい: cramped, 124
せわ: care, 140; せわを する: take care (of), 140
せん: line, 236
せんしゅ: player (on a sports team), athlete, 27
せんじつ: the other day, 143
せんせい／先生: teacher, 26
せんたく: laundry, 61; せんたくを する: do laundry, 61
ぜんはん／前半: the first half, 156
ぜんぶ: all, 220
せんよう／専用: exclusive use, 235

そうしんする: send (electronically), 224
そう そう: that is right, 42
そうだん: consultation, 77; そうだんする: consult, 77; そうだんにのる: give asked-for advice, 165
そうべつかい／そうべつ会: farewell party, 91
そうむ: general affairs, 110
そつぎょう: graduate, 101; そつぎょうする: graduate, 101
そこ: there, 241
そと／外: outside, 140
その あと／その 後: after that, 188
そのころ: at that time, 129
その ばあい: in that case, 227
そふ: (one's own) grandfather, 26
ソフト: software, 218
そぼ: (one's own) grandmother, 26
そら／空: sky, 203
それでは: well then, 181
それなら: if so, if that is the case, 151
それに: in addition, 230
それに する: I'll take that one, 19
それより: more than that, 218

ダイエット: diet, 63

だいがくせい／大学生: university student, 118

だいざい: material, subject matter, 193

だいじ（な）／大事（な）: important, precious, 83

だいじょうぶ（な）: okay, all right, fine, 90

たいしょく: retiring, 107; たいしょくする: retire, 107

だいすき（な）: like very much, 13

たいせつ（な）: important, 173

だいとうりょう: president, 210

ダイビング: diving, 64

だいぶ: quite a bit, 116

だいぶつ: large statue of Buddha, 74

たいへん（な）: tough, rough, hard, 62

ダウンロードする: download, 218

たかい／高い: tall, high, 19; たかさ／高さ: height, 193

たからくじ: lottery, 204

タクシーだい: taxi fare, 212

〜だけ: (part.) just, only, 218

たしかに: certainly, 193

だす／出す: send, issue, 88; let out, 242; put out (trash), 247; ねつをだす／ねつを 出す: develop a fever, 244

たすかる: be a help, 165

たずねる: (R2) visit, 211

ただいま: (polite form) right now, 190

たたく: beat, play (drums), 64

〜たち: (suff.) (added to nouns referring to people to create a plural), 70

たてもの: building, 125

たのしみ: delight, 93

たのしむ: enjoy, 175

たのむ: call on (for help), 218

たびたび: repeatedly, often, 225

たべほうだい: all-you-can-eat, 63

たべもの: food, 13

たまご: egg, 137

たまに: occasionally, 58

だめ（な）: no good, 218

〜たら: when, if, 181

たりる／足りる: be sufficient, 238

だれか: someone, anyone, 4

ダンサー: dancer, 211

だんだん: gradually, 127

たんぼ／田んぼ: rice paddy, 124

ちいさ（な）／小さ（な）: small, 42

チーズバーガー: cheeseburger, 92; チーズバーガー・セット: cheeseburger combo, 92

チーフ: chief 5

チェックイン: check-in, 22

チェックする: check, 105

チェロ: cello, 141

ちがう: differ, 63

ちきゅう: Earth, 212

チケット: ticket (for an event), 78

ちこく: being late, 230

ちちおや／父親: father, 143

チャイナドレス: Chinese (silk) dress, 139

ちゃいろ: brown, 43

〜ちゃく／〜着: arriving at . . . , 175

チャレンジ: challenge, 193

〜ちゃん: (suff.) (informal title of courtesy used toward women younger than oneself, or toward children), 116

ちゃんと: properly, 141

〜ちゅう／〜中: (suff.) during, throughout, 77

ちゅうい: attention, heed, 213; ちゅういする: watch out (for), be careful (of), 213

ちゅうがく／中学: junior high school, 105

ちゅうし: cancellation, being called off, 205

ちゅうしゃけん: parking ticket, 159

ちゅうしゃじょう: parking space/spot, 183

ちゅうじゅん／中じゅん: the middle ten days of the month, 156

ちゅうしょく／昼食: lunch, 188

ちょうし: condition, 89

ちょうしょく／朝食: breakfast, 219

ちょうせん: challenge, 140; ちょうせんする: test oneself against, 140

ちょうど: exactly, just, 76; ちょうどいい: just right, 229

〜ちょうめ: district, 111

ちょくせつ: directly, 238

ちらし: advertising flyer, 161

ツアー: tour, 79

つうやく: interpreter, 210

つかう: use, 51

つかれる: (R2) get tired, 70

つき／月: month, 58

〜つき: with . . . , including . . . , 93

つぎに: next, 188

つく: (intr.) attach (to), come with 37; come on (of electricity), 242

つくえ: table, 43

つける: (R2) put (sauce etc.) on (food), dip (food) in (sauce, etc.), 187

つごう: convenience, 160

つづける: (R2) continue (with), 108

つつむ: wrap, 19

つめたい: cold, 41

つよい: strong, 93

つり: fishing, 27

つれていく／つれて行く: take (someone) somewhere, 244

〜で: (part.) because of, 108

であう／出会う: meet, encounter, 140

ていえん: garden, 175

ディスプレイ: display, 25

データ: data, 88

デート: date, 205; デートをする: go on a date, 205

でかける／出かける: (R2) go out, set out, 143

できる: (R2) get done, 88; be built, 124; can, 151; できれば: if possible, 246

テコンドー: tae kwon do, 143

デザート: dessert, 5

デザイン: design, 129

〜でしょう: right? 83; 〜でしょうか: might it be?, 33

デスク: desk, 39

テスト: test, 153

てつだい: help, 187

てぶくろ: glove, 39

デュッセルドルフ: Düsseldorf, 93

テラス: terrace, 42

でる／出る: (R2) come out,

89; be issued, 201; 〜に で
る／〜に 出る: go to, attend,
92; appear,181; （でんわに）で
る／（電話に）出る: answer
(the phone), 190
テレビかいぎ／テレビ会議:
teleconference, 56
てんいん／店員: salesperson,
clerk, 19
てんきん: being transferred, 108
てんしょく: changing jobs, 107; て
んしょくする: change jobs, 107
でんとう: tradition, 175
てんぷする: attach (a file), 224
てんぷファイル: attached file,
225

〜と: when, 235
〜という: called . . . , 193
トイレ: toilet, bathroom, 159
とうさん: bankruptcy, 191; とう
さんする: go under, go bank-
rupt, 191
とうし: investing, 214; とうしす
る: invest, 214
どうしたら 〜か: how, 193
どうしたんですか: what is
wrong?, 90
どうすれば いいですか: what
should I do?, 218
どうぞ おさきに／どうぞ お先
に: please go ahead, 92
とうちゃく: arrival, 176; とう
ちゃくする: arrive, 176
どうぶつ: animal, 140
どうりょう: colleague, 26
どうろ: road, 124
とおくに: far away, 193
とおり: avenue, 240
〜どおり: (suff.) street, avenue,
65; just as . . . , 246
とおりすぎる: go past, go by, 241
とおる: pass, go over, 241
とかい: big city, 143
とき／時: time, when, 101
ドキドキする: be nervously
excited, 127
とくに／特に: especially, 143;
とくに ない／特に ない:
not(hing) in particular, 227
とくべつ（な）／特別（な）: spe-
cial, 201

どこか: somewhere, anywhere, 3
どこでも: anywhere, 241
どこも: anywhere, nowhere, 3;
everywhere, 12
とざん: mountain climbing, 193
どちら: which one (of the two),
6; どちらも: both, either, 11
とつぜん: suddenly, 212
どっち: (informal) which, 235
とどく: be delivered, 137
となりの ひと／となりの 人:
next-door neighbor, 26
とぶ: fly, 204
とまる: stay overnight, 135
とまる: (intr.) stop, 229
ドライブ: drive, 61; ドライブを
する: go for a drive, 61
トラブル: trouble, 239
とりに いく／とりに 行く: come
and get (lit., "go to get"), 33
とりにく: chicken (meat), 186
とりひきさき: client, 239
とりもどす: take back, 193
とる: take, get, 33; take, have, 157
トルコ: Turkey, 79
トレーニング: training, 64
どろぼう: thief, robber, 191

〜なあ: (part.) I wish . . . , 201
ナイロン: nylon, 39
なおす: fix, cure, 243
なおる: get better (of injury, disease), 242
なか／中: inside, middle, 78
ながい／長い: long, 24
なかごろ／中ごろ: around the
middle, 156
なかなか 〜ない: not easily, 143
ながめ: view, 79
ながれる: (R2) flow, 129
なくす: lose, 135
なくなる: disappear, 124
〜なければ ならない: must, 235
なぜなら 〜から: the reason
why is because . . . , 193
なつかしい: nostalgic, 101
〜など: and so on, 175
なにか／何か: something, any-
thing, 3
なふだ: tag, 37
なべ: pot, 74; なべりょうり: meal
cooked in a pot at the table, 74

なまもの／生もの: perishables, 159
ならぶ: line up, 129; おならびく
ださい: (polite form) please line
up, 188
なる: become, 70
なんとか／何とか: somehow,
one way or another, 141
なんども／何度も: many times,
190

〜に: (part.) for, 11; per, 51
にえる: (intr.) cook (in liquid),186
におい: smell, 187
にかい／2回: twice, 51
にく: meat, 171
にし／西: west, 176
〜について: about, concerning, 43
にっき: diary, 231
ニックネーム: nickname, 141
にもつ: package, 219
にゅうがくする／入学する:
enter school, 107
ニュース: news, 60
にゅうりょくする: input, 224
〜によって: depending on, due
to, according to, 247
にる: (trans.) cook (in liquid), 186
にんきが ある／人気が ある:
be popular, be fashionable, 3

ぬぐ: take off (clothes, shoes), 54

ねがい: wish, hope, 92
ねつを だす → だす
ねぶそく: sleeplessness, 89
ねぼう: getting up late, 172; ねぼ
うする oversleep, 172
ねむい: sleepy, 89
ねむる: sleep, 209
ねる: (R2) go to bed, 60
ねんだい: age group, 141
ねんれい: age, 141

〜の あたりに: near, in the general area of, 33
〜の そばに: beside, by, 159
のちほど: later on, 241
のびる: (R2) extend, grow, 201;
be prolonged, 245
のぼる／上る: climb, go up
(something), 65
〜の まま: just as it is/was, 125

のみかい／飲み会: drinking party, 91
のみもの: beverage, 5
のんびりする: relax, 61

は: tooth/teeth, 60
〜ば: if, 218
ばあい: case, instance, 227
パーセント: percent, 208
バーベキュー: barbecue, 61; バーベキューを する: have a barbecue, 61
ばい／倍: times, double, 201
バイオテクノロジー: biotechnology, 110
ばいてん／売店: stall, kiosk 120
ばいに なる／倍に なる: be doubled, 208
はいる／入る: go/come in, enter, 25; はいっている／入っている: be in/inside, 33
はく: wear (shoes, pants, etc. over the feet), 9
〜はく／〜ぱく／〜泊: (counter for nights spent a hotel or an inn), 160
ハクション: (sound of sneezing), 83
はこ: box, 37
はし: bridge, 124
はじまる／始まる: (intr.) begin, 151
はじめ／初め: beginning, at first, 79; はじめに／初めに: to begin with, 188
はじめて／初めて: for the first time, 101; はじめての／初めての: first, first-time, 140; はじめての こと／始めての こと: new things, 140
はじめる／始める: (trans., R2) begin, start, 60
はしる: run, 65; (of car), 231
はずかしい: embarrassing, 172
バスケットボールせんしゅ: basketball player, 27
パスポート: passport, 204
パスワード: password, 237
はたけ: field, patch (of land), 124
はたち: twenty years old, 118
はたらく／働く: work, 152
〜はつ／〜発: departing . . . , 175

バッグ: bag, 37
パック: carton, 247
パッケージ: package, 33
はっしんおん: beep (on an answering machine), 190
はで（な）: colorful, gaudy, 24
はな: nose, 41
はな（みず）: runny nose, 89
はなす／話す: talk, speak, 54
はなみ／花見: cherry blossom viewing, 91
はなれる: leave, 127
はやい: fast, 20; early, 51; はやく: quickly, early, 83
はやし: grove, 124
はらう: pay, 137
はる: spring, 117
バルコニー: balcony, 37
バレエ: ballet, 109
はれる: (R2) clear up, 203
ハワイ: Hawaii, 123
ばん: night, evening, 76
バンクーバー: Vancouver, 27
はんたい: opposite, 229; はんたいがわ: opposite side, 229
はんとし／半年: half a year, 112
はんぶん／半分: half, 208

ひ／日: day, 23
ひ／火: flame, 243
ビーチ・リゾート: beach resort, 175
ひがえり／日帰り: day trip, 175
ひがし／東: east, 176
ひく: play (an instrument), 64; catch (a cold), 89; pull, 237
ひくい: low, short, 24
ひげ: beard, mustache, 41
ひざ: knee, 41
ひさしぶり（です）: it has been a long time, 101
ひじ: elbow, 41
ビジネス: business, 214
ひじょうよびだしボタン: emergency call button, 213
ひたい: forehead, 41
びっくりする: be surprised, 173
ひっこし: moving (from one home to another), 93; ひっこす: move (from one home to another), 107
ひつよう（な）: necessary, 123

ひとたち／人たち: people, 70
ひとびと／人びと: people, 193
ビニール: vinyl, 39
びょうき: illness, disease, 118
ひらく: open (a file), 224
ひろい: spacious, 22
ひろう: pick up, 120
びん: bottle, 247

〜ぶ／〜部: department (in a company), 51
ファッションエリア: fashionable part of town, 129
ファッションビル: stylish building containing boutiques and other fancy shops, 129
ファンドマネージャー: fund manager, 214
ファンヒーター: fan heater, 243
ふうけい: landscape, 211
フードフェア: food fair, 77
ふえる: (intr., R2) increase, 124
フォワード: forward (position in a game), 111
ぶか／部下: junior staff, 26
ふく: clothes, 93
ふぐ: blowfish, 201
ふくろ: sack, bag, 33
ふざいつうち: notice of attempted delivery, 226
ふた: lid, 236
ぶたにく: pork, 186
ふたりとも／二人とも: both of them (referring to people), 27
ぶちょう／部長: department manager, 63
ふつかよい: hangover, 89
ぶつり: physics, 110
ブティック: boutique, 129
ふとい: wide, 24
ふとる: gain weight, 221
ふね: boat, 177
ふべん（な）: inconvenient, 124
ふみきり: railroad crossing, 240
ふゆ: winter, 118
フライドポテト: french fry, 37
ブラジル: Brazil, 7
プラスチック: plastic, 39
ブランドショップ: store selling brand-name apparel, 129
〜ぶり: (suff.) after an interval of . . . , 126

フリーズする: freeze (of computer), 224

ふりこむ: make a direct deposit into a bank account, 158

ふる: fall (of rain, snow), 183

フレーム: frame, 43

ふろ: bath, 60

プロ: professional, 211

ブログ: blog, 141

プログラマー: programmer, 110

プロジェクト: project, 5

プロフィール: profile, 141

ぶんか: culture, 140

ぶんがく: literature, 110

へいじつ: weekday, 12

へえ: oh, really? 51

ペット: pet, 159

ペットボトル: plastic bottle, 247

ベビーカー: baby carriage, 158

へや／部屋: room, 4

へる: (intr., R2) decrease, 124

へん（な）: strange, odd, 230

へんかする: change, 193

へんじ: response, answer, 88

べんとう: box lunch, 38

～ほうが いい: should/should not . . . , 83

ぼうねんかい／ぼうねん会: end-of-the-year party, 91

ぼうはん: crime prevention, 243; ぼうはんライト: security light, 243

ほうりつ: law, 110

ほお: cheek, 41

ボーナス: bonus, 201

ホームシックに かかる: get homesick, 212

ホームステイ: homestay, 101

ホームページ: website, 181

ぼく: I/me (informal; used by men and boys), 63

ほしい: want to have, 122

ポジション: position, 111

ぼしゅう: recruitment, 132; ぼしゅうする: recruit, 132

ポスト: (public) mailbox, 237

ホストファミリー: host family, 127

ほそい: thin, narrow, 24

ほぞんする: save (a file), 224

ボタン: button, 236

ポット: thermos jug, 187

ほど: about (lit., "to the extent of"), 151

ほどうきょう: pedestrian bridge, 240

ほとんど: almost, 59

ポルトガル: Portugal, 7

ほろびる: (R2) be destroyed, 212

ぼんおどり: Bon Festival dance, 74

ほんだな: bookshelf, 39

ま（あ）: well, in any case, 209

マーク: mark, 40

マーケティング: marketing, 101

まい～／毎～: (pref.) every, 62; まいつき／毎月: every month, 62; まいとし／毎年: every year, 122; まいねん／毎年 → まいとし／毎年

まいります: (humble form) go, come, 181

マウスパッド: mouse pad, 10

～まえ／～前: (suff.) to . . . , before . . . , 76; ～まえに／～前に: before, 33

マグカップ: mug, 10

まける: lose, 172

まじめ（な）: serious, 41; まじめさ: serious-mindedness, 192

まず: first of all, 188

まちがえる: (R2) mistake, make a mistake about, 172

マック: McDonald's (short for マクドナルド), 92

マッサージ: massage, 219

まっちゃ: thick, bitter green tea used in tea ceremony, 74

マット: mat, 51

マニア: mania, 193

まにあう／間に合う: be on time, make it, 132

マフラー: scarf, 39

まゆ（げ）: eyebrow, 41

まよう: be at a loss, 165

まわる／回る: travel around, go around, 65

マンションの かんりにん／マンションの かんり人: apartment manager, 26

みえる／見える: (intr., R2) be visible, can see, 165

みがく: brush, 60

みぎがわ／右側: right side, 235

みじかい: short, 24

みち: road, way, 119

みちあんない: giving directions, 236

みちに まよう: get lost, 212

みつかる／見つかる: be able to find, 42

みどり: green, 124

みなさん: (polite from) everyone, the others, 91

みなみ／南: south, 176

みみ: ear, 41

みんな: everyone, 85

むかう: head to, 188

むかえに いく／むかえに 行く: go to meet, 56

むかえに まいります: (humble form) go to meet, 181

むかえる: (R2) meet, welcome, 56

むかし: back in the old days, 125

～むけ: (suff.) geared toward, for, 13

むし: insect, 212

むね: chest, breast, 41

むり（な）: impossible, 83

むりょう: free, does not cost money 159

むりを する: force oneself, overdo it, 83

めい: (one's own) niece, 26

～めい／～名: (counter for people), 181

めいごさん: (someone else's) niece, 26

めいしょ: place of interest, 176

メインストリート: main street, 129

メートル: meter, 155

メールする: send e-mail, 91

めがね: glasses, 39

メキシコ: Mexico, 136

めしあがる: (honorific form) eat, 187; めしあがってください: (honorific form) please eat, 187

メッセージ: message, 190

めの まえ／目の 前: right in front of one, 237

めん: noodles, 236

メンテナンス: maintenance, 92
メンバー: member, 132

〜も いる: there are also those who . . . , 132
もうしこむ: apply, 161
もうすぐ: in a few minutes, 76
もえる: (R2) burnable, 247
もし: if, 204
もじばけする: become garbled (of e-mail), 224
モダン (な): modern, 129
もちろん: of course, 108
もっと: more, 19
モデル: model, 27
もどる: go/come back, 77
もの: (concrete) thing, 140
ものがたり: story, tale, 129
〜も 〜も: both . . . and . . . , 125
もり: forest, 124
もんだい: question, 168; prob-lem, 193

やおや／八百屋: fruit and veg-etable dealer, 129
やきゅうチーム: baseball team, 223
やく: (trans.) roast, 186
やく／約: approximately, 193
やくそく: appointment, promise, 77; やくそくする: promise, 108
やけい: city lights, 143
やける: (intr., R2) roast, 186
やさしい: gentle, kind, 41
やせい: the wild, 174; やせいど うぶつ: wild animals, 174
やせる: (R2) get slim, 219
やっと: at last, finally, 42
やね: roof, 237
やま／山: mountain, 64
やまのぼり／山のぼり: moun-tain climbing, 64
やめる: (R2) quit, 27
やる: do, 111
やわらかい: soft, 24; flexible, 228

ゆ: hot water, 186
ゆうがた／夕方: evening, 76
ゆうしょく／夕食: dinner, 188
ゆうじん／友人: friend, 133
ゆうはん／夕はん: dinner, 185
ゆうひ／夕日: evening sun, 139

ゆうびんうけ: home mailbox, mail slot, 226
ゆうべ: last night, 122
ユーモア: humor, 161
ゆかた: informal cotton kimono, 3
ゆっくり: slowly, leisurely, 153
ゆび: finger, 89
ゆめ: dream, 210
ゆれる: (R2) sway, shake, 243

〜よう／〜用: for use as, 19
よういする／用意する: prepare, get (something) ready, 181
ようし: paper, 225
ようじ／用事: things to do, errands, 70
ようしょく: Western-style food, 219
ようす: appearance, situation, 213; ようすを みる／ようすを 見る: gauge the situation, 213
ヨガ: yoga, 51
よかったら: if you would like, 165
よく ありません: not good, 83
よてい／予定: plan, schedule, 77; よていどおり／予定どおり: as planned, as scheduled, 246; よて いひょう／予定ひょう: plan-ning calendar, 157
〜よね: (part. comb.) right? 125
〜より: (part.) than, 6
よる: stop off, 60
よる／夜: night, evening, 76
よろこぶ: be pleased, be delighted, 132
よろしい: (polite form) good, 151
よろしいですか: would it be all right?, 133

らいきゃく: having a visitor, 241
ライト: light, 243
らいにち／来日: coming to Japan, 157
ライフスポーツ: lifetime sport, 143

りこん: divorce, 107; りこんする: get divorced, 107
リサイクル: recycling, 247
リスク: risk, 214
リスト: list, 8
りゅうがくせい: foreign stu-

dent, 203
りょうかい: I understand, 245
りょうきん: fare, 176
りょうしん／両親: (one's own) parents, 26
りょうてい: an elegant and expensive traditional Japanese restaurant, 201
りょうほう／両方: both, 11
リラックスする: relax, 75

ルーマニア: Romania, 7
るす: being away from home, 205
るすばんでんわ／るすばん電 話: answering machine, 190

れい／例: example, 5
レジ: cash register, 33
レシート: receipt, 159
レシピ: recipe, 27
れつ: line, 143
レッスン: lesson, 5
レバー: lever, 237
れんしゅう: practice, 132
レンタカー: rental car, 174; レンタカー・プラン: rental car option, 175
レンタルショップ: rental shop, 29
れんらく: contact, connection, 92; れんらくする: contact, get in touch (with), 92
れんらくさき: contact informa-tion, 181

ろくおん: recording, 190; ろくお んする: record, 190
ロシア: Russia, 7

わかす: (trans.) boil, 186
わく: (intr.) boil, 186
わける／分ける: (R2) divide, separate, 247
わしつ: Japanese-style room, 138
わしょく: Japanese-style food, 219
わすれもの: thing left behind, 34
わすれる: (R2) forget, leave behind, 33
わだいこ: Japanese drum, 64
わたす: hand over, 238
わたる: cross, 236
ワンサイズ: one size, 2

The following abbreviations are used:

adj.	adjective
intr.	intransitive (verb)
n.	noun
trans.	transitive (verb)
v.	verb

about: (concerning) 〜について, 43; (lit., "to the extent of") ほど, 151; about like this: このぐらい, 19

access: アクセスする, 224

accessories: アクセサリー, 129

accident: じこ, 168; get into an accident: じこに あう, 191

according to: 〜によって, 247

accounting: けいり, 110

actress: じょゆう, 108

actually: じつは, 83

addition, in: それに, 230

address book: アドレスちょう, 10

adult: おとな, 176

advertising flyer: ちらし, 161

after: 〜から, 101; after that: その あと／その 後, 188

age: (of person) ねんれい, 141; (in history) じだい, 193

age group: ねんだい, 141

ahead (of): さき／先, 83; (polite form) おさきに／お先に, 83

air: くうき／空気, 124

air conditioning unit: クーラー, 205

all: ぜんぶ, 220

all day: いちにちじゅう／一日中, 214

all right: だいじょうぶ (な), 90

all sorts: いろいろ (な), 140

all-you-can-eat: たべほうだい, 63

allergy: アレルギー, 89

almost: ほとんど, 59

always: いつも, 58

and moreover . . . : 〜し 〜し, 165

and so on: など, 175

animal: どうぶつ, 140

annoying: うるさい, 168

answer: (n.) (reply) へんじ, 88; (v.) (the phone) (でんわに) でる／(電話に) 出る, 190

answering machine: るすばんでんわ／るすばん電話, 190

anyone: だれか, 4

anything: なにか／何か, 3

anytime: いつでも, 247

anywhere: どこか, 3

anywhere: どこも, 3; どこでも, 241

apartment: アパート, 37; apartment manager: マンションの かんりにん／マンションの かんり人, 26

apologize: あやまる, 231

appear: 〜に でる／〜に 出る, 181

appearance: ようす, 213

apply: もうしこむ, 161

appointment: やくそく, 77

approximately: やく／約, 193

architect: けんちくか, 110

Argentina: アルゼンチン, 7

arm: うで, 41

arrival: とうちゃく, 176; arrive: とうちゃくする, 176; arriving at . . . : 〜ちゃく／〜着, 175

ask a favor of: おねがいする, 92

assistant: アシスタント, 26

at first: はじめ／始め, 79

at last: やっと, 42

athlete: せんしゅ, 27

attach: (attach to, stick to) つく, 37; (a file to an e-mail) てんぷする, 224; attached file: てんぷ ファイル, 225

attend: (〜に)でる／(〜に) 出る, 92

attention: ちゅうい, 213

aunt: (one's own) おば, 26; (someone else's) おばさん, 26

automatic: じどう〜／自動〜, 243; automatic door: じどうドア／自動ドア, 240

avenue: (〜)どおり, 65, 240

away from home, being: るす, 205

baby: あかんぼう, 106

baby carriage: ベビーカー, 158

bag: ふくろ, 33; バッグ, 37

balcony: バルコニー, 37

ballet: バレエ, 109

bankrupt, go: どうさんする, 191; bankruptcy: とうさん, 191

barbecue: バーベキュー, 61; have a barbecue: バーベキューを する, 61

baseball team: やきゅうチーム, 223

basketball player: バスケットボールせんしゅ, 27

bath: (お)ふろ, 60

bathroom: トイレ, 159

be: (polite form) ございます, 159; (humble form) おります, 181

beach resort: ビーチ・リゾート, 175

beard: ひげ, 41

beat: たたく, 64

beautiful: うつくしい, 193

because of: 〜で, 108

become: なる, 70

beef: ぎゅうにく, 186

beep: (on an answering machine) はっしんおん, 190

before . . . : 〜まえ／〜前, 76; 〜まえに／〜前に, 33

begin: (trans.) はじめる／始める, 60; (intr.) はじまる／始まる, 151; to begin with: はじめに／初めに, 188

beginning: はじめ／初め, 79; beginning level: しょきゅう, 161

beloved, my: あいよう, 141

beside: 〜の そばに, 159

best, do one's: がんばる, 51

beverage: のみもの, 5

bicycle: じてんしゃ, 65

biotechnology: バイオテクノロジー, 110

blood type: けつえきがた, 141

blog: ブログ, 141

blowfish: ふぐ, 201

boat: ふね, 177

body: からだ, 140

boil: (intr.) わく, 186; (trans.) わかす, 186

Bon Festival dance: ぼんおどり, 4

bonus: ボーナス, 201

bookshelf: ほんだな, 39

borrow: かりる, 29

both: どちらも, りょうほう／両方, 11; both . . . and . . . : ～も～も, 125; both of them: (referring to people) ふたりとも／二人とも, 27

bottle: びん, 247

boutique: ブティック, 129

box: はこ, 37

box lunch: (お)べんとう, 38

boyfriend, my: かれ, 108

Brazil: ブラジル, 7

break: (intr.) こわれる, 172

breakfast: ちょうしょく／朝食, 219

breast: むね, 41

bridge: はし, 124

bring up: (children) そだてる, 204

brown: ちゃいろ, 43

brush: みがく, 60

Buddha, large statue of: だいぶつ, 74

building: たてもの, 125

building manager: かんりにん／かんり人, 226; building manager's office: かんりにんしつ／かんり人しつ, 226

built, be: できる, 124

burnable: もえる, 247

business: きぎょう, 208; ビジネス, 214; business productivity: ぎょうせき, 208

but . . . : けど, 141

button: ボタン, 236

by: ～の そばに, 159

cabinet: キャビネット, 37

café: カフェ, 60

cafeteria: しょくどう, 188

cake shop: ケーキや／ケーキ屋, 245

calendar: カレンダー, 10

call me . . . : ～と よんでください, 111

call on: (for help) たのむ, 218

called . . . : ～という, 193

can: (able to) できる, 151; (container) かん, 247

Canada: カナダ, 3

cancellation: ちゅうし, 205

capital: しきん, 214

Cappadocia: カッパドキア, 79

care: せわ, 140

care for: きにいる／気に入る, 139

careful (of), be: ちゅういする, 213

carton: パック, 247

case: (container) ケース, 201; (situation) ばあい, 227; if that is the case: それなら, 151; in any case: ま(あ), 209; in that case: そのばあい, 227

cash: げんきん, 25

cash register: レジ, 33

castle: (お)しろ, 74

catch: (a cold) ひく, 89

cell phone case: けいたいケース, 10

cello: チェロ, 141

certain . . . , a: ある～, 212

certainly: たしかに, 193

certification: しかく, 210

challenge: チャレンジ, 193; ちょうせん, 140

chance: きかい, 70; chance at a perfect photo: シャッターチャンス, 193

change: (intr.) かわる, 124, へんかする, 193; (trans.) かえる, 243; (clothes) きがえる, 60; (exchange: money) かえる, 158; change jobs: てんしょくする, 107; changing jobs: てんしょく, 107: for a change of mood: きぶんてんかんに／気分てんかんに, 227

chat: おしゃべりをする, 61; chatting: おしゃべり, 61

check: チェックする, 105

check-in: チェックイン, 22

checkup: しんだん, 86

cheek: ほお, 41

cheerful: あかるい, 41

cheers: かんぱい, 235

cheeseburger: チーズバーガー, 92; cheeseburger combo: チーズバーガー・セット, 92

cherry blossom: さくら, 165; cherry blossom viewing: はなみ／花見, 91

chest: むね, 41

chicken (meat): とりにく, 186

chief: チーフ, 5

child, have a: こどもが うまれる／子どもが 生まれる, 107

Chinese (silk) dress: チャイナドレス, 139

choose: えらぶ, 176

chop: きる, 186

Christmas party: クリスマスパーティー, 91

city: し, 247; big city: とかい, 143; city lights: やけい, 143; within the city: しない, 175

civic/civil: しみん, 141

civil servant: こうむいん, 110

clear up: (of weather) はれる, 203; clearing up (of trouble, etc.): かいしょう, 246

clerk: てんいん／店員, 19

click: クリックする, 143

client: とりひきさき, 239

climb: のぼる／上る, 65

clock in: しゅっしゃする／出社する, 151

close: しまる, 219

clothes: ふく, 93

cloud: くも, 124

club: グループ, 143

coach: コーチ, 223

coffee shop: コーヒーショップ, 241

coin locker: コインロッカー, 158

cola: コーラ, 12

collect: あつめる, 247

cold: (adj.) (of weather) つめたい, 41; (n.) (illness) かぜ, 83

collapse: おちこむ, 208

colleague: どうりょう, 26

colorful: はで(な), 24

combo: セット, 92

come: (humble form) まいります, 181

come and get: とりにいく／とりに 行く, 33

come back: もどる 77

come in: はいる／入る, 25
come on: (of electricity) つく, 242
come out: でる／出る, 54
come with: つく, 37
coming to Japan: らいにち／来日, 157
community center: コミュニティーセンター, 66
company: ～しゃ／～社, 20; company employee: しゃいん／社員, 13
compare: くらべる, 116; compared to . . .: ～と くらべて, 116
complete: すませる, 239
complexion: かおいろ, 83
computer: コンピューター, 123; computer science: コンピューターサイエンス, 110
concern: しんぱいごと, 227
concerning: ～について, 43
condition: (physical) ちょうし, 89
congratulations: おめでとうございます, 108
congregate: あつまる, 188
connect (to): せつぞくする, 224
connection: れんらく, 92
considerably: ずいぶん, 116
consult: そうだんする, 77; consultation: (ご)そうだん, 77
consultant: コンサルタント, 110
consulting: コンサルティング, 111
contact: (n.) れんらく, 92; (v.) れんらくする, 92; contact information: れんらくさき, 181
continue with: つづける, 108
contract, can get a: しごとが とれる／仕事が とれる, 209
convenience: (ご)つごう, 160
conversation: かいわ, 104
conveyor-belt sushi restaurant: かいてんずし, 227
cook: (intr.) にえる, 186; (trans.) にる, 186
cookie: クッキー, 11
cool: すずしい, 118
cough: せき, 89
countryside: いなか, 210
cover (with): かぶる, 193
cram school: じゅく, 116
cramped: せまい, 124
credit card: クレジットカード, 25; credit card company: カード

がいしゃ／カード会社, 86
crime prevention: ぼうはん, 243
cross: わたる, 236
crosswalk: おうだんほどう, 240
crowded, become: こむ, 12
culture: ぶんか, 140
cure: なおす, 243
curtain: カーテン, 231
customer: (polite form) おきゃくさま, 56
cut: きる, 186; (a bonus) カットする, 209
cute: かわいい, 24
cycling: サイクリング, 64

dancer: ダンサー, 211
dangerous: あぶない, 151
dark: くらい, 117
darling: こいびと, 212
data: データ, 88
date: デート, 205; go on a date: デートを する, 205
day: ひ／日, 23; back in the old days: むかし, 125; the day before yesterday: おととい, 152; day trip: ひがえり／日帰り, 175; one day: あるひ／ある日, 212
decide: きめる, 91; be decided: きまる, 247
decrease: へる, 124
deep-fry: あげる, 186
delete: さくじょする, 224
delight: たのしみ, 93; be delighted: よろこぶ, 132
delivered, be: とどく, 137
depart: しゅっぱつする／出発する, 176; departing . . .: ～はつ／～発, 175; departure: しゅっぱつ／出発, 176
department: (in a company) ～ぶ／～部, 51; department manager: ぶちょう／部長, 63
depending on: ～によって, 247
deposit into a bank account, make a direct: ふりこむ, 158
design: デザイン, 129
desk: デスク, 39
dessert: デザート, 5
destroyed, be: ほろびる, 212
determined, be: きまる, 247
development: かいはつ, 13
diaper: おむつ, 159

diary: にっき, 231
die: しぬ, 53
diet: ダイエット, 63
different: ちがう, 63
dining room: しょくどう, 188
dinner: ゆうはん／夕はん, 185; ゆうしょく／夕食, 188
dinner party: しょくじかい／食事会, 91
dip (food) in (sauce etc.): つける, 187
diplomat: がいこうかん, 110
directly: ちょくせつ, 238
directory: (in a building) あんないばん, 240
dirty: きたない, 124
disappear: (of inanimate object) なくなる, 124; (of animate object): いなくなる, 212
disappointed, be: がっかりする, 172
disease: びょうき, 118
dish: (お)さら, 10
dislike: きらい (な), 117
display: ディスプレイ, 25
district: ～ちょうめ, 111
divide: わける／分ける, 247
diving: ダイビング, 64
divorce: りこん, 107; get divorced: りこんする, 107
do: やる, 111; (humble form) いたします, 188
document: しょるい, 37; document envelope: しょるいぶくろ, 39
doing away with: かいしょう, 246
double: ばい／倍, 201: be doubled: ばいに なる／倍に なる, 208
download: ダウンロードする, 218
dramatically: きゅうに／急に, 125
draw: かく, 64, 211
dream: ゆめ, 210
drinking party: のみかい／飲み会, 91
drive: (n.) ドライブ, 61; (v.) うんてんする, 213; driving: うんてん, 213; go for a drive: ドライブを する, 61
drop: おとす, 86
due to: ～によって, 247
during: ～ちゅう／～中, 77

Düsseldorf: デュッセルドルフ, 93
duties: きんむ, 101; on duty (in): ～きんむ, 101

each: ～ずつ, 11
ear: みみ, 41
early: はやい, 51
Earth: ちきゅう, 212
earthquake: じしん, 168
easily, not: なかなか ～ない, 143
east: ひがし／東, 176
eat: (honorific form) めしあがる, 187; eating out: がいしょく／外食, 62
economics: けいざい, 110
education: きょういく, 111
egg: たまご, 137
either: どちらも, 11
elbow: ひじ, 41
elementary school: しょうがっこう／小学校, 106
elevator corridor: エレベーターホール, 240
embarrassing: はずかしい, 172
emergency call button: ひじょうよびだしボタン, 213
empty, become: すく／空く, 56
encounter: であう／出会う, 140
end: (v.) おわる／終わる, 43; (n.) おわり／終わり, 156; the end of the month: げつまつ／月末, 156
end-of-the-year party: ぼうねんかい／ぼうねん会, 91
energetic: げんき (な), 41
engaged, get: こんやくする, 107; engagement: こんやく, 107
English conversation: えいかいわ, 104
enjoy: たのしむ, 175
enter: はいる／入る, 25; enter school: にゅうがくする／入学する, 107
enterprise: きぎょう, 214
entrance exams, taking: じゅけん, 109; studying for entrance exams: じゅけんべっきょう, 109
environment: かんきょう, 193
errands: ようじ／用事, 70
especially: とくに／特に, 143
evening: ゆうがた／夕方, 76; ばん、よる／夜, 76
evening sun: ゆうひ／夕日, 139

ever (since): ずっと, 104
every: まい～／毎～; every month: まいつき／毎月, 62; every year: まいとし／毎年, 122
everyone: みんな, 85; (polite form) みなさん, 91
everywhere: どこも, 12
exactly: ちょうど, 76
exam: しけん, 107; take an exam: しけんを うける, 107
example: れい／例, 5
exchange: かえる, 158
excited, be nervously: ドキドキする, 127
exclusive use: せんよう／専用, 235
exercise: うんどう, 65; うんどうを する, 65
exist: (polite form) ございます, 159
experience: けいけん, 132
explain: せつめいする, 85; explanation: せつめい, 85
extend: のびる, 201
eyebrow: まゆ (げ), 41

fabulous: すばらしい, 79
face: かお, 60
facilities: せつび, 223
fail: おちる, 172
fairly: なかなか, 143
fall: (n.) (season) あき, 118; (v.) おちる, 213; (of prices etc.) さがる／下がる, 208; (of rain, snow) ふる, 183
family: (someone else's) ごかぞく, 8
fan heater: ファンヒーター, 243
fantastic: すばらしい, 79; すごい, 201
far away: とおくに, 193
fare: りょうきん, 176
farewell party: そうべつかい／そうべつ会, 91
fashionable, be: にんきが ある／人気が ある, 3; fashionable part of town: ファッションエリア, 129
fast: はやい, 20
father: ちちおや／父親, 143
fatty tuna: おおトロ, 227
favorite, my: あいよう, 141

feeling: きもち, 127
female: じょせい, 112
fever, develop a: ねつを だす／ねつを 出す, 244
few: すくない／少ない, 9
field: はたけ, 124
field trip: けんがく／見学, 161
finally: やっと, 42
find, be able to: みつかる／見つかる, 42
fine: だいじょうぶ (な), 90
finger: ゆび, 89
finish: (intr.) おわる／終わる, 43; (trans.) すませる, 239; be finished: すむ, 185
first: はじめての／初めての, 140; first of all: まず, 188; the first: さいしょ, 156; the first half: ぜんはん／前半, 156; the first ten days of the month: じょうじゅん／上じゅん, 156; the first week of the month: いっしゅうめ／1週目, 156
first-time: はじめての／初めての, 140; for the first time: はじめて／初めて, 101
fish dealer: さかなや／さかな屋, 129
fishing: つり, 27
fitting room: しちゃくしつ, 25
fix: なおす, 243
flame: ひ／火, 243
flexible: やわらかい, 228
flow: ながれる, 129
flu, the: インフルエンザ, 89
fly: とぶ, 204
folding/fold-up: おりたたみ, 40
food: たべもの, 13
food fair: フードフェア, 77
for: ～に, 11; (geared toward) ～むけ, 13
forbidden, it is: いけない, 221
force oneself: むりを する, 83
forehead: ひたい, 41
foreign country: がいこく／外国, 22
foreign student: りゅうがくせい, 203
foreigner: がいこくじん／外国人, 22
forest: もり, 124
forget: わすれる, 33

format: しょしき, 224

forward: (position in a game) フォワード, 111

four seasons, the: しき, 28

fragrance: かおり, 139; be fragrant: かおりが する, 139

frame: フレーム, 43

free: (does not cost money) むりょう, 159; (unrestricted) じゆう, 188

freeway: こうそくどうろ, 213

freeze: (of computer) フリーズ する, 224

french fry: フライドポテト, 37

friend: ゆうじん／友人, 133

frightening: こわい, 79

front entrance: しょうめんげんかん, 240

fruit and vegetable dealer: やおや／八百屋, 129

fund manager: ファンドマネージャー, 214

funds: しきん, 214

furnished: かぐつきの, 93

gain weight: ふとる, 221

garbled, become: もじばけする, 224

garden: ていえん, 175

gardening: ガーデニング, 27

gas station: ガソリンスタンド, 124

gather: (intr.) あつまる, 188; (trans.) あつめる, 247; gathering place: かいじょう, 157

gaudy: はで (な), 24

gauge the situation: ようすを みる／ようすを 見る, 213

geared toward: ～むけ, 13

general affairs: そうむ, 110

general area: あたり, 33; in the general area of, ～の あたりに, 33

gentle: やさしい, 41

get: とる, 33; (a virus): かんせんする, 224

get better: (of injury, disease) なおる, 242

get done: できる, 88

get to know: しりあう, 108

get up: おきる, 60

girlfriend: ガールフレンド, 79; my girlfriend: かのじょ, 219

give: (flowers) おくる, 167; give to (someone) to look after: あず

ける, 158

give asked-for advice: そうだんに のる, 165

give back: かえす, 158

give birth to: うむ／生む, 210

giving directions: みちあんない, 236

glad: うれしい, 172

glass: グラス, 37; one glass: いっぱい, 209

glasses: めがね, 39

glide around: すべる, 143

gloomy: くらい, 191

glove: てぶくろ, 39

go: (humble form) まいります, 181

go around: まわる／回る, 65

go by: とおりすぎる, 241

go back: もどる, 77

go down: (intr.) (of prices) さがる／下がる, 208; (trans.) (a hill etc.) くだる／下る, 241

go in: はいる／入る, 25

going home: かえり／帰り, 70

go out: (leave) でかける／出かける, 143; (of electricity): きえる, 242

go past: とおりすぎる, 241

go to: (～に)でる／(～に)出る, 92

go to bed: ねる, 60

go under: (go bankrupt) とうさんする, 191

go up: (climb) のぼる／上る, 65; (rise) あがる／上がる, 208

good-bye: おつかれさま, 70

gourmet: グルメ, 175

grade: せいせき, 208

gradually: だんだん, 127

graduate: そつぎょうする, 101; graduation: そつぎょう, 101

grandfather: (one's own) そふ, 26; (someone else's) おじいさん, 26

grandmother (one's own): そぼ, 26; (someone else's) おばあさん, 26

Greece: ギリシャ, 139

green: みどり, 124

green tea: まっちゃ, 74

group: グループ, 143

grove: はやし, 124

grow: のびる, 201

guidance: あんない, 56

guide: あんないする, 56

guidebook: ガイドブック, 103

hair: かみ (のけ), 41

half: はんぶん／半分, 208

half a year: はんとし／半年, 112

hand over: わたす, 238

hangover: ふつかよい, 89

happy: うれしい, 172

hard: たいへん (な), 62

hard: (of surface) かたい, 24

hard time, have a: こまる, 168

have: とる, 157

Hawaii: ハワイ, 123

hay fever: かふんしょう, 89

he: かれ, 108

head to: むかう, 188

health: けんこう, 86; health checkup: けんこうしんだん, 86

hear, be able to: きこえる／聞こえる, 168

heavy: おもい, 24

heed: ちゅうい, 213

height: たかさ／高さ, 193; (of person) せ, 19

help: (n.) (お)てつだい, 187; (v.) (humble form): おてつだいする, 187; be a help: たすかる, 165

her: かのじょ, 219

here: こちら, 12

heritage site: いさん, 174

high: たかい／高い, 19

hill: さか, 240

him: かれ, 108

hmm . . . : あのう, 19; ええと, 42

hobby: しゅみ, 143

homesick, get: ホームシックに かかる, 212

homestay: ホームステイ, 101

homework: しゅくだい, 185

hope: ねがい, 92

host family: ホストファミリー, 127

hot-air balloon: ききゅう, 79

hot chocolate: ココア, 221

hot water: (お)ゆ, 186

house: いえ, 124; the entire house, throughout the house: いえじゅう, 106

housewife: しゅふ, 129

housing: じゅうたく, 124

how: どうしたら ～か, 193

however: しかし, 193
huh?: ええっ, 235
human resources: じんじ／人事, 110
humor: ユーモア, 161
hurry: いそぐ／急ぐ, 167; in a hurry: いそいで／急いで, 231

I: (informal; used by men and boys): ぼく, 63
ice hockey: アイスホッケー, 173
if: 〜か どうか, 165; 〜たら, 181; もし, 204; 〜ば, 218; if so: それなら, 151; if you would like: よかったら, 165; if possible: できれば, 246
illness: びょうき, 118
important: だいじ（な）／大事（な）, 83; たいせつ（な）, 173
impossible: むり（な）, 83
impression: かんそう, 161
including . . .: 〜つき, 93
inconvenient: ふべん（な）, 124
increase: ふえる, 124
inform: しらせる, 91
injured, get: けがを する, 89
injury: けが, 89
in-line skating: インラインスケート, 143
input: にゅうりょくする, 224
insect: むし, 212
inside: なか／中, 78; be inside: はいっている／入っている, 33
inside, the: うち／内, うちがわ／内側, 226
install: インストールする, 224
instance: ばあい, 227
instant noodles: カップめん, 236
interest: しゅみ, 143
interest: きょうみ, 176
interest, have an: きょうみが ある, 176
international relations: こくさいかんけい, 110
Internet, the: インターネット, 214
interpreter: つうやく, 210
interval of, after an . . .: 〜ぶり, 126
invest: とうしする, 214; investing: とうし, 214
investigate: しらべる, 54
invitation: （お）さそい, 160; invite: さそう, 160

irritating: うるさい, 168
issue: だす／出す, 88; be issued: でる／出る, 201
item for sale: しょうひん, 33

Japanese drum: わだいこ, 64
Japanese-style food: わしょく, 219
Japanese-style room: わしつ, 138
jet lag: じさぼけ, 89
job assignment: きんむ, 101
job, get a: しゅうしょくする, 107; getting a job: しゅうしょく, 107
junior high school: ちゅうがく／中学, 105
junior staff: ぶか／部下, 26
just: 〜だけ, 218; ちょうど, 76; just as . . .: 〜どおり, 246; just as it is/was: 〜の まま, 125
just now: さっき, 40
just right: ちょうど いい, 229

karaoke: カラオケ, 60
karate: からて／空手, 64
key card: カードキー, 226
key holder: キーホルダー, 10
kimono: きもの, 21
kind: (adj.) (of personality): やさしい, 41; (n.) しゅるい, 247
kiosk: ばいてん／売店, 120
knee: ひざ, 41

landscape: ふうけい, 211
largest amount: さいこうがく, 214
last, the: さいご, 156; the last ten days of the month: げじゅん／下じゅん, 156
last night: ゆうべ, 122
late, be: おくれる, 172; being late: ちこく, 230; getting up late: ねぼう, 172
later: あとで／後で, 3; 〜ご／〜後, 112; later on: のちほど, 241
latter half, the: こうはん／後半, 156
laundry: せんたく, 61; do laundry: せんたくを する, 61
law: ほうりつ, 110
learn: おぼえる, 223
leather: かわ, 39
leave: (separate from) はなれる, 127; leave (something somewhere): おいてくる, 221; leave

behind: (forget) わすれる, 33
lecture presentation: こうえんかい／こうえん会, 138
leisurely: ゆっくり, 153
lesson: レッスン, 5
let out: だす／出す, 242
lever: レバー, 237
lid: ふた, 236
life: せいかつ, 143
lifetime sport: ライフスポーツ, 143
light: (adj.) (lightweight): かるい, 24; (n.) ライト, 243
like: きに いる／気に 入る, 139; like very much: だいすき（な）, 13
line: (queue) れつ, 143; (mark) せん, 236; one line: いちれつ／一れつ, 188
line up: ならぶ, 129
list: リスト, 8
literature: ぶんがく, 110
little: すくない／少ない, 9; a little: すこし／少し, 79, (polite form) しょうしょう, 40; little by little: すこしずつ／少しずつ, 129
live: くらす, 210
lock: (become locked) かぎが かかる, 226
long: ながい／長い, 24; it has been long time: ひさしぶり（です）, 101
look for: さがす, 40
look into: しらべる, 54
lose: (mislay) おとす, 86, なくす, 135; (fail in a match) まける, 172
loss, be at a: まよう, 165
lost, get: みちに まよう, 212
lot, a: おおい／多い, 9
lottery: たからくじ, 204
low: ひくい, 24
lunch: ちゅうしょく／昼食, 188; おひる／お昼, 221

mailbox: (at home) ゆうびんうけ, 226; (public) ポスト, 237
main street: メインストリート, 129
maintenance: メンテナンス, 92
make a phone call: でんわを／電話を かける, 238
make it (on time): まにあう／間に 合う, 132
make-up: （お）けしょう, 105;

make up (one's face): （お）け しょう を する, 105

management: けいえい, 110

mania: マニア, 193

many: (of things) おおい／多い, 9; (of people): おおぜい／大ぜ い, 193; many times: なんども ／何度も, 190

mark: マーク, 40

market: いちば, 56

marketing :マーケティング, 101

married, get: けっこんする, 107

massage: マッサージ, 219

mat: マット, 51

material: だいざい, 193

mathematics: すうがく, 110

matter: こと, 140

may: ～かもしれません, 181

may be: ～でしょう, 83

McDonald's: マック, 92

me: (informal; used by men and boys): ぼく, 63

mean: いじわる（な）, 41

meat: にく, 171

medical science: いがく, 110

medium (size): Mサイズ, 25

meet: むかえる, 56

meet: (by chance) であう／出 会う, 140; go to meet: むかえ に いく／むかえに 行く, 56, (humble form) むかえに まい ります, 181

member: メンバー, 132

membership dues: かいひ, 223

memorize: おぼえる, 223

memory: おもいで／思い出, 127

merchandise management: しょ うひんかんり, 110

message: メッセージ, 190

meteorite: いんせき, 212

meter: メートル, 155

Mexico: メキシコ, 136

middle: なか／中, 78; around the middle: なかごろ／中ごろ, 156; the middle ten days of the month: ちゅうじゅん／ 中じゅん, 156

might :～かもしれません, 181

might it be?: ～でしょうか, 33

mild-mannered: おとなしい, 41

milk: ぎゅうにゅう, 247

minutes, in a few: もうすぐ, 76

mistake: まちがえる, 172

model: モデル, 27

modern: モダン（な）, 129

moment ago, only a: さっき, 40

month: つき／月, 58

more: もっと, 19

more than . . .: ～いじょう, 159

more than that: それより, 218

morning: あさ／朝, 76; during the morning: ごぜんちゅう／ 午前中, 77; morning sun: あさ ひ／朝日, 193; this morning: け さ, 40; one morning: あるあ さ／ある朝, 212

mountain: やま／山, 64; moun- tain climbing: やまのぼり／山 のぼり, 64; とざん, 193

mouse pad: マウスパッド, 10

mouth: くち／口, 41

move: (trans.) うごかす／動か す, 140; (intr.) うごく／動く, 141; (from one home to another) ひっ こす, 107; moving (from one home to another): ひっこし, 93

movement: うんどう, 193

mug: マグカップ, 10

music, piece of: きょく, 143

must: ～なければ ならない, 235

mustache: ひげ, 41

narrow: (thin) ほそい, 24

national bond: こくさい, 214

nature: しぜん, 174

near: ～の あたりに, 33

necessary: ひつよう（な）, 123

neck: くび, 41

neighborhood: きんじょ, 129

nephew: (one's own) おい, 26; (someone else's) おいごさん, 26

never mind: いいです, 25

new: しん～／新～, 33; new things: はじめての こと／始 めての こと, 140

news: ニュース, 60

New Year: しょうがつ, 122; New Year party: しんねんかい／ 新年会, 91

next: つぎに, 247

next-door neighbor: となりの ひと／人, 26

next time: こんど／今度, 38

nickname: ニックネーム, 141

niece: (one's own) めい, 26; (someone else's) めいごさん, 26

night: ばん, よる／夜, 76; stay of one night: いっぱく／１泊, 160

no good: だめ（な）, 218; it is no good: いけない, 221

no thank you: いいです, 63

noisy: うるさい, 168

none except for: ～しか ～ない, 218

noodles: めん, 236

north: きた／北, 176

nose: はな, 41

nostalgic: なつかしい, 101

not good: よく ありません, 83

notice: きづく／気づく, 212

notice of attempted delivery: ふ ざいつうち, 226

not(hing) in particular: とくに／ 特に ない, 227

nowhere: どこも, 3

number: かず, 203; number one: いちばん, 8

nurse: かんごし, 110

nursing room: じゅにゅうしつ, 158

nylon: ナイロン, 39

observation: かんさつ, 140; observe: かんさつする, 140

occasionally: たまに, 58

occur: おきる, 212

odd: おかしい, 225; へん（な）, 230

of course: もちろん, 108

office: じむしょ, 93; じむしつ, 138

oh, I see: ああ, 19

oh, really?: へえ, 51

oil: あぶら, 186

oil: オイル, 186

okay: だいじょうぶ（な）, 90

omelet, Japanese-style: (floury and containing vegetables and meat or seafood) おこのみやき, 74

one way or another: なんとか／ 何とか, 141

oneself: じぶん／自分, 143

one size: ワンサイズ, 23

one-way: かたみち, 176

only: ～だけ, 218

open: (intr.) あく, 242; (a file): ひ らく, あける, 224; (of business): オープンする, 129; open up: あ く／空く, 181

opera: オペラ, 161

opportunity: きかい, 70

opposite: はんたい, 229; opposite side: はんたいがわ, 229

orchestra: オーケストラ, 132

other day, the: せんじつ, 143

outside: そと／外, 140

overdo it: むりを する, 83

overseas: かいがい, 13

oversleep: ねぼうする, 172

overtime work: ざんぎょう, 63; do overtime work: ざんぎょう を する, 63

package: パッケージ, 33; (tour package) セット, 175; (item sent in the mail) にもつ, 219

paint: かく, 211

painter: がか, 210

paper: かみ, 33; ようし, 225

paper bag: かみぶくろ, 33

parents (one's own) りょうしん／両親, 26; (someone else's) ごりょうしん／ご両親, 26

parking space/spot: ちゅうしゃじょう, 183

parking ticket: ちゅうしゃけん, 159

participant: さんかしゃ, 189

participate: さんかする, 79

pass: (an exam) ごうかくする, 172; (go over: railroad tracks) とおる, 241; (of time) すぎる, 76; passing an exam ごうかく, 172

passenger: じょうきゃく, 229

passport: パスポート, 204

password: パスワード, 237

past: (the hour) ～すぎ, 76

patch: (of land) はたけ, 124

pay: はらう, 137; payment: （お）しはらい, 25

pedestrian bridge: ほどうきょう, 240

people: ひとたち／人たち, 70; ひとびと／人びと, 193; people at the office: かいしゃの ひと／会社の 人, 11

pepper: こしょう, 186

per: ～に, 51

percent: パーセント, 208

perfume: こうすい, 139

period: (in history) じだい, 193

perishables: なまもの／生もの, 159

person: (polite form) かた／方, 19

personal history: けいれき, 112

pet: ペット, 159

physics: ぶつり, 110

pick up: ひろう, 120

place of interest: めいしょ, 176

plain: (of color) じみ（な）, 24

plan: よてい／予定, 77; as planned: よていどおり／予定どおり, 246

planning: きかく, 110; planning calendar よていひょう／予定ひょう, 157; planning meeting: うちあわせ／打ち合わせ, 151

plastic: プラスチック, 39; plastic bottle: ペットボトル, 247

play: (an instrument) ひく, 64; (drums) たたく, 64

player: (on a sports team) せんしゅ, 27

pleased, be: よろこぶ, 132

police officer: けいかん, 110

pond: いけ, 124

popular, be: にんきが ある／人気が ある, 3

population: じんこう／人口, 202

pork: ぶたにく, 186

Portugal: ポルトガル, 7

position: ポジション, 111

possible, if: できれば, 246

pot: なべ, 74; meal cooked in a pot at the table: なべりょうり, 74

practice: れんしゅう, 132

precious: だいじ（な）／大事（な）, 83

pregnant, become: こどもが できる／子どもが できる, 107

preliminary inspection: したみ, 157

preparation: じゅんび, 56; do preparations じゅんびを する, 56

prepare: よういする／用意する, 181

president: (of a country) だいとうりょう, 210

press: おす, 213

primary school: しょうがっこう／小学校, 106

print: いんさつする, 224

problem: もんだい, 193

product: しょうひん, 33; new product: しんしょうひん, 33

professional: プロ, 211

profile: プロフィール, 141

profits: うりあげ／売り上げ, 201

programmer: プログラマー, 110

project: プロジェクト, 5

prolonged, be: のびる, 245

promise: (n.) やくそく, 77; (v.) やくそくする, 108

properly: ちゃんと, 141

public relations: こうほう, 110

pull: ひく, 237

push: おす, 213

put: おく, 221; (sauce etc. on food): つける, 187

put on: (clothes) きる／着る, 9; (a hat) かぶる, 36; (a necktie) （ネクタイを）する, 36; (glasses): かける, 119; (music) かける, 214

put out: (trash) だす／出す, 247

qualification: しかく, 210

qualified, get: しかくを とる, 210

question: もんだい, 168; that is a good question: そうですねえ, 211

quickly: はやく, early, 83

quit: やめる, 27

quite a bit: だいぶ, 116

railroad crossing: ふみきり, 240

rain: あめ／雨, 9; it does not rain much: あめが すくない／雨が 少ない, 9; it rains a lot: あめが おおい／雨が 多い, 9

ramen noodles: ラーメン, 236

ready, get (something): よういする／用意する, 181

realized, be: じつげんする, 193

really?: えっ, 42

reboot: さいきどうする, 224

receipt: レシート, 159

receive: うける, 107; (humble form) いただく, 151; (e-mail etc. electronically) じゅしんする, 224

recently: さいきん, 3

recipe: レシピ, 27

record: ろくおんする, 190; recording ろくおん, 190

recruit: ぼしゅうする, 132; recruitment: ぼしゅう, 132

recycling: リサイクル, 247

red: あか, 12

reference room: しりょうしつ, 138

regrettable: ざんねん（な）, 143

くやしい, 172; regrettably: ざん
ねんな ことに, 193

relax: のんびりする, 61; リラッ
クスする, 75

rent: かりる, 29

rental car: レンタカー, 174; rental
car option: レンタカー・プラ
ン, 175; rental shop: レンタル
ショップ, 29

repeatedly: たびたび, 225

reporter: きしゃ, 108

researcher: けんきゅうしゃ, 110

residential area: じゅうたくち,
129

response: へんじ, 88

rest area: きゅうけいじょ, 158

retire: たいしょくする, 107; retiring: たいしょく, 107

rice ball: おにぎり, 13

rice cooker: すいはんき, 243

rice paddy: たんぼ／田んぼ, 124

rich, the filthy: おおがねもち, 210

right?: 〜でしょう, 83

right, that is: そう そう, 42

right away: いまから／今から, 33

right in front of one: めの まえ／
目の 前, 237

right now: (polite form) ただい
ま, 190

right side: みぎがわ／右側, 235

right there: (close to one) すぐ, 241

rise: あがる／上がる, 208

risk: リスク, 214

river: かわ／川, 124

road: みち, 119; どうろ, 124

roast: (intr.) やける, 186; (trans.)
やく, 186

robber: どろぼう, 191

Romania: ルーマニア, 7

roof: やね, 237

roof garden: おくじょう／屋上,
219

room: へや／部屋, 4

rough: たいへん（な）, 92

roundtrip: おうふく, 176

run: はしる, 65; (of car), 231

runny nose: はな（みず）, 89

rural area: いなか, 210

Russia: ロシア, 7

sack: ふくろ, 33

sad: かなしい, 172

safe: (n.) (storage box for money)
きんこ, 37; (adj.) (not hazard-
ous) あんぜん（な）, 214

salary: きゅうりょう, 208

sales amount: うりあげ／売り
上げ, 201

sales and marketing: えいぎょう,
110

sales trends: うれゆき／売れ
行き, 201

salesperson: てんいん／店員, 19

salt: しお, 186

same: おなじ, 25

save: (a file) ほぞんする, 224

scarf: マフラー, 39

schedule: よてい, 77; as scheduled よていどおり／予定どお
り, 246

screen: スクリーン, 29; がめん, 237

search for: さがす, 40

seashell: かいがら, 139

seashore: かいがん, 214

seaside: うみべ, 214

season: シーズン, 193

seat: せき, 40

section chief: かちょう／課長, 151

section: か／課, 70

security guard: ガードマン, 240

security light: ぼうはんライト, 243

see, can: みえる／見える, 165

see (someone) off: おくりに い
く／おくりに 行く, 43

sell: うれる／売れる, 201

send: おくる, 43; だす／出す, 88;
(e-mail etc. electronically): そう
しんする, 224; send e-mail:
メールする, 91

senior high school: こうこう／
高校, 105

separate: わける／分ける, 247

serious: (of personality) まじめ（な）,
41; (of illness) おもい, 191;

serious-mindedness: まじめさ, 192

service: サービス, 22

set: (configure) せっていする,
224; (a timer): セットする, 243

set out: でかける／出かける,
143

setting(s): せってい, 224

several: いくつか, 33

shake: ゆれる, 243

she: かのじょ, 219

shirt: シャツ, 37

shoe: くつ, 9

shopping: かいもの, 12; shopping
street: しょうてんがい, 124

short: (low to the ground) ひく
い, 24; (not having much length)
みじかい, 24

should . . . : 〜た 〜ほうが いい,
83; should not . . . : 〜ない ほ
うが いい, 83

show (someone) around: あんな
いする, 56

shower: シャワー, 60

shut down: しゅうりょうする,
224

shuttle bus: シャトルバス, 75

siblings: (one's own) きょうだい,
26; (someone else's) ごきょう
だい, 26

sick of, be: きらい（な）, 117

side: 〜がわ／〜側, 226

sightseeing: かんこう, 175; sightseeing within the city: しないか
んこう, 175

simple: かんたん（な）, 22; シン
プル（な）, 24

sing: うたう, 60

Singapore: シンガポール, 62

sink: (into water) しずむ, 139

sit: すわる, 36

situation: ようす, 213

size: サイズ, 19

skate: すべる, 143; skating:
スケート, 143

sketchy: あやしい, 225

sky: そら／空, 203

sleep: ねむる, 209

sleeplessness: ねぶそく, 89

sleepy: ねむい, 89

slim, get: やせる, 219

slope: さか, 240

slowly: ゆっくり, 153

small: ちいさ（な）／小さ（な）, 42

smell: (v.) (smell good) かおりが
する, 139; (n.) におい, 187; (fragrance) かおり, 139

smoked salmon: スモークサー
モン, 11

smoking area: きつえんじょ, 158

smoking lounge: きつえんしつ, 138

sneeze: くしゃみ, 89

snowboarding: スノーボード, 64

soccer player: サッカーせんしゅ, 42

soft: やわらかい, 24

software: ソフト, 218

sold out: うりきれ, 25

somehow: なんとか／何とか, 141

someone: だれか, 4

sometime: いつか, 4

somewhere: どこか, 3

song: うた, 60; きょく, 143

south: みなみ／南, 176

soy sauce: （お）しょうゆ, 186

spacious: ひろい, 22

Spain: スペイン, 7

Spanish: スペインご／スペイン語, 155

spare key: スペアキー, 226

speak: はなす／話す, 54

special: とくべつ（な）／特別（な）, 201

spectacular: すばらしい, 79

speech: スピーチ, 173

spend (time): すごす, 140

spring: (season) はる, 117

stall: ばいてん／売店, 120

start: はじめる／始める, 60

start up: (a computer) きどうする, 224

starting now: これから, 51

station building: えきビル／駅ビル, 124; in front of the station: えきまえ／駅前, 160

stature: せ, 19

stay overnight: とまる, 135

stiff: かたい, 228

stir-fry: いためる, 186

stock prices: かぶか, 208

stop: とまる, 229

stop off: よる, 60

story: ものがたり, 129

strange: おかしい, 225; へん（な）, 230

strawberry: いちご, 129; strawberry patch: いちごばたけ, 129

street: ～どおり, 65

stress: ストレス, 227

strict: きびしい, 41

strike: (labor strike) スト, 204

strong: つよい, 93

stubborn: がんこ（な）, 41

student: せいと, 161

stylish: おしゃれ（な）, 130

subdued: (of color) じみ（な）, 24

subject matter: だいざい, 193

suburbs: こうがい, 27

such . . . as this: こんな, 218

suddenly: きゅうに／急に, 125; とつぜん, 212

sufficient, be: たりる／足りる, 238

suit: スーツ, 60

suitcase: スーツケース, 37

superior: じょうし, 26

supermarket, large: おおがたスーパー, 124

surprised, be: おどろく, 172; びっくりする, 173

sushi: （お）すし, 13

suspicious: あやしい, 225

sway: ゆれる, 243

sweetheart: こいびと, 212

swim: およぐ, 53

switch: スイッチ, 243

symbolize: しょうちょうする, 129

system notebook: システムてちょう, 43

systems department: システムぶ／システム部, 51

table: つくえ, 43

tae kwon do: テコンドー, 143

tag: なふだ, 37

take: (pick up) とる, 33; (have) とる, 157; (a shower) あびる, 54; (someone somewhere): つれていく／つれて行く, 244

take back: とりもどす, 193

take care (of): せわを する, 140; take care of yourself: おだいじに／お大事に, 83

take off: (clothes, shoes) ぬぐ, 54

tale: ものがたり, 129

talk: はなす／話す, 54; おしゃべりを する, 61; talking: おしゃべり, 61

tall: たかい／高い, 19

tall: (of person) せが たかい／せが 高い, 19

tavern: いざかや, 60

taxi fare: タクシーだい, 212

tea ceremony: さどう, 64

teacher: せんせい／先生, 26; きょうし, 110

teleconference: テレビかいぎ／テレビ会議, 56

temperature: おんど, 243

terrace: テラス, 42

test: しけん, 107; テスト, 152; test oneself against: ちょうせんする, 140

than: ～より, 6

thanks: おかげさまで, 90; thanks to . . . : おかげで , 143

there: そこ, 241

thermos jug: ポット, 187

thick: あつい, 24

thief: どろぼう, 191

thin: (narrow) ほそい, 24; (of cloth, paper, etc.): うすい, 24

thing: (abstract) こと, 140; (concrete) もの, 140; thing left behind: わすれもの, 34; things to do: ようじ／用事, 70

think about: かんがえる, 193

this/this one (here): (polite) こちら, 19

throughout: ～じゅう／中, 106

throw away: すてる, 223

ticket: (for an event) チケット, 78

tidy up: かたづける, 61

time: (the time when . . .) とき／時, 101; (in a broad sense) ころ, 129; at that time: そのころ, 129; be on time: まにあう／間に合う, 132; the whole time: ずっと, 104

time(s): (expressing frequency) ～かい／回, 51

times: (double) ばい／倍, 201

tired, get: つかれる, 70

to . . . : (telling time) ～まえ／～前, 76

toilet: トイレ, 159

tooth/teeth: は, 60

touch (with), get in: れんらくする, 92

tough: たいへん（な）, 92

tour: ツアー, 79

trading company: しょうしゃ, 111

tradition: でんとう, 175

traffic jam: じゅうたい, 220

training: トレーニング, 64; training session: けんしゅう, 157

transferred, being: てんきん, 108

transportation, means of: こうつうきかん, 124

trash: ごみ, 193

tree: き／木, 124

triple: さんばい／３倍, 208

trouble: トラブル, 239; be troubled: こまる, 168

trust: しんらいする, 214

Turkey: トルコ, 79

twenty years old: はたち, 118

twice: にかい／２回, 51

type: しゅるい, 247

uh . . . : あのう, 19; ええと, 42

uncle: (one's own) おじ, 26; (someone else's) おじさん, 26

understand, I: りょうかい, 245; (polite form) しょうちする, 181

unfortunate: ざんねん（な）, 143

university student: だいがくせい／大学生, 118

us: うち, 201

use: つかう, 51; for use as: ～よう／～用, 19

vacant, become: あく／空く, 181

vacation: きゅうか, 151; take a vacation: きゅうかを とる, 157

Vancouver: バンクーバー, 27

vanish: きえる, 221

various: いろいろ（な）, 140; in various ways: いろいろ, 12

view: ながめ, 79

vinegar: す, 186

vinyl: ビニール, 39

virus: ウィルス, 224

visible, be: みえる／見える, 165

visit: (lit., "play") あそぶ, 38; (humble form) うかがう, 132; (go to see) たずねる, 211

visitor: (polite form) おきゃくさま, 56; having a visitor: らいきゃく, 241

voice: こえ, 168

waist: ウエスト, 41

want to have: ほしい, 122

ward: (of a city) く, 247

warm: あたたかい, 118

wash: あらう, 60

watch out (for): ちゅういする, 213

way: みち, 119; way of ——ing: ～かた／～方, 161

we: うち, 201

wear: (shoes, pants, etc. over the feet) はく, 9

website: ホームページ, 181; ウェブサイト, 224

week: しゅう／週, 51; per week: しゅうに／週に, 51; the week after next: さらいしゅう／さ来週, 156

weekday: へいじつ, 12

weight training: ウエイトトレーニング, 66

welcome: むかえる, 56; welcome party: かんげいかい／かんげい会, 91

well: ま（あ）, 209; well then: じゃあ, 86; それでは, 181

west: にし／西, 176

Western-style food: ようしょく, 219

whale: くじら, 177

what?: あれっ, 63; ええっ, 235

wheelchair: くるまいす, 158

when: とき／時, 101; (speaking of likely or unlikely occurrence) ～たら, 181; (speaking of natural, habitual, or inevitable result) ～と, 235

whether: ～か どうか, 165

which: どっち, どちら, 235; which one (of the two): どちらも, 4

white: しろ／白, 12

wide: (thick) ふとい, 24

wild, the: やせい, 174; wild animals: やせいどうぶつ, 174

win: (a match) かつ, 172; (a lottery) あたる, 204

winter: ふゆ, 118

wish: ねがい, 92; I wish . . . : ～なあ, 201

with . . . : ～つき, 93

withdraw (money): おろす／下ろす, 158

woman: じょせい, 112

wonder . . . , I: ～かな（あ）, 246

wonderful: すごい, 201

wool: ウール, 39

work: はたらく, 132; can get work しごとが とれる／仕事が とれる, 209; work of art: さくひん, 188

world, the: せかい, 174; all over the world せかいじゅう／せかい中, 129; world heritage site: せかいいさん, 177; world natural heritage site: せかいしぜんいさん, 174

worried: しんぱい（な）, 93

worrywart: しんぱいしょう, 191

would it be okay?: (polite form) よろしいでしょうか, 151

wow: うわあ, 28; あっ, 125

wrap: つつむ, 19

wristwatch: うでどけい, 39

yawn: あくび, 89

year before last, the: おととし, 79

year, within the: ことしじゅう／今年中, 123

years old: ～さい, 106

yellow: きいろい, 122

yoga: ヨガ, 51

Index

abbreviations, 116, 235. *See also* contractions

able to see/hear, 165

adjectives: adverbial forms of, 84; conditional forms of, 222; in the -te form, acting as conjunctions, 35; negative form 〜くありません instead of 〜ない, 83; plain forms of, 121; stems of, followed by さ, 192; used in indirect questions, 170; used to construct modifying clauses, 134; used with かもしれません, 182; used with とき, 106; used with なります, 117; used with んです, 88

adverbs: adverbial forms, 84, 117; for expressing frequency, 58; ずいぶん vs. だいぶ, 116; ずっと, 104; そろそろ, 70

advice, asking for, 20, 218

after, 〜てから, 104

agreement, expressing with そうでしょう, 116

assertions, expressing with よね, 235

be, exist: humble form おります, 181; polite form ございます, 159

before, まえ (に) ／前 (に), 103

become, 〜く／になります, 117

can see/hear, みえます／きこえます, 165

case, if that is the, それなら, 151

cause/reason: indicating with から／ので, 152; indicating with で, 168; indicating with the -te form, 133, 168; conditional (〜ば) form, 222

change in state, describing a, 117, 202

coming/going/returning to do something, 38

comparisons, making, 6, 8, 21, 23

completion: expressing with 〜たら, 194; expressing with 〜てしまう, 218

conditional/if- statements, 222

conjunction, the -te form acting as a, 34–35. *See also* ので and から *under* particles

contractions/abbreviations, 206–07

contrast, 3, 101

conversations, starting up, 3, 51

counter: for age, 106; for buildings, 245; for nights spent at a hotel or an inn, 106; for ordinal numbers, 143; for people, 181; for times, 51, 58

cram schools, 116

decisions, expressing with にします, 23

desu/masu style: 201, 206

dictionary form, 53

duty, *see* necessity

explanations/explaining, 51, 55, 57, 83, 88

experiences, past, 〜ことがある, 73

family, 26

favors, asking, 151

frequency, 58

giongo, 83

going somewhere to do something and coming back, 85. *See also* coming

gratitude, expressing with たすかります, 165

guess, expressing with とおもう, 133

hesitation: expressing with あのう, 19; expressing with さあ, 3; expressing with んです, 83

honorific forms: ごらんください, 198; めしあがる／めしあがってください, 187

honorific language: 206

humble forms: いたします, 188; いただく, 151; うかがう, 133; おてつだいする, 187; おります, 181; まいります, 181

hypothetical/if- statements, 204

inside groups vs. outside ones, 201

interjections: ああ, 19, 33; あのう, 19; えっ, 42

interpretations, confirming with そうなんです, 102

interrogatives, *see* question words

intonation: falling, 3; rising, 83, 116

invitations, preceded by よかったら, 165

just, だけ, 218

linking related reasons, excuses, thoughts with し, 165

modifying clauses, 134–35

nominalizing/nominalizer, 136, 210

necessity, expressing with 〜なければ なりません, 238

not yet, 〜ていません, 87

obligation, *see* necessity

object: nominalized sentence segments serving as, 136; が used to mark instead of を, 165

occurrence, likely or highly unlikely, expressing with 〜たら, 184

omission: in general, 19; of topic／わたし, 3; of part of a question, 3, 151; of particles, 4, 33, 103, 206; of のなか／の中, 8; of どうか in indirect questions, 170

ongoing action, expressing with 〜ています, 36

only, だけ／しか, 218

opinion, expressing with とおもう, 133

particle combinations: 101, 207

particles: emotive, 206; omitting, 3, 4, 59, 206; が, 36, 101, 136, 165; から, 101; だけ, 218; で, 34, 108, 168; と, 236; なあ, 201; など, 175; に, 11, 33, 51, 58, 70; の, 19, 136, 207; は, 101, 136; ほど, 151; よね, 125; よね, 213; わ／わよ, 206; を, 59, 101, 165

periods of time, 58

plain forms: 52–53, 71–72, 121; before かもしれません, 182; before と in quotations, 122; before とき, 119; before の in nominalized sentences, 136;

before ので, 152; before んです, 56; in indirect questions, 170; in modifying clauses, 134; in sentence-final position, indicating tense and informality, 193

plain style: 52

polite language: 19, 52, 152, 181

polite forms: おきゃくさま, 56; おさきに／お先に, 83; おすごしください, 198; おつまりください, 188; おならびください, 188; おまちください, 40; ございます, 159; ございません, 40; ごしょうかいいたします, 101; しょうしょう, 40; ただいま, 190; 〜ましょう, 166; 方／かた, 18; こちら, 19

polite prefix: ご〜, 181

potential form, 154

prefixes: honorific ご〜, 8; まい〜, 62; polite ご〜, 181; しん〜, 33

questions: ending in んですか, 55; for asking someone's preference, 5; indirect, 170; omitting part of, 3, 19, 57; stalling rather than answering, 3; straightforward vs. soft-sounding, 33; using sentence fragments when asking, 19

question words: followed by か to refer to indefinite places, things, or people, 4

quotation, direct and indirect, 122

reasons, indicating with んです, 83. See also cause

requests: implying, 20; softening, 19

results: indicating with から／ので, 168; indicating with 〜たら, 219; natural or habitual, indicating with と, 236

returning, see coming

ryokan charges, 181

some——/any——, 4

school, elementary and junior high, 116

spaces between kana/kanji, absence of in written Japanese, 129

states in effect, indicating with 〜ています, 36

stopping in mid-sentence, 57, 83

subject: changing the, 218; nominalized sentence segments serving as, 136; specifying in an indirect question, 170

suffixes: 〜かた／〜方, 151; 〜じゅう, 106; 〜たち, 70; 〜ちゅう, 77; 〜どおり, 65, 246; 〜ぶり, 126; 〜まえ, 76; 〜むけ, 13

suggestions; asking for, 5, 218; declining, 57; giving, 86, 218; preceded by よかったら, 165

supposition, もし used to express, 204

surprise: expressing with すごい, 201; expressing with あれっ?, 218

talking to oneself, 201

time: expressions for telling, 76; time frames, 156. See also when

titles of courtesy: さん, 51; ちゃん, 116; くん, 157

topic maker/particle は: omitted, 33; not used within a modifying clause, 135; が replacing, 133

topics: in sentences that express a comparison, 21; nominalized sentence segments serving as, 136; noun phrases identified as, 135

try and . . . , 〜てみます, 9

uncertainty, expressing with かもしれません, 182

verbs: conjugations of, 53; conditional (〜ば)forms of, 222; dictionary forms of, 53; intransitive and transitive, 186, 242; plain forms of, 52–53, 71–72, 121; potential forms of, 154; -te forms of, 71; volitional forms of, 166

volitional form, 166

want to have, がほしい, 122

way of ——ing, 〜かた／〜方, 161

when, とき, 106, 119

（改訂第3版）コミュニケーションのための日本語　第2巻　テキスト
JAPANESE FOR BUSY PEOPLE II: Revised 3rd Edition

2007 年 1 月　第 1 刷発行
2008 年 1 月　第 3 刷発行

著　者　　社団法人 国際日本語普及協会

挿　画　　角 愼作

発行者　　富田 充

発行所　　講談社インターナショナル株式会社
　　　　　〒112-8652　東京都文京区音羽 1-17-14
　　　　　電話　03-3944-6493（編集部）
　　　　　　　　03-3944-6492（営業部・業務部）
　　　　　ホームページ　www.kodansha-intl.com

印刷・製本所　大日本印刷株式会社